THE AD GAME

By the same author:

The Business of Show Business

THE AD GAME

A Complete Guide to Careers
in Advertising, Marketing
and Related Areas

JUDITH A. KATZ

BARNES & NOBLE BOOKS
A DIVISION OF HARPER & ROW, PUBLISHERS
New York, Cambridge, Philadelphia, San Francisco,
London, Mexico City, São Paulo, Singapore, Sydney

FIRST EDITION

Designer: Sidney Feinberg

Library of Congress Cataloging in Publication Data
Katz, Judith A.
    The ad game.
    Includes index.
    1. Advertising—Vocational guidance.   2.   Marketing—Vocational guidance.   I.   Title.
HF5828.4.K38   1984   659.1'023'73   83–48792
ISBN 0–06–015299–0   84 85 86 87 88 10 9 8 7 6 5 4 3 2 1
ISBN 0–06–463576–7 (pbk.) 84 85 86 87 88 10 9 8 7 6 5 4 3 2 1

For my mother and father

And for the job-seekers of the future . . .
Jamie, Lauren W., Max B., Max C., Gaby, Tara,
Celeste, Lauren & Jessica, Joshua, Jordon,
Michele, Robert K., Noah, Ezra, Aaron, Erica,
Alec and Walden

"To be what we are, and to become
   what we are capable of becoming is
   the only end of life."
                        —ROBERT LOUIS STEVENSON

In an effort not to genderize the job descriptions, the author uses the universal *he* throughout.

Contents

Acknowledgments

My gratitude to the following people:

First of all to those who opened their professional lives to me: Gordon Weaver, Amil Gargano, Ken Angel, Jeanne Harrison, Jerry Fields, Judy Wald, Peter Tafti. Thanks for your time, truthfulness and words of wisdom.

And to so many others who were willing to tell me what they did or knew, and help me put *The Ad Game* together, forgive me if I've left any of you out: artists' representative Darwin Bahm; illustrator Peter Cross; Ogilvy & Mather senior vice-presidents Fran Devereus and Cliff Angers; BBD&O senior vice-president Charles Buck; McCann-Erickson senior VP and copy head, Penny Hawkey; Miller, Addison, Steele president and staff: Ken Miller, Asa Miller, Pat Kaye, Jim Schaus, Ellie Ritter; ABC director of network news sales, Bill Breen; *New York* magazine ad manager, David O'Brasky; Macy's advertising exec, Fern Rodriquez; Paramount Pictures' Jackie Torrence; Ally & Gargano's Patty Weber, Yvonne Gloede, Marsha Cohen, Barbara Schnabel, Linda Sapanaro; Wm. Douglas McAdams's Cheryl Shelton; Della Femina, Travisano & Partners' senior VP, media, Ned Gelband; Air Power president, Elaine Whalen; accountant Don Talbot; Colarossi-Griswold TV commercial producer, and my first boss, Dusty Rossell; David Falcon, president of David Falcon, Inc., N W Ayer's Robin Kavanaugh; Clio Awards' Michael Demtriads; the staff of *Adweek;* the Advertising Club of New York; Direct Mail/Marketing Association; Public Relation Society of America; the ANA, especially Rosemary Collins; ABC's research exec, Leslee Green; Barbara Keleman, president of Keleman Associates, research specialists.

And a special thanks to Adele Marano.

Introduction

September, 1968: *Me with the KM&G Personnel Director*

"So, you want to get into advertising," he said to me as he chomped on his cigar.

"Well, I'm very interested in it. That is, I think I am. What I mean to say is, advertising sounds like it might be for me."

"Exactly what kind of advertising work *might* you be interested in? Media? TV? Print? Account work? Are you sure you want to work for an advertising agency? Maybe you'd be more suited to work in marketing, on the client side, or for a TV production company."

"I don't know. I mean, I'm not sure I know enough to say which I'm interested in. But, of course, I could learn anything. Is there a job where I could get an overview of everything that goes on and learn what the jobs are so that I could decide which I'm interested in? Or must I choose one department?"

"This is an advertising agency, Ms. Katz, not a school."

Fifteen years later: *Me with My Cousin, the Advertising Novice*

"So, you want to get into advertising," I said to him as I munched on my cottage cheese and fruit.

"Well, I think so. I think I'd be good at it."

"In which direction do you want to go? Art, copywriting, media, marketing, research, production—nod when I hit a vein."

"I don't know. To tell the truth, I'm not sure I even know what those are. Is there a way for me to find out?"

The Ad Game was written to provide advertising novices with that way to find out. It's a "what-is" rather than a "how-to" book. On the following pages are your options, laid out before you on a silver platter. Here are job descriptions of most every job in advertising, not only with agencies but with corporations, production companies, model agencies, the media, and

other places. Don't try to read them all at once. Consider them
slowly, a few at a time. After narrowing down the jobs to the
few you are really interested in and qualified for, you can begin to figure out how to get one of them.

Here also you will find career profiles of people working in
key areas of advertising: one at a motion picture studio, one in
account services at an agency, one at the top of a creative department, one at a TV production company. These profiles will
give you a good idea of what the people who have these jobs
actually *do* in their daily work. They will also show you that
there is more than one way to have a successful career in advertising. With so many arenas to choose from, you need not
be a creative genius like Amil Gargano, profiled in Part IV.
Your claim to fame might be in marketing, or working with
small budgets, or working in a corporate environment. The
profiles also show how varied are the portals of entry to the
field of advertising. One person fell in, then climbed the ladder
step by step. Another very deliberately set out to do just what
he's doing now. A third thought he'd never work in advertising
until he learned he could do so with creativity and integrity. A
fourth changed her career midstream. None allowed himself to
be taken over by mediocrity—something of an accomplish-
ment in a business one person described as "overrun with dull-
ness."

Mediocrity is not the worst quality that has been attributed
to people who work in advertising. From *The Man in the Gray
Flannel Suit* to television's *Bewitched* to *The Hucksters*, admen
have been portrayed as slaves and conformists, somewhat silly
slaves and conformists at that. Although advertising is a much-
maligned profession, there is some truth to this. Many companies do insist that their management, if not their "creatives,"
present a certain image and that all their employees be a thousand percent committed to their work. ("I never heard of nine
to five," said the founder of Grey Advertising. "Anyone who
works those hours and expects to succeed is a dumbbell.") Advertising is one of the highest stress industries; the job-hopping
and burnout rates give proof of that. It's not surprising that a
lot of people working in advertising are dying to get out. But
for all those dying to get out there are twice as many dying to
get in. And many who are in dearly love what they do and
wouldn't—in fact, couldn't—do anything else.

One final word. You may have wondered about the title of this book. Considering the long hours put in and the tremendous amount of money spent on advertising, it is anything but a game. So why the ad "game"? Three days into my first job in advertising, half the people in my department were fired in what's referred to in the industry as a bloodbath. "Why?" I asked my boss.

"We lost an account," he said.

"How come?" I really wanted to know.

"Who knows how come? That's why they call it the ad game. Sometimes winning, sometimes losing has more to do with where the wheels stop than with whether you're doing a good job."

There are some who find the gamble unbearable; others who find it challenging, even enticing. Only you know which of these types you are. It's my sincere hope that if you are one of the second variety, *The Ad Game* will help you begin a long and successful career in advertising.

PART I

AN OVERVIEW

1 How Advertising Became an Industry

Advertising has actually existed forever, and in one form or another, it probably always will. The very first kind of advertising was word of mouth (one caveman telling another where to go for good hunting!). But there is evidence that printed advertising existed at least three thousand years ago in Egypt. Also, the ancient Athenians and Romans, enterprising merchants that they were, got the idea of using objects and signs to notify people of the availability of a product. For instance, a wine shop was indicated by a bush over the door. The Greek merchants also employed town criers, carefully selected for their clear enunciation and pleasing voices, to shout their wares to passersby. Sometimes they were even accompanied by musicians. During the Middle Ages in England, signboards became a part of the national tradition. And, with the invention of printing in the fifteenth century came the earliest printed handbills. When a public press was introduced in the seventeenth century, merchants began selling their wares through commercial notices inserted in newsletters with other items of news. These were known as "puffs."

This, of course, is a far cry from the slick TV commercials, four-color ads, billboards and direct mail we know as "advertising" today, but it was a beginning. A beginning with a long start in coming, for while advertising has existed forever, the advertising industry has not. It didn't evolve until someone managed to get paid for giving advice on how and where to advertise. That first occurred but a short 150 years ago. That's when the first "adman" (Volney B. Palmer was his name) appeared on the scene. His idea was to represent newspapers as a sales agent, charging merchants a commission for his "expert" advice. Before that time, when newspapers first gained popularity, merchants would place ads directly through the media—that is, through the newspapers. One of the merchants' problems was where to place the advertisements to do the most good. Volney's advice was welcomed, and pretty soon

other experts followed suit. Before long, "accepting and con-
spicuously posting advertisements" became a lucrative and
quite popular vocation. The advertising agent was born; only
then they were known as "newspaper agents," and many
charged as much as 30 to 40 percent commission for their service. Competition was fierce. One agent, N. W. Ayer, decided
he would, as an extra enticement to use his agency, offer to
compose as well as post advertisements. Little did he know he
would be setting a precedent that would launch the first full-
service advertising agency (which today still exists and is, as
N W Ayer, Inc., among the twenty largest agencies in the
world) and, in effect, set in motion the entire advertising industry. Eventually, of course, all agents offered art and copy to
their clients, becoming *advertiser's* (or advertising) agents, rather
than newspaper agents.

At just about this time, in the late 1890s, the newspapers
also organized themselves, and decided to give a discount *only*
to recognized advertising agents. By the 1920s most media had
adopted the still-prevalent standard 15 percent discount/com-
mission, which they provide for all recognized advertising
agencies.

2 The Industry Today

Why advertising is created today is basically the same as in the
past—a company with something to sell decides it wants to sell
it to a lot of people. However, *when* and *how* advertising is
created today is markedly different and much more complicated. Four stages are involved: marketing objectives are determined, marketing strategies are developed, creative plans
are made and, finally, the advertising is produced and placed.
Some of this process is done by the advertiser, some by the
advertising agency and some by outside suppliers.

Most times, the advertiser (known as "the client"), through
its marketing department, determines what the advertising is
to accomplish—that is, the marketing objectives. Ad agency
management and/or account services works with the client in
determining what to say in the advertising (for instance, "Lis-

termint lasts longer than any other mouthwash"). Ad agency "creatives" decide how to say it (for instance, referring to Listermint as *Laster*mint in an advertisement). And outside suppliers (printers, engravers, TV production companies) produce the advertising. Media people, working for an ad agency, advertiser and/or independent media company, place the advertising in the various media, print and broadcast. Also involved throughout is marketing and advertising research, which provides all sorts of information for the marketing people, account service, creative and media staff. For example, using the above concept, research might have found that what concerns people most about mouthwash is not how it tastes or what color it is, but how long it lasts. In testing the word *Lastermint*, research might find consumers aren't getting the message, or that they are.

This is a rather simplified version of why and how advertising is created. But enough to give you some idea of all that is involved. As you read the job descriptions and profiles that follow, you will get a much clearer and more specific idea of the process.

Before any of that takes place, an advertiser must decide who will prepare and place his advertising. He has three options here. He can retain one or more full-service ad agencies to do it all—that is, prepare, place and produce. He can form a strong advertising department within his corporation, which will then utilize any number of agencies and other sources (graphic arts companies, free-lance artists and writers, media-buying services) on an à la carte basis. Or he can establish an in-house agency that functions just like an ad agency, except that it has only one client—its parent organization. If the corporation is very large, it might do all three. Once an agency is assigned a piece of business, it stays with it until the job is done or the corporation stops making the product or offering the service, or until a contract has expired and a new agency lures the account away. This could be for decades or for a few months.

Most companies, when they plan on using an advertising agency for serious, expensive service (for instance, to launch a new product), shop around before selecting the one for them. They might even invite a number of agencies to prepare a com-

petitive, speculative advertising campaign to show what kind
of advertising they would run for the company if they were
hired.

There is more than one reason why a corporation would decide to advertise a product or service (more on those later),
and more than one way they could accomplish this. For the
most part, however, particularly in the case of big business, the
job of planning, preparing and producing advertising is left to
one or another kind of advertising agency.

The advertising industry today is a $60 billion business, and
it's estimated that by the year 2000, $780 billion will be spent
by advertisers on advertising; and many, many more people
than today will be employed to keep it functioning. Media
planning and placement, and even N. W. Ayer's "extras"—art
and copy—are a mere few of the many sophisticated services
advertising agencies today offer their clients. Among the many
others are: marketing consultation, research, package design,
logo design, new product development, public relations, television production, international expertise, conference and exhibition direction. Advertising today is not only the business
that places and produces advertising to sell products, it is also
the business that often develops marketing strategies, develops
new products and, some would say, even creates differences
between products that are basically the same. In the past, the
main function of advertising was to announce the availability of
a product. Then, through their research and new product development departments, advertising began encouraging product innovations and product differences. Today, with so many
parity products, it's often up to the advertising industry to *give*
a product an apparent difference in the marketplace—often a
product is literally "created" by its advertising.

To advertise a product today is no simple task; to do it successfully and honestly is a real challenge—a challenge that is
met quite often by an industry that, as the slogan goes, has
"come a long way, baby." Early advertising innovators would
be astonished to learn how important advertising is to the
world economy and the degree of creative and marketing ingenuity advertising professionals have developed.

3 Types of Advertising Agencies

There are anywhere from forty-five hundred to eight thousand advertising agencies* in the country today. Of those, there are various types of agencies, with an agency's type being classified in one of two ways—by the kind of advertising it handles, and by its size. There are about forty "big" agencies and fifty-four "medium-size" agencies in the country; the remaining four thousand to eight thousand are so-called small agencies. Incidentally, don't let these statistics mislead you regarding your chances of finding employment. The fact is, over half the people employed by advertising agencies work for the ninety-odd large and medium-size shops. (This statistic is of course greatly influenced by the tendency in the past fifteen years toward conglomeration—that is, large agencies' gobbling up of smaller ones. One reason for that is, once a big agency reaches a certain size, the easiest way for it to increase its billings is to buy a smaller company with a strong client list, or one which services a part of the country where the bigger agency has no clients. There is also the inducement to acquire another agency so that if a major client leaves the bigger agency, the blow won't be felt so hard.)

In the advertising industry, the terms "small," "medium" and "big" have more specific meanings than an outsider might think. Big agencies are called so because they bill over $15 million and usually much more. (A few agencies bill in the billions. For example, in 1983 Young & Rubicam billed $2.5 billion.) Medium agencies bill from $5 million to $15 million, and small agencies are called "small" because they bill less than $5 million. And the terms go even beyond these definitions. Big agencies have big clients and big offices. Medium agencies may also have big clients and gorgeous offices. Small

---

*The Directory of Advertising Agencies, which counts only recognized agencies, lists 4,500; the U.S. Department of Commerce, which lists all existing agencies, no matter how small, counts 8,000.

agencies rarely have big clients, although they may have a small division of a big client. (In advertising there are, of course, exceptions to every rule. Backer & Spielvogel, for instance, is a so-called small agency known for its big clients and large profits.) Today, big agencies are more than likely to be super-agencies, or mega-agencies—that is, several agencies under one umbrella or holding company. Medium and small agencies are more than likely today to be subsidiaries of a big agency. Carrying the definition even further, big and medium-size agencies are usually generalists while small agencies are usually specialists—that is, agencies with expertise in a particular type of advertising or client.

Working for one "type" of agency—say, a general consumer super-size agency—is quite different from working for another, say, a small direct-response agency. For one thing, with a large corporate-type agency, you'll start out in one department and may never learn what's going on in the others— while at a smaller agency, even at an entry-level job, you'll get an overview of what everyone else is doing. On the other hand, at the larger agency you may be trained and carefully groomed to move up the ladder of your department, while at the smaller agency you probably won't be formally trained at all. Then there're the clients you'll work with at the various types of agencies. At a big or medium-size general consumer agency you'll work for a wide variety of "important" clients, with big budgets and in every media, the most important being broadcast advertising. At a small or medium specialty shop you'll be working with one kind of maybe-not-so-big client, and you may only work in one medium. Probably it won't be broadcast. But you'll get to know your client's business as well as he does, an important mark for anyone in the "category-oriented advertising business."

The rest of this section gives a more detailed picture of the two basic types of advertising agency—the general consumer agencies and the specialized agencies.

The General Consumer Agencies

These are what most people think of when they think of an advertising agency: super-size, big, medium, and a very few small general consumer ad agencies throughout the world.

Most, if not all, have an office in New York. General consumer ad agencies, known as generalists, have as clients a variety of accounts, including some of the world's largest corporations. Generally speaking, the larger the agency, the larger the client—big business hires big advertising agencies. A typical general consumer ad agency client roster might include a packaged goods manufacturer, i.c., food, drug, toiletry or household product; a tobacco company; a large clothing manufacturer; and maybe an airline. It's not unusual for such an agency to handle only part of an advertiser's business while another general consumer agency handles another piece of the client's business. For instance, a huge tobacco company like R. J. Reynolds might have one of its brands with one agency—perhaps one with a strong creative department—and another brand with an agency known for its marketing ability. General consumer ad agencies are hired by advertisers for a variety of reasons: to launch and position a new product or service; to add value to a product or service (new and improved) or to reposition and promote an existing product or service. Most general consumer ad agencies are run very businesslike and have a corporate-type environment. They are divided into various departments (more on those later) and have some sort of management board set up to administer the agency and assure it makes a profit. Some of the very large agencies are multi-million-dollar publicly owned corporations. Among the largest and better-known general consumer ad agencies are: Young & Rubicam; J. Walter Thompson Company; McCann-Erickson; Ogilvy & Mather; Ted Bates & Company; BBD&O (Batten, Barton, Durstine & Osborn); Leo Burnett Company; Foote, Cone & Belding; Doyle Dane Bernbach; Grey Advertising; Benton & Bowles; Compton Advertising; Dancer-Fitzgerald-Sample; N W Ayer, Inc.; Kenyon & Eckhardt, Inc.; KM&G International, Inc.; Della Femina, Travisano & Partners; Ally & Gargano; McCaffrey & McCall. For additional, more specific information on these agencies and others see Appendix C, page 228.

The Specialized Agencies

Like so many other things, advertising, in the past few years, has evolved into a highly specialized industry. That is, in addi-

tion to the general consumer-type agencies, there are those
"specialists" which cater to one type of account or specialize
in a particular mode of advertising. Following you will find
descriptions of the various types of agencies that exist today.

   *Direct Marketing (a.k.a. Direct Response) Advertising Agen-
cies.*   Direct marketing advertising is quickly becoming one of
the most popular ways to advertise—perhaps because it is the
most easily tested, the most direct and not the most expensive
way, particularly when it's direct *mail*. Therefore, direct market advertising agencies are booming. These medium and
small-size shops specialize in the type of advertising in which a
company offers goods or services *directly* to its potential customers through the media. The customers make their response
directly to the company. The dominant direct marketing medium is the mail, although direct response advertising can be
done through TV, radio, newspapers, supplements, magazines,
coupons and business publications. Organizations making
heavy use of direct marketing ad agencies include mail-order
catalog companies, publishing houses, fund-raising organizations, record clubs and political activists. Employees of direct
response agencies are generally experienced in this type of advertising, especially the account people and copywriters. (As a
matter of fact, direct response copywriters often work independently and do a very lucrative business.) Because direct
marketing advertising is so thoroughly tested, those with skills
in and knowledge of statistics and research might want to consider this field. One of the largest direct response advertising
agencies is Wunderman, Ricotta & Kline, New York—acquired
by Young & Rubicam in 1973.

   Recruitment Advertising Agencies.   There are a number of
agencies known as recruitment specialists. Such agencies offer
corporate personnel departments a way to effectively recruit
qualified job applicants. In other words, it's the job of recruitment specialists to persuade people to apply for jobs. It is a
very specialized field requiring skills having little to do with
most other forms of advertising. Recruitment advertising tends
to be factual rather than creative, utilizes copy but little art
and employs account executives to solicit as well as manage
clients. (Most earn a commission of 7.5 percent on all advertising they place.) As the *New York Times* and other Sunday

papers close their classified sections Thursday evenings, Wednesday and Thursday are very busy days at recruitment advertising agencies. While this is not a glamorous area of advertising, it can be quite lucrative. Some recruitment ad agencies also serve their clients as recruitment consultants, advising clients on all staffing matters and even screening potential candidates . . . so it could be a viable area for those in the personnel field who are interested in moving over to advertising. Some of the largest recruitment agencies are North American Advertising; Deutsch, Shea & Evans; and Thompson Recruitment, a division of the JWT Group.

Business-to-Business (a.k.a. Trade or Industrial) Advertising Agencies. Business-to-business ad agencies specialize in advertising to people at their work, and communicating to them in their job function rather than as individuals. They don't advertise to the general consumer, but to businesses which might use or buy the product or service they are advertising. Trade agencies specialize in knowing about all elements involved in the business purchase. At one time, business-to-business advertising was considered second-rate advertising, and the top people in the field didn't want to work on it. While this is less true today, business-to-business is still less competitive than consumer advertising and therefore a good place for the neophyte to look for work. Business-to-business ad agencies employ the same kinds of advertising personnel that consumer agencies do: account, creative and media; one difference is that there is much less broadcast advertising done at business-to-business ad agencies. There are independent shops which specialize in industrial advertising; also, there are subsidiaries of big agencies and some general consumer agencies doing this kind of advertising—which means there is a wide arena to choose from and move around within, for those with interest and expertise in business-to-business advertising. Business-to-business is most definitely a growing field. Nearly $2 million were spent in business publications in 1980, and by now the figure has surely increased. Marsteller, Inc., a division of Young & Rubicam, is a worldwide leader in business-to-business advertising.

Financial Advertising Agencies. There are quite a few small ad agencies specializing in advertising for financial organizations—that is, banks, brokerage firms, and mortgage compa-

nies. This is a particular type of advertising, and requires
knowledge of the financial community as well as of the style of
advertising that financial institutions tend to favor.

Entertainment Industry Advertising Agencies. There are
also quite a few small independent shops and medium-size subsidiaries that specialize in entertainment advertising, that is, in
advertising theatrical events, motion pictures and other forms
of entertainment. They have as their clients theatrical producers, filmmakers, movie studios and distributors. Entertainment
industry ad agencies employ the same kinds of people that
most agencies do, and in addition, the full-service agencies may
also have a public relations arm. To get employed by any of
these shops, it helps to have a thorough knowledge and understanding of the entertainment business in addition to whatever
advertising skills you can offer. Two creations unique to entertainment advertising are the theatrical trailer—a sort of long
commercial that is shown in movie houses to preview a film—
and the theatrical poster, generally designed by an illustrator
specializing in theater posters. (Paul Davis is among the most
prestigious of those.) With more and more producers choosing
to advertise their shows and films on TV, entertainment advertising has been burgeoning in the past few years. As a matter of
fact, movie advertising on network TV increased by 61 percent
in 1980, making it the fastest-growing category of advertising
on the networks, according to Broadcast Advertisers Report.
Typically, entertainment ad agencies specialize in either
theater or movie advertising. Serino, Coyne & Nappi is one of
the more successful theatrical ad agencies; and Diener-Hauser-
Bates, the entertainment subsidiary of Ted Bates, is quite successful in movie advertising.

Health-Care (a.k.a. Pharmaceutical) Advertising Agencies.
These agencies specialize in marketing pharmaceutical and
health-care products to doctors, to health-care professionals
and, sometimes, in the case of over-the-counter items, to the
consumer. Health-care ad agencies maintain the same type of
staff that consumer agencies do, as well as a staff of doctors to
check all outgoing copy and art, for such agencies are regulat-
ed by the FDA. There are, within the field, some agencies
which specialize in pharmaceuticals and others which have all
kinds of health-care accounts, i.e., surgical equipment and lab
equipment. It's not always necessary, but those interested in

this kind of advertising would do better to have some experience in the health field. William Douglas McAdams, Inc., is one of the oldest and largest agencies in the health-care field.

Hotel, Resort and Travel Advertising Agencies.   Not many, but a few agencies do specialize in hotel, resort and travel advertising. Travel ad agencies have as clients hotels, resorts and tourist bureaus. They service them the way any agency services a client—that is, with marketing, creative and media advice. As travel clients tend to use much collateral material, e.g., brochures, stationery and postcards, this could be a good area for graphic designers and art directors. It is not uncommon for hotel advertising executives to have a background in the hotel industry or even be a graduate of the Cornell School of Hotel Administration or similar institution. The biggest independent agency in the field is Needham & Grohmann, servicing clients throughout the country as well as the Caribbean, Far East, Latin America and Europe.

Political Advertising Agencies.   While there is a good deal of controversy over the merits of political advertising (there are those who say it has changed the rules of the game from letting the better candidate have a chance to win to letting the most appealing candidate with the biggest ad budget win), it exists and is fast becoming a specialty that many advertising people are interested in. The big agencies do handle some political advertising, often in conjunction with a political media consultant (the most famous being David Garth). A great deal of political advertising is consulting—that is, the overseeing and supervising and hiring of individuals and services as they're needed. As there is much research conducted for any political campaign, those interested in the field would do well to work for a research company which specializes in doing surveys for politicians. Besides consultants and the big agencies, there are small shops that specialize in political advertising. One such agency is Dailey & Associates in Los Angeles (recently acquired by the Interpublic Group of Companies), which established Campaign '80 and the November Group, the former being Ronald Reagan's ad agency, the latter Nixon's in 1972. Both were set up and operated as long as those two Republican presidential campaigns ran.

Miscellaneous Specialty Advertising Agencies.   This is the age of specialization, and advertising is not immune to that

fact. More and more specialty shops are becoming a growth
area in the industry. While there may not be hundreds of each
specialty mentioned, there are enough (even one is enough)
for them to be mentioned here for your consideration. There
are agencies specializing in *corporate advertising*, that is, in
building corporate identification. One such shop is FCB/Cor-
porate, a division of Foote, Cone and Belding. There are agencies specializing in *real estate*, marketing and advertising con-
dominiums, office space, shopping centers, real estate brokers.
In New York, Miller, Addison, Steele, Inc., specializes in this
type of work. There are agencies specializing in the *home fur-
nishing industry*, the *fashion industry*, the *publishing industry*.
Lately there are even agencies specializing in marketing to certain ethnic groups, most noticeably, the Hispanic market. What
all this means to the neophyte in advertising, particularly the
career-changer, is an opportunity to bring one's previously
learned skills and experience to a new field—the "specialty"
advertising industry.

4   How Advertising Agencies Are Organized

The structure of an ad agency will vary, depending on the kind
of and the amount of business it handles. However, most agencies are divided into the following departments: *administration,
account services, creative, media, print production, traffic, finance*
and *bookkeeping.* Even very small agencies are divided this way,
with maybe one person in each department, or the same person operating more than one department. Large and medium-
size agencies have these additional departments: *television production, research, personnel.* They may also have departments
for *public relations, broadcast business administration, international business, conferences and trade shows, sales promotion, new
business, new product development, TV syndication.* Below is a
description of each department and some explanation of what
goes on within each. The various jobs in each department are
defined and described throughout the book. Learning about
the various departments should help you take your first step in
deciding which advertising career, if any, is right for you. It's
important that you decide from the beginning what part of

advertising you feel most comfortable in, because advertising is a business of specialists. Rarely, except in very small agencies, do advertising people change hats. From very early on, you are "typed" as an account, creative, media, production, research or management person. So the sooner you find your niche, the faster you'll be able to climb the appropriate ladder.

The Various Departments Within an Advertising Agency

Administration (a.k.a. General Management) Department. All agencies, no matter the size, require direction and management. It's the job of those in administration to provide that and to run the agency smoothly, efficiently and, most important, profitably. An agency's administrative department might consist of one person (in that case, almost always the president and founder of the agency) or several people (usually the agency principals and co-founders) or a board of directors, one of whom will be managing director and ultimately responsible. Many of the larger agencies depend on planning and review boards and executive committees to make major decisions. Members of these boards are generally departmental heads and agency executives—for example, a senior vice-president in charge of finances or internal operations or creative services. Regardless of how many administrators an agency has, this department's job is to set policy and to make the major management decisions such as deciding who works on which accounts and what work gets presented to the clients. Additionally, it's often management's responsibility to service the very big accounts, go after new business, set financial goals, monitor the accomplishments of the agency and pursue opportunities for profitable investment and expansion. It is most unusual for anyone to go straight into an upper-level or middle-level administrative job without working in another area of the business, unless of course it's his own agency.

Account Service Department. The account service department of an agency is responsible for gathering relevant information; analyzing marketing problems; preparing, along with the client, a marketing strategy; and coordinating the services of the various departments so that the agency's clients are best served. If it is the job of the creative and production people to decide *how* to say something, it's the job of the account service department to decide *what* to say. At some agencies the title "account executive" is given to all account people; at other agencies there are various titles and responsibilities—for example, management supervisor, senior account executive, junior account executive. Depending on an account person's level, he will communicate with his client match. For example, at the most senior level, the president of the company will only communicate with the president of the agency or a member of the executive committee. The account manager at an agency will communicate with the client's marketing director, and so on. In some cases, the account service department actually functions as a client's marketing department, with full responsibility for a product. In those cases, the account people apply themselves to the full range of their client's business: product development, pricing, distribution, sales. In other cases, the account department functions as a marketing partner to the client, and decisions and strategies are planned together. There are also cases where an account department has very little say regarding strategy, and in those cases, the account people function pretty much like glorified messengers, shuttling work between client and agency—getting approvals from the client. At some ad agencies, particularly recruitment agencies, account people are responsible for soliciting as well as handling accounts. But at most large agencies, new business is handled by a separate group of people. Because account people "have" or "run" a piece of business, but don't actually *do* anything (as opposed to other departments, where the advertising is created and placed), many advertising neophytes think these are the easiest jobs in advertising. They're wrong. Account people work hard, have a lot of responsibility (if not so much power) and are the most vulnerable when a piece of business is lost. They are the ones most often fired. So account people must have tough skins and tenacious attitudes. They should also have management skills, a love of and interest in people, an ability to learn everything they can about someone else's business and, above all, a talent for communicating to many different types of people.

Account people do a lot of talking—at client meetings, internal meetings, business breakfasts, lunches and dinners; a lot of reading—research material, sales figures; and a lot of writing—contact reports, strategy statements, memos, letters, budgets. A career in account work can be high-paying and exciting, but it's almost always at high risk.

Creative Department. The creative department of an ad agency is by far the most crucial to its success. Clearly, creative is what advertising is all about. It's here, in the creative department, where an agency's ultimate product, its advertising, is created. As previously mentioned, it's the creative department that decides how to say something once the account department decides what to say. The creative department is headed up by a creative director and maybe a few associate creative directors, and consists of copywriters, art directors, assistants, secretaries and gofers. It's their job to turn marketing strategy into advertising. Everything is taken into account before the creative department sits down to work. They meet and meet and meet with the account department, and sometimes even the client, and they learn about the target market, competition, pricing, packaging, consumer opinion, positioning—the way a product will be marketed, for instance, the *strongest* detergent, or the *mildest* detergent, or the *cleanest-smelling* detergent. Once the creative department comes up with something they believe is "on target," they confer with the account department. If at first everyone agrees that the work is good (which is *very* rare), it goes on to be approved by agency management and, eventually, by the client. A much more common scenario is constant meetings, contentions, alterations—between the creative and the account departments—before anything gets approved and sent on to the production department to be actually produced. Once that occurs, the creative department supervises the work and must approve everything (photographs, illustrations, retouching) before an ad is produced. In the case of TV commercials, a producer is brought in from the TV department, but the creative department still keeps tight control of what the spots look like. Creative departments are organized in various ways. In some agencies, creative teams work on an assignment together; in others (and this is an old-fashioned way), copywriters write the ad first, then hand it over to an art director to "visualize." In some agencies, specifically the larger agencies, senior creative teams work on TV commercials; medium-experienced teams work on consumer

print ads; and junior teams work on trade ads. Some agencies
don't make such distinctions, and assign all work to all creative
people. Because creative is the most visible and, some would
say, appealing department to work in, it's also the most competitive job-wise. Some of the larger agencies have training
programs (see Part VI, "Finding a Job," for more information),
and there are entry-level jobs as assistant, gofer, junior art director or copywriter. However, they're tough to come by.
Anyone interested in this area must have a portfolio or work to
show the creative manager, director or whoever hires creative
people (almost never the personnel department). A guide has
been written to help people prepare their portfolio, or "book,"
as it's called in the industry. It's *How to Put Your Book Together
and Get a Job in Advertising,* by Maxine Paetro. See Appendix B,
page 217, for details.

Media Department.   The media department is where print
space and television and radio time is bought and placed. It is
an updated version of the original advertising agency—that is,
it's where advertisers turn for advice on where to place advertising so that it will do the most good at the best price. What
happens here is that a strategy is developed (by the client, the
account people and the top media people), for instance, to
reach single women between the ages of 18 and 34. Then the
department functions on two levels: planning and buying. The
planning consists of analyzing all media available, figuring out
the cost and recommending a plan to the client and/or account
group. This sounds much easier than it actually is. Many questions must be answered before a good plan, i.e., one that allo-
cates the client's media funds to reach the maximum potential,
is developed. Media people ponder such questions as: which
markets are best for a particular product; how much money
must be spent in each market in order to make the advertising
effort worthwhile; how many times, in which media; in which
markets are the competition doing best, worst, etc. Once a plan
is completed and approved by the client, the media department's job is to execute it—that is, carry out the buying of
space and time at the lowest possible price. Again, it sounds
easier than it is, for there's a tremendous amount of wheeling,
dealing and negotiating of prices. At some agencies, media
people work on specific accounts; at others they work on a
variety of accounts but within specific markets. Some agencies

believe in specialization, and have media specialists in planning, network negotiations, spot buying, magazines, newspapers, outdoor advertising (billboards). Some agencies buy print space directly from the media while they buy broadcast time through a media-buying service. At very small agencies, they often buy all the media through a media-buying service. And some clients—those who spend a tremendous amount of money on advertising—buy their own media, in order to take advantage of the 15 percent discount. The media department is often a good place for a beginner to look for his first job in advertising. There are more entry-level jobs here than in many other departments, and while most veteran media people don't move to other departments, it is possible for those with one or two years' experience to make a lateral move into another department. Also, media can be a satisfying, lucrative and less risky career than other more "glamorous" areas of advertising.

Print Production Department. This department is responsible for turning the creative department's work into tangible advertising. People in print production buy the type the art- or type-director specified; they buy engravings for color printing; they buy the printing (that is, they choose which printing company will do the work). They make certain an ad is properly prepared for a magazine or newspaper. In some agencies, the print production department is integrated into the traffic department; in others, particularly in the larger ones, they're two separate departments. The person in charge of the production department is called the production manager, and is one of the unsung heroes of advertising. His work is never identified as his, yet is so very important to how an agency functions. At the large agencies there are various jobs in the production department having to do with specific production techniques, i.e., the person in charge of color retouching, the person in charge of printers' bidding, etc. This is not one of the most competitive advertising occupations; however, the catch in getting a job here is that you must have some production experience in order to get hired. Some people accomplish this by working for a typographer, printer, publisher or graphic arts company, or by starting in an agency as a production assistant or even secretary to the print production department. It's not unusual for people in production to move from one industry to another.

Traffic Department. The traffic department keeps track of

the creative and production work, plans the flow and scheduling of work in progress and makes sure that everyone does his work on time in order to meet deadlines and closing dates. It is a vital department to any agency. Without it, chaos would surely prevail. There are two ways agencies handle traffic departments. One way is to keep the department autonomous, with a hierarchy of jobs, such as traffic trainee, traffic planner, traffic manager–print production, traffic director, etc., and, ultimately, the head of the traffic department. The other way is to have traffic executives assigned to a piece of business, working within the account group. For entry-level people, it is best to look for the first type of agency, as they're more apt to hire and train inexperienced people. Working in "traffic" is one of the best ways to gain experience while learning the agency business. And, because traffic is such a pivotal department (it's their job to keep track of all agency functions—including copy, art, production and media), it's an excellent place to get a bird's-eye view of agency activities and come in contact with (and get the opportunity to impress) people from other departments. It's not at all unusual for traffic people to make lateral moves into account work, media, or even the client side of advertising. More and more advertising agencies are utilizing computers to help keep the traffic moving smoothly and on schedule, so those interested in this area might consider a computer course.

Finance and Bookkeeping Department. This department is responsible for collecting money from clients and paying the media and other creditors. Under the directorship of a chief financial officer (who is often on the board of directors or other managing board), the department is also responsible for financial forecasting and cost controls. It's also the department which pays the salaries, produces the company's annual report when necessary, and is in charge of all tax reports. People in this area are specialists, and rarely do they move around to other industries. This could be because the major problems facing agencies are so specific to the advertising industry.

For instance, cash flow: In order for an agency to take advantage of its commission from the media, it must pay that media within a given amount of time. However, most clients rarely pay on time, leaving the agency to lay out tremendous amounts of income before it comes in. Or production charging: Who pays for unacceptable work? How much commission should be tagged on to work done outside an agency?

While the financial problems here are germane to advertising, this is not the place for anyone interested in an advertising career. However, for someone interested in the financial side of advertising with ambitions toward a career as a financial officer, this is the department to look into.

Television Production (a.k.a. Broadcast) Department. It's the job of the TV production department to supervise the making of the agency's commercials. Depending on the staff and facilities, the TV department of an agency will either be minimally involved in this process—leaving almost all the work to whatever TV production company is chosen for the job—or they may remain quite involved from casting through post-production work. A TV production department at a small agency where little TV is done might consist only of an art director/producer, responsible for art direction as well as for the supervision of TV production. Or it may (and often does at the large agencies) consist of a complete staff of producers, directors, broadcast business administrators, casting people and production assistants. Technical people (e.g., electricians, makeup, carpenters), even at the very big agencies, are supplied on a free-lance basis or by the production company; they are never employed full-time by TV production departments. Some agencies, however, do have actual studios where they shoot auditions and some production work—in which case they will employ some technical people full-time. In general, TV commercial departments exist to coordinate and liaison between the creative department and the production companies. It is a highly popular department and so, once again, competitive as far as job opportunities are concerned. However, there are some entry-level jobs: production assistant, production secretary, casting assistant, assistant to a producer and production bidder. (For a related area, see the section "TV Syndication Department," page 25.)

Research Department. The research department's function is to plan and execute marketing and advertising research that will hopefully minimize the client's mistakes in the marketplace and enable the ad agency to create efficient, successful, on-target advertising. Basically, they deal with market research, product research and copy research. In market research, they ask: Who are the buyers? What are they thinking?

Why do they do what they do? In product research, they find
out how the public relates to a particular product. Does it accomplish what people want? How does the packaging appeal
or distract? Which price is most acceptable? In copy research,
they are concerned with how effective the advertising is. Do
people notice the message? Are they motivated by the words?
Does the jingle work? If not, why not? And, most important,
the research department is responsible for passing what they
learn along to the account, media and creative departments.
Because, before any effective advertising can be created, the
marketing, media and creative people must know exactly who
it is they are talking to and how they are communicating to
them. The research department determines what information
must be secured, then figures out how to get it. They develop a
variety of programs, implement or have implemented a broad
range of studies, analyze the information that has been gathered and pass along their recommendations. Some marketing
departments function as the market research arm for the client.
Others function more to help make their company's advertising as effective as possible. Again, the size and importance of
the research department varies greatly from agency to agency,
with some small agencies farming out all their research to independent research companies and other large agencies maintaining full research staffs. Also, the way research departments
are structured varies from one agency to another. At some,
there are research groups, similar to account groups in that a
group of people concentrate on one client or product. At others, research personnel work on a project-to-project basis on
all agency business. Now, agencies are luring research people
away from other areas of research and from research companies. Increasingly, research specialists (copy research people,
marketing research, statisticians) are found in research departments of ad agencies. There are also many research generalists.
As advertising becomes less and less a hunch/instinct industry
and more and more businesslike, research departments will be
more numerous and important.

Personnel (a.k.a. Human Resources) Department. In general, the personnel area has become a more influential, effective and complex part of the business world and, in particular,
of advertising. The personnel department is responsible for
more than ever before. While the primary responsibility of

most advertising personnel departments is still recruitment, many have expanded their services to staff welfare and training—making it a more interesting and appealing sphere of work. Although personnel is still not considered actual advertising work, it has become, at many agencies, a department more integrated into the scheme of things. This is because the large agencies, as other sectors of American business, have begun to understand the importance of training and the entire human resources area. Also, advertising is a "people-oriented business," with an agency's strength lying in its staff. Therefore, personnel departments of advertising agencies can be most influential. Generally, only large and medium-size agencies have separate personnel departments. Jobs range from secretary to highly paid and educated vice-presidents of personnel.

Public Relations. Most agency public relations divisions are run as independent subsidiary companies. However, some agencies do offer public relations services to their clients: sometimes through a public relations free-lancer who may service more than one ad agency; sometimes through a small internal department of the agency (usually a one- or two-man band); and sometimes through what is called a *corporate communications department* where some public relations functions are handled (e.g., the writing of corporate newsletters, speeches, corporate ads).

Broadcast Business Administration and Operations. These functions fall either within a television production department, an accounting department, a traffic department, or to an independent department. What goes on here is the administration and trafficking of television and radio commercials from pre-production through final broadcast use and reuse. The people in this department liaison with the account groups, production and creative departments, accounting staff, legal staff and outside; with talent agents, union officials, network clearance and continuity people, et al. They are concerned with finding the most efficient and economical ways to produce radio and television commercials and with making sure every project is completed on time and with the necessary approvals and clearances. It's their job to keep track of commercials bids, cost estimates and actuals, to check compensation for talent in commercials, to interpret and administer radio and television talent and labor contracts and to act as liaison to the various labor unions. Jobs range from administrative to supervisory to entry level, with various concentrations: talent payment, labor relations, business control and record-keeping, network clearance and traffic. This is not a well-known area and therefore less competitive than others.

International Department.   Most agencies don't have separate international departments. They handle international clients through the regular channels, that is, by the account group assigned to the business or through a wholly owned subsidiary of the agency (for instance, the JWT Group handles its international clients through J. Walter Thompson International and Euro-Advertising). But in the agencies where an international department does exist to service both American clients in the international marketplace and international clients, the department functions generally to coordinate the agency's international efforts and to deal with its parallel department in the client's organization—that is, the client's international marketing department.

Conference and Trade Show Department.   Again, few agencies maintain a separate department to help their clients put together a conference or exhibit at a trade show. But some do, and in those cases the department functions either by becoming very involved in its client's projects or—and this is more common—by recommending a conference and trade-show specialist for the job and then overseeing that company's work. This is a highly specialized area, and only agencies servicing clients with a need for this maintain such a department. Many agencies are able to handle their client's needs in this area through a sales promotion department or specialist.

Collateral/Sales Promotion Department.   Most advertisers use various kinds of collateral and sales promotion materials, e.g., labels, logos, catalogs, P.O.P. (point of purchase) displays, trade show exhibits, packaging, mailings, brochures, etc. In some cases this material is created and produced the same way ads are, through the creative and production departments; in other cases, the advertiser itself will take responsibility for having such material produced; and sometimes a separate department or subsidiary is set up to handle below-the-line promotions and collateral material for an account. Such departments vary from agency to agency, and might consist of a full staff of graphic designers, sales promotion experts and production people, or one or two traffic people, or maybe one expert in this area. For more information on this field, see Chapter 5, "Places to Work 'in Advertising' Other than an Advertising Agency," page 26.

New Business Department.   A few of the super-size agencies have departments focusing on the very important function of obtaining new business. However, most agencies integrate new business activities into existing channels, with the top people at the agency being responsible for attracting business. At some agencies, particularly recruitment specialists, all account executives are encouraged to solicit new business and are given a commission on any business they do bring into the agency. While there are some people in the industry with particular expertise in the new business area, they are generally experienced, even seasoned advertising veterans, making new business not a good place—at least at the large agencies—for the newcomer.

New Product Development.   In most cases, new product development is handled by advertisers or by companies specializing in the field, or new product development is integrated into other departments. But in a few cases—again, at the very large agencies—departments are set up to help clients generate new products and line extensions. The department, along with the account group, is responsible for scrutinizing the environment in which the new product will have to survive. And, along with the research department, it is also responsible for testing the idea of the product and for working with the creative department in creating and testing advertising concepts. When it is finally clear that the product will be launched, new product development feeds other departments (i.e., the account group, media) involved in that launch with all pertinent data.

TV Syndication Department.   A number of agencies have these departments, whose function it is to buy and/or develop TV programming from independent production companies and then sell it to stations. They sell the TV programming in a variety of ways: on a barter basis, in exchange for commercial time; for cash; or for use as a showcase for their advertiser clients. Some agencies set their syndication arm up as part of a media department, others as a separate department, and quite a few of the super-size agencies set it up as an independent subsidiary of the agency. For example, DDB/Storyteller is a subsidiary of Doyle Dane Bernbach; Lexington Broadcast Services is a subsidiary of Grey Advertising; Dancer Fitzgerald Sample has its Tomorrow Entertainment. Benton & Bowles has gone as far as establishing an independent production company, Telecom Entertainment, where original programming is developed and produced.

More or less, that's the way advertising agencies are structured: into various departments, each one separate but not so equal, dependent on the others to get the work done, requiring particular abilities from its crew. Within an agency itself you will find many different choices and career paths to take. And, there are diversified kinds of advertising agencies to choose among. And, to augment the choice even further, the advertising *industry* consists of a great deal more than just advertising agencies. As a matter of fact, only one-third of the people working in advertising work for the agencies. The rest work for corporations, media houses, production companies, magazine publishers, printers, public relations companies, graphic design companies, premium and incentive companies, etc. Throughout *The Ad Game*, particularly in Chapter 13, "Supporting Service Job Descriptions," you'll find advertising jobs mentioned that are not necessarily with ad agencies. Below is a description of just some of the places these jobs can be found. Needless to say, this is not a complete listing. For that, you'll have to do your own research . . . but it is comprehensive enough to give you a good idea of how large-scale the advertising industry is.

5   Places to Work "in Advertising" Other Than an Advertising Agency

Public Relations Companies. The uninitiated often confuse advertising and public relations. In fact, they are two distinct (yet related) fields. Advertising is the business of convincing the public, through *paid* communications, to buy a product or service. Public relations is the business of spreading the good word. Probably the first public relations effort on record took place to get the Constitution ratified, in 1787. Certainly, politics was one of the first fields to see the benefit of getting favorable "press." And show business was a fast second. We've all seen or read about the importance of the press agent during the heyday of the movies in the 1920s and 1930s. The greatest growth of public relations, however, came during and after World War II. Business and not-for-profit organizations began to see a need for professional help in making certain their messages were reaching the public's attention. Often, the need for professional public relations people was emphasized (and still is) when circumstances created unfavorable reaction from the public. Today, virtually every sector of business and government employs the services of one or another sort of public relations company. While an advertising agency and a PR firm might work together, combining their efforts for the same client, the work is not exactly the same. Public relations organizations are concerned with how an individual or company is viewed by others; it's their job to present their client to the public in whichever way that client wants. Nor are the methods PR firms use to reach their goal the same as the methods employed by advertising. Special events, positive newspaper and magazine articles, speeches, public appearances, etc., are what public relations firms are about. At times, a public relations campaign will include advertising—mostly corporate identification and issue- or advocacy-type advertising. Of course, the tools required in the two fields are often alike: research, writing, imagination, art, media placement. (However, placement of PR material is quite different from media placement in advertising: In the first case, it's placing *unpaid* stories and blurbs.) As of late, the trend has been to uncouple public relations from advertising (although a few agencies still have public relations departments, and some PR firms employ advertising types to produce corporate ads, collateral material, etc.). It is much more common, however, that a large ad agency will own a public relations subsidiary to service its clients—the way the JWT Group owns Hill and Knowlton, or Foote, Cone & Belding owns Carl Byoir & Associates. Public relations agencies are hired by a company or person for a long-term comprehensive program or a one-time, focused project. The larger PR firms are divided into various departments, such as a public issues department, financial relations department, product publicity department, entertainment department. They might have a broadcast and video service department to train clients for television interviews and a research department where they both monitor important news stories that might affect a client's PR program as well as provide data regarding the public's attitude toward a client, and evaluate publicity campaigns. (One PR agency, Ketchum Public Relations, a subsidiary of KM&C International, uses a computer system to measure the effectiveness of its campaigns.) So, the types of jobs available with PR firms are as extensive as with ad agencies. There's creative, account, media, research, production work and more (for specifics, see Parts II–V of this book). Some firms have offices throughout the country (especially in Washington, to assist clients dealing with legislation and to provide lobbying and government relations support). Recently, several PR agencies have expanded their offices outside this country, where it has not been an established function for some time, to Europe, Japan and South America. While there aren't as many types of PR firms as there are ad agencies, there are quite a few different categories. There are the small, medium and large independent PR firms; the subsidiaries of the large ad agencies; the one-person consultants; the press agents servicing the theatrical industry (of those, there are very small offices, medium-size offices and consultants); and there are the specialists who cater to one industry—say, publishing, politics, not-for-profit organizations, or the entertainment industry.

The Media.   Every TV station, radio station, consumer magazine, trade magazine, consumer and trade newspaper employs an advertising staff, to sell advertising and to support the advertising effort. While most jobs are sales—that is, selling time and space to advertising agencies, independent media houses and advertisers—there are also advertising-related jobs with the media in sales promotion, research, public relations and doing actual advertising work, i.e., copywriting and art direction.

TV Commercial Production Companies.   TV commercial production companies are where TV commercials are actually made. They are hired by an ad agency to produce, direct, shoot, edit and score the commercial. Sometimes they actually perform all these tasks themselves; other times, they oversee the work of others, such as independent editors, musical scoring companies or music libraries. Production houses are the places to seek work for those interested in making TV commercials (not writing them—that's handled by the ad agency). Most production companies hire union and non-union technicians (gaffers, grips) on a free-lance project-to-project basis. They also employ some full-time on-staff people. Depending on their size, and the amount of work, that might include one or several producers, directors, casting directors, stylists, production managers and production assistants. Production houses are located in California, Florida and throughout the country—especially where the weather is decent year-round—and in New York.

√*Large Organizations.* Virtually every large corporation, from motion picture studios to breakfast cereal manufacturers, maintains some sort of advertising department, with a marketing director and a full advertising staff. It's their job to do one or the other or both of the following: act as liaison between the company and the company's ad agency or actually produce the company's advertising and sales promotion material. And, at the very top level, to determine marketing and advertising strategy. Large organizations handle their advertising/marketing in one of three ways. One way (the least common) is by forming an in-house agency responsible for all or some of the advertising. Primarily, this is done when a company spends huge amounts of money on its advertising effort and believes it would be more cost-efficient to handle the work itself. By "being" an advertising agency—albeit one with only one client—it can save the approximately 17 percent that agencies charge clients above all production costs and gain the 15 percent commission offered by the media to ad agencies. Far more common is a large organization that has either a marketing/advertising department or product manager system and utilizes the services of one or more advertising agencies to prepare and place its advertising. Where there is a marketing/advertising department (this is usually the case with service organizations such as airline companies), there will be many jobs headed by an advertising manager, and various divisions in that department. For instance: marketing services, media, sales promotion. In the product manager system, there is no advertising department per se, but individuals are in charge of particular brands, with their responsibilities including *all* phases of the marketing of such brands. For instance: development, package design, research and advertising. There will also be an advertising manager who functions as an advertising adviser to those brand managers. In the product manager system, as well as the advertising department system, everybody is in contact with the advertising agency, at their own particular level: the president of the company with the president of the agency, the marketing director with the management supervisor, the group product manager with the account supervisor, the product manager with the account executive, etc. Unless some advertising preparation or placement is done by the organization, most marketing jobs are of the administrative variety. As is often the case, people working in marketing departments of huge corporations do move to the agency side, mostly in account service–type jobs . . . also the reverse is true with advertising account people moving over to marketing departments or brand management jobs with large organizations. The third way large organizations handle their advertising/marketing is on an à la carte basis—that is, forming an in-house agency and using it for certain products (perhaps those which require a lot of creative work but which would not be profitable for an agency to handle) and retaining the services of advertising agencies to handle other products.

Retail Stores. All major department stores (Saks, Bloomingdale's, Macy's) have fully staffed advertising departments to produce much of their advertising, catalogs and other collateral material. With daily ads, and as many as one million catalogs going out monthly, large staffs are required. Some in-house department store advertising departments are larger than many ad agencies. And they employ just about every type of advertising person: senior VPs in charge of advertising, art directors, layout artists, copywriters, mechanical artists, production managers, traffic managers (often called coordinators), media people (known as schedulers), retouchers, PR directors.

Some department stores, like Macy's in New York, even have their own type shop and employ typesetters; and their own photo studios where they employ on-staff photographers; and their own broadcast department where they employ TV commercial producers, directors and various assistants. Most retail advertising departments are divided into various sub-departments with one group of people working on daily newspaper ads, another on catalogs, another on special projects. At any rate, the wide variety of jobs available with retail department stores certainly make them worth consideration by an advertising job-seeker.

Printers. There are several large printing firms and related organizations (e.g., color labs, typesetters, retouchers) that employ people in advertising jobs, most of them in the production area. It's their job to convert mechanicals into actual printed matter: brochures, catalogs, leaflets, sales promotion material. Most jobs with printers are highly technical (e.g., printing machine operators, typesetters), but there are others. Printing companies employ production managers, and salespeople known as "reps." Both these jobs require an interaction with advertising agencies and a tremendous knowledge of the production side of the business. In other words, they are very much a part of the industry.

Graphic Arts and Package Design Companies (a.k.a. Art Studios, Commercial Design Studios). In many ways these organizations are similar to advertising agencies. The big difference is that graphic arts companies are usually not concerned with helping their client formulate a marketing strategy or media plan. They are only concerned with the print creative side of the business. They design logos, collateral material, posters and other visuals. At times they even design ads. There also exist *marketing/design companies* that do get involved in the client's marketing and packaging. And there are companies that specialize in food packaging, such as Lippincott & Margulies, the New York organization that designed the Taster's Choice package. Graphic art, food packaging and marketing design companies are very good places for artists of all sorts to look for work. For those interested in the field, there is a book called *Packaging: The Sixth Sense,* by Ernest Dichty.

Independent Research Supply Firms (a.k.a. the Supplier). Most advertising agencies don't have research departments large enough to conduct actual research—that is, the field work. So they hire independent research companies to do it for them. In other cases, ad agencies use such firms to do all their research work—that is, develop, design and analyze the research as well as conduct it. While some of these independent research supply firms specialize, most do all types of research: market research, political research, broadcast and communications research, attitude and opinion research and, of course, advertising research. Most also use various research methodologies (e.g., telephone research, in-person, focus groups) and service a wide spectrum of clients: ad agencies, PR firms, the media, the advertisers themselves. One of the larger research companies with a major presence in the advertising industry is Yankelovich Skelly and White, Inc.

Miscellany   There are even more spheres of work related to the industry but hardly thought of by the neophyte job-seeker (unless he is lucky enough to know some savvy person). To name just a few: There are the trade associations (see Appendix B, page 219, for specific names) and the award organizations like the Clios; there is the premium and incentive industry (often referred to as "specialty advertising"), and companies which specialize in sweepstakes, contests, games and promotions—Ventura Associates is one of the biggest of these, with offices in New York and Boston; there is the conference and exhibition industry, which has recently been budding since more and more agencies stopped handling this type of work for their clients and have passed it on to specialists; and there's the $700 million outdoor advertising industry—that is, billboards, which can be found as far away as Saudia Arabia (courtesy of United Outdoor Advertising of Saudia Arabia) and throughout the rest of the world (in France, much movie advertising is done this way).

In addition to the above-mentioned TV commercial production companies, there are animation houses, industrial filmmakers, filmstrip and slide presentation companies—and lately there are many new computer graphic companies coming up. In Los Angeles, there is even a company—Associated Film Promotions—that induces film companies to use their clients' products in their movies. They scour film scripts to find scenes where their clients' products might be used (for instance, a can of beer in Burt Reynolds's hand), and then persuade the movie company to use their brands. There are various kinds of talent agencies, representing print models and commercial actors. In New York, there's a company specializing in subway train-card and station posters. The list goes on and on. There are also quite a few advertising professions where you can work on a free-lance basis for all sorts of organizations. Among those are: illustrator, direct mail copywriter, photographer, stylist, home economist, jingle writer, mechanical artist, etc. There are many places, other than ad agencies, for the advertising neophyte or advertising career-changer to look for and find work. All it takes is good research skills, interest and tenacity—but more on that in Part VI, "Finding a Job." Or it may take having the courage to start a business of one's own.

6   Where Is the Advertising Industry?

Advertising is just about everywhere. And everywhere there is advertising, there is the advertising industry. It's truly a worldwide network. Which means, those of you living throughout the country and the world won't necessarily have to move to New York City to find employment. But it should be mentioned here that the capital of advertising is still New York (if not Madison Avenue, from which a lot of agencies have moved due to rent increases!). Most of the major ad agencies have their main offices in New York. Most supporting services are located there, e.g., the media, printing industry, commercial production companies, model agencies. And New York continues to be, as it has always been from the beginning of the ad game, a mecca for young, burgeoning advertising talent. This is not to say, however, that other cities and even countries don't have fine advertising agencies and supporting services. Because they do. And some New York–based agencies have fully staffed branch offices in several cities: for instance, J. Walter Thompson in Chicago, which is as big as if not bigger than the New York office. And Foote, Cone & Belding in San Francisco. There are at least four or five New York agencies with branches in Boston. And several more with some kind of office in Los Angeles. McCann-Erickson has a big office in Atlanta, the business capital of the South and the home of Coca-Cola, one of their major clients. In the same vein, BBD&O has an office in Minneapolis for its client 3M. Other agencies have their main office in whatever city their major client is located and only a branch office in New York. For instance, there's Campbell-Ewald with its home office in Detroit to service the automobile industry; and Ketchum Advertising with a home base in Pittsburgh. As for TV commercial production, while 65 percent of advertising spots are produced in New York, a lot of business is done in Los Angeles and Florida, where the weather is more conducive to year-round location shooting.

America is the birthplace of marketing and advertising, but many European countries and Japan are catching up, at least in the amount of money spent on advertising. In a 1983 study done of eighty-six countries, by Starch INRA Hooper, a research firm, and the International Advertising Federation, it was found that the United States has 51 percent of the world's advertising but that Japan, in second place, was catching up and West Germany was up 38 percent from its past year. What all this means to the job-seeker is an expanded job market-place—a marketplace, however, that in recent years has changed quite a bit, making competition a lot tougher. In the 1960s, many creative people went to Europe and Japan to show agencies there the American way to solve problems. Today, many Europeans and Japanese are coming here to show us a thing or two. The influx is powerfully apparent in the "new wave" TV commercials (e.g., like Chanel No. 5's "Enjoy the Fantasy" spot) that are so ubiquitous. As Europeans achieved a good understanding of what advertising can accomplish, they became more accomplished in the art of advertising, giving Americans interested in working abroad some real competition. Still, there are ways for Americans to find work overseas. One is to work for a U.S. agency with international offices, of which there are many: McCann-Erickson, with 4,465 overseas employees; J. Walter Thompson with 4,769; Ogilvy & Mather with 3,840. While the majority of the world-wide offices of American companies are staffed almost entirely by natives, there are a few jobs left over for Americans—that is, for Americans who speak the language (even minimally) and have American advertising know-how—those who have been trained by an American company.

To sum up, the advertising industry is far-reaching and can be found in practically every corner of the world (even in developing countries: Brazil, for instance, has some very sophisticated agencies). Certainly it can be found in the major American cities. But the center is still New York, and for those hoping to make it big, the center is where they belong.

PART II

CLIENT MARKETING

The Client Marketing Jobs

The advertising industry exists to service its clients, the advertisers. Advertisers employ people within their organizations to market their products or services. These employees act as a link between the company and its sales force on the one hand, and the advertising agency on the other. Representing their company, these people are advertising's *raison d'être* and the provocation of all that happens.

Note: Marketing/advertising job responsibilities on the client side vary greatly from one corporation to another. Mainly dependent on how a corporation utilizes the services of an ad agency: giving them total responsibility, using them and other suppliers on an à la carte basis—that is, using only certain of their services—or not using them at all, preferring an in-house agency. Also, jobs on the client side are influenced by whether a corporation practices the *product brand manager system* (whereby one person and his assistants run the marketing of a single brand as if it were an independent company) or some other system—usually a version of an advertising department, with individuals being responsible for specific functions: collateral material, media payment, etc. Therefore, the following jobs aren't as "neat" or definitive as those in other parts of the book, particularly Parts III and IV.

7 Client Marketing Job Descriptions

Advertising Assistant.   Several large corporations have some sort of entry-level advertising job, either as assistant brand manager or advertising assistant. The job of advertising assistant is basically a training position providing knowledge of and initial experience in responsibilities of an advertising executive. It gives supervisors an opportunity to observe the assistant and appraise his performance, with particular attention to his creative and innovative abilities. The person reports to an advertising manager, promotions manager, brand manager, marketing manager, etc. In order to qualify for such a position a person must have a basic understanding of the function of advertising and promotion in marketing, and of the business of the corporation. This understanding can have been gained in an academic environment.

Advertising Manager.   The advertising manager reports to the marketing director and is regarded, depending on the company's structure for the management of the advertising function (i.e., the product manager system or advertising department), as the staff specialist with decision-making authority, or the link between the company's marketing director and sales force on the one hand and the ad agency on the other. In both cases the ad manager influences how advertising is made, but he doesn't make it—the agency does that. In the product manager system, the advertising manager serves as an adviser to all product managers. That is, since the product managers have other duties in addition to advertising, and are rarely advertising experts, the advertising manager provides advice and counsel on all matters pertaining to advertising (creative, media, sales promotion) and usually enjoys greater influence within the organization on such matters. Every marketing plan and advertising plan is submitted to him for critical review and comment. He participates in all meetings with the product manager and the advertising agency, and expresses his agreement or disagreement with any agency recommendations. He

37

is involved in creative and media approvals, and often serves as a technical adviser to the marketing director. When there is an advertising department, the advertising manager is head of that department and supervises all its activities and personnel (i.e., approval systems, budget control, work flow). He is accountable only to the marketing director of the company. Many marketing directors come from the ranks of advertising managers. In some corporations, there exists the job of *assistant advertising manager*, perhaps being in charge of a particular liaison with the agency: for instance, media payment, production, creative.

Brand (a.k.a. Product) Manager. The brand manager has complete responsibility for the success of his brand or product. For example, a brand manager working for R. J. Reynolds Corporation might be responsible for the complete marketing of Camel cigarettes, while a different brand manager will be responsible for another of Reynolds's brands. A *group brand manager* (known as a "grouper") is responsible for more than one brand and oversees the brand manager. Brand managers are responsible for all aspects of their brands' marketing: advertising, product development and research, package design, sales promotion, business forecasting, etc., and they generally have *assistant brand managers* and internal staff members to help them (chief among those is the advertising manager). Specific product management responsibilities include: development of marketing plans and the building of objectives and strategies for sales and profit; control and supervision of the implementation of brand plans; reviewing brand objectives, advertising and promotional expenditures, and approval and control of financial commitments; recommending brand sales and profit goals to management; development and analysis of trends of product categories, competitive product entries and consumer usage and attitudes in liaison with marketing research, sales and advertising agencies; recommending long-range brand plans; approving copy and media objectives in conjunction with advertising agencies and ad manager and approving and directing the execution of those strategies; directing the development and coordination of brand promotions with the promotion and sales departments; developing and recommending packaging form and design with packaging design department and/or agency; developing and recommending selling prices;

recommending sales forecasts from which production schedules and costs of goods are determined.

Product managers hold important positions and must have all-around marketing know-how. Most start their careers as assistant product managers or assistant account executives with an ad agency. (The two jobs, account executive and brand manager, are similar and interface on a close daily basis.) These days a brand manager is expected to have an MBA.

Consultants. Large organizations sometimes employ consultants with various expertise to advise and/or oversee specific operations. For instance, a company might employ someone to consult on TV production costs, to review their agency's recommendations and provide an outside opinion. Or they might employ a research consultant to oversee field work and to supplement their own and/or their agency's research department. Some corporations employ former agency people as advertising consultants when they are looking for a new advertising agency. This work is usually part-time or temporary, and only for those with expertise in a particular discipline—usually gained while working in a previous career. It is a potentially lucrative occupation, but again, only for the experienced, even a seasoned career-changer.

Corporate Media Manager. Some corporations that are being serviced by advertising agency media departments employ someone to act as a prime contact between the company and its agencies in media matters. It's this person's responsibility to give direction to agency media planners, to review all media plans developed by the agency and to administer the execution of all media buying by the agency. Media managers regularly measure the performance of media and agencies to be certain that objectives and plans are being met. They maintain financial control over media budgets by reviewing expenditures and future plans. They review all media plans to ensure they conform to brand requirements, and obtain management approval of each recommendation prior to allowing the agency to proceed with a purchase. Media managers stay abreast of latest media developments via trade magazines, contacts with media representatives and agency media personnel, and advise and support the advertising manager or director on all matters pertaining to media. For related jobs, see the section "Media Jobs," page 69.

Corporate Production Manager.   Some corporations employ
a print production staff to be responsible for the production of
all printed promotional material. This production staff functions very much like an agency production and/or traffic staff
(see Chapter 11, "Agency Creative and Production Job Descriptions," page 95). They schedule production of all advertising material (booklets, catalogs, house newsletters) as well as
ads, correlating the time schedules with the production facili
ties. They oversee the work of engravers, advertising agency,
printers and other suppliers. They conduct follow-up with artists, photographers and printers to ensure proper progress of
the various jobs. A corporate production manager must be an
individual with a broad knowledge of the mechanics of printing
and engraving. This experience can be gained at an ad agency,
art studio or printing company.

Corporate Public Relations Executive.   This job varies from
one corporation to another. In some it holds full responsibilities; in others, it's an internal public relations job; and in others
it's more of a customer relations than a public relations job.
And sometimes, when a public relations firm or arm of an
agency is heavily involved, it's a liaison job. At any rate, the
following is a description of a public relations job with full
responsibilities. It's the public relations director's job to prepare various forms of communication to internal and external
audiences, in order to create public awareness of the company
as a leading producer of quality products or services, as a desirable member of the community, and—when the company is a
public corporation—as a choice investment. In short, to create
a corporate image. He prepares and disseminates corporate,
product and operational news material to trade and consumer
media. He prepares shareholder communications (including
quarterly and annual reports), working with officers of the
company and creative staff. He writes speeches and prepares
material for presentation by officers of the company. He supervises community and employee relations activities, including
preparing and producing an internal newsletter and employee
information material. He writes and assists other executives to
write booklets, pamphlets, handbooks, newsletters and similar
internal and external communications. He helps plan, organize
and publicize major press conferences and special events, and
he maintains good relations with members of the press. He may

be assisted in his duties by a *public relations writer/assistant,* and may work with outside public relations counsel and/or an advertising director in developing programs and publicity. For further information, see the section "Public Relations Jobs," page 76.

Corporate Research Director. The marketing research director and staff (e.g., *analysts, assistants*) of a corporation might function on a number of levels. They could be employed primarily to act as an in-house service arm of an advertising agency. Or they could be employed to plan, suggest and implement research programs, working either with an outside supply firm or with internal staff who conduct the actual research. (Some corporations maintain huge research staffs.) Also, they could be employed to work with new product managers and others concerned with research and development. In any case, the basic job descriptions are similar to those research jobs described in Part III, "Agency Administration and Account Services," and Part V, "Supporting Services," with the major difference being, it's the corporate research person's responsibility to communicate with all internal departments in order to ascertain research needs. For instance: with the product manager to acquire information on product changes, promotional policies, marketing activities and views on sales and expected returns from various programs; with the sales department to acquire competitive activity information; with the advertising manager to acquire information on advertising formats, themes and media.

All corporate research positions require knowledge of and experience in research techniques. A good entry-level job here is that of *marketing trainee.* However, most research jobs on the client side are not on an entry level. Those can be found with the suppliers (see Part V, "Supporting Services") and with those few giant corporations that have large staffs.

Creative Scientist. A few of the major advertisers (e.g., Standard Brands) as well as advertising agencies employ biochemists, pharmacists and others to translate information on products and competitors' products into layman's language for the creative staff and/or product managers to help them to develop marketing and creative strategies. A good example of this work is what happened when Maybelline wanted to play up that their polish was chip-resistant. It was a "creative scien-

tist," Stanley De Nisco at Ted Bates, who thought up the idea
of painting Ping-Pong balls with the nail polish and playing
Ping-Pong with them in a TV commercial. In addition to working with the creative staff, creative scientists work closely with
a company's legal department, since it's the responsibility of an
agency and client to make only true claims. Also, creative
scientists work closely with new product development people.
This job is obviously only for the well trained scientist with a
creative flair. It might be good for scientists looking for a career change.

In-House Agency Jobs.   An in-house agency is one set up as
an autonomous arm to a large corporation. It functions just as
any agency does, with one exception: it serves but one client,
itself. In some cases an in-house agency will be responsible for
all advertising for its company; in other cases—for instance,
Revlon's in-house agency—some assignments will be handled
in-house while others will be delegated to an outside agency.
Sometimes, only an in-house creative department will exist—
this to save the 17.65 percent additional charges ad agencies
bill their clients over and above production costs. Other times,
only an in-house media department will exist, again to save
money. Depending on whether the agency is full-service, there
will be a full or partial staff. In a full-service situation, there is a
media, creative, production, promotion, marketing and *public relations* staff, just as one would find at an ad agency. For specific
job descriptions, look throughout this book.

Marketing Director.   The marketing director of a corporation has complete responsibility for the market function—in
most cases answering only to the chief executive officer or general manager of that company. It is the marketing director's
awesome responsibility to formulate marketing objectives, to
build and operate a smoothly functioning marketing organization, to approve or sometimes formulate the marketing strategy by which the objectives are to be achieved (this in conjunction with his ad agency) and to work with the special
groups within his organization and without that carry out the
various marketing activities. One of his most important responsibilities is the selection and supervision of his aides: the advertising director, the product managers, the promotion manager,
the research director and sometimes the sales manager. (In
some organizations the sales manager has status equal to the

marketing director's.) Another crucial task of the marketing director is his selection of an ad agency or agencies. And while the marketing director isn't always an advertising expert, he must thoroughly understand advertising and know how it works and what it can accomplish. For it is his job not only to decide the specific objectives of the advertising, but also to delegate authority and to give final approval of all advertising preparation and placement. Who the marketing director gives authority to depends largely on how the company is organized—whether there is a centralized department or a product management system. In the first case, the advertising director is given line responsibility for the advertising function and has the authority to make the day-to-day advertising decisions (see the section "Advertising Manager," page 37); in the second case, the product manager, in consultation with an ad director, has the responsibility (see the section "Brand (a.k.a. Product) Manager," page 38). The job of marketing director is top-of-the-line on the client side of advertising, and as such, requires much experience and knowledge of marketing. Not only must the marketing director know about the product or service his organization offers, he must know about pricing, packaging, distribution, advertising, selling, promotion and research. For further information on this job, see Chapter 8, "Profile of a Marketing Director," page 46.

New Product Development Manager. Several people are usually employed by a company to be responsible for new product development and research. These individuals work with the marketing research department, packaging development department, product managers and advertising agencies to ensure that new product plans are being influenced by the best thinking available on particular issues. They are responsible for determining feasibility, cost and timing on new items and products. They work with the company's sales force to ensure effective development and implementation of pricing, packaging, promotional programs and new product introductions. They outline—usually for the head of their company—new product opportunities and participate in the development of overall long- and short-range business strategies on new products. To minimize the risk of a new product failure, the new product development manager works with his own staff, the advertising agency research staff and/or a new product development company (see Part V, "Supporting Services," for more on that) to test and rate all new product ideas. The first stage of this testing usually includes marketing research. At the second stage of product development, actual samples of the new product are made up and used for consumer testing. If the product passes this stage, test-marketing begins. In test-marketing, the product is marketed to consumers as though it were actually being introduced to the public. But instead of marketing it throughout the country, it is sold only in several small "test" markets. Sales statistics are then gathered and carefully analyzed. At this point, the new product development manager makes his final recommendation. While this is not an advertising job per se, it is a job that interfaces with many advertising functions.

Package Design Manager. The package design manager and his staff are responsible for planning, directing and coordinating package design projects from concept development through to finished design production. He collaborates with the *product managers, package design research experts, package designers* and creative agencies in the development of package structure and design—for new products and for modification of existing packaging. He evaluates each design proposal for feasibility, compatibility with marketing strategies, effectiveness in promoting sales and projection of desired corporate image to consumers. He conducts cost analyses, develops and monitors package design budgets and establishes timetables for projects. It's his job to get sample packages made—for marketing, advertising and sales promotion tests—and to supervise the work of the internal package designer and production department. Or, if creative package design companies are used, he selects those, as well as photographers, printers, etc., and directs and approves all creative activities in connection with design projects. Because packaging operates under rapid change and increased government regulation, the packaging manager must also understand the environment in which the packaging will compete and all regulations affecting advertising and packaging.

Product Manager. See the section "Brand (a.k.a. Product) Manager," page 38.

Retail Store Jobs. Most retail stores prepare and place their own advertising and maintain an advertising/promotion department, with a vice-president in charge. All kinds of advertising jobs can be had here: marketing, creative, media, production, publicity. (For specific job descriptions, see Parts III–V of this book.) The head of the department establishes budgets and determines what kind of advertising can be most effectively used. He may work with an outside ad agency, free-lancers and production houses to produce the advertising, depending on his staff and needs at a particular time. One of the most consuming retail advertising jobs is that of preparing the enormous quantities of the frequently used store catalog.

Sales Promotion Manager. The sales promotion manager of a corporation, and his staff (*display manager, promotion supervisors* and *assistants*), are responsible for the coordination, development and execution of corporate sales promotion and promotional events. They may have the assistance of an advertising agency sales promotion department and/or an outside sales promotion company. Corporate sales promotion people work closely with product managers, ad managers and the sales staff in determining their company's sales promotion needs. They develop promotional approaches and concepts within the framework of overall marketing objectives and then select agencies, outside vendors, free-lance artists, or whatever and whoever is necessary for implementing their concepts. (Concepts might include a sweepstakes, contest, novelty gifts, giveaways, premiums, displays, exhibitions, collateral material.) Heavy daily contact with outside vendors to discuss and supervise production of promotions is usually a large part of this job. The position generally requires sales promotion experience, gained either at an advertising agency, supplier or other corporation. For further information, see the section "Sales Promotion Manager," page 106.

Specialty Jobs. There are jobs in advertising on the client side that are germane to a particular industry. For instance, in movie marketing departments there is a person responsible for the creation of "trailers," two- to three-minute previews of a movie shown to movie audiences. It would be impossible to mention all of these jobs here, but if you are interested in a particular industry and want to work in its marketing division, pay close attention to the ways in which they advertise and figure out what these specialty jobs are. For more on ways to research a job title, see Part VI, "Finding a Job."

8 Profile of a Marketing Director

Gordon Weaver, President, Worldwide Marketing, Paramount Pictures

Every large company in the United States employs someone to be ultimately responsible for its marketing and advertising. Sometimes that person is referred to as the "advertising manager," other times as the "director of marketing," or maybe "senior vice-president in charge of marketing." Whatever the title, it's this person's awesome responsibility to ensure that every product his company produces is effectively and successfully marketed and that the advertising agency he chooses to help in this task does the best possible job. Gordon Weaver has that responsibility at Paramount Pictures.

Because the product his company produces is motion pictures, it's Gordon's job to develop strategies and choose publicity and advertising that will sell people on Paramount films. Since, lately, in most cases it costs as much to market a film as it does to make one, and since advertising and marketing are crucial to a movie company, being head of marketing at a movie company is as important and pressured a job as you're likely to find, certainly on the client side of the advertising industry.

Like his counterpart at a packaged goods company, a movie company marketing president works with his organization's sales force and development people, his own internal staff, and with outside ad agencies (that he has chosen) in order to sell his company's wares. Unlike his packaged goods counterpart, he is dealing with maybe twenty "new" products a year (as opposed to two or three); he has the opening weekend of a movie in which to make or break it; and in essence he is selling nothing but an experience, an intangible. Also, there's this added pressure: good advertising can't save a bad product, but it can save a risky movie, or at the very least, help recover its costs.

Gordon Weaver describes the job this way:

"It's my job to expose people to the possibility, if they come to see a particular film, of touching magic. What I do is show them they can, for two hours, be isolated from the world and experience things and emotions that they've never experienced before . . . and make that a very attractive thing for the audience. I'm selling magic. You can't touch it, feel it or smell it, and you can't take it home with you. Whenever anyone asks what it is I do, I say, 'Anything you read or hear or know about Paramount Pictures, I have caused to happen. So, if you see a billboard somewhere or a leaflet, or a TV commercial, or [hear] a radio spot or have seen someone on a talk show or read a newspaper advertisement, it has emanated from Paramount's marketing department. As head of that department, I initiated and/or supervised its appearance.'"

Movie advertising is a job Gordon wanted since he was a boy—back in Farmerville, Louisiana. He knew that even before he knew that it was called marketing.

"I grew up in Farmerville, population two thousand. For some strange reason, I decided, when I was in the ninth grade, that what I wanted to be was the person at a motion picture company who created the ads and publicity. I had no idea what that person was called, nor did anyone in my family. Certainly no one at school knew anything about it. Farmerville was the kind of town where most forms of entertainment were considered dirty; even dancing in public was frowned upon. But for some reason I had this interest. When I was fourteen or fifteen I convinced my father, who ran a small restaurant, the kind you'd find in *The Last Picture Show*, to advertise in the weekly local paper. My idea was to reprint the menu, without changing a thing, in French. Of course, no one in town spoke a word of French, but suddenly the menu was something special and his business tripled. Also, as a youngster, I was always volunteering to do the publicity for the 4H Club or for the school dance. And I was forever hanging around the local radio station in nearby Monroe to find out what this magic was all about and how people sell things."

It's a long way from the Farmerville 4H Club to Paramount Pictures; and Gordon knew, somehow, that his first steps should be toward the center of advertising and the entertainment industry . . . New York.

"No one at Louisiana Tech knew a thing about what I wanted

to do, so I knew it was up to me to make it my business to find out. I applied to NYU, to their business school, for marketing and advertising, got accepted and came to New York. NYU was real good for me in a number of ways. One, it was a terrific way to make the transition from small town to big city. Two, it certainly taught me some basic crafts. And three, and perhaps most important, it enabled me to be exposed to ad agencies, theaters, movies, television and all the other media of which New York is the center. I made it a point to find out all I could about each area. So while I came to study at NYU, I ended up studying the city as well. My goal never changed and I knew it was important for me to soak up as much as possible while I was in this transitional stage.

"I was very short on money and had to work seven days a week while going to school. I reached the point where I couldn't handle that schedule and had to quit NYU before graduating. I took the first job I could get, which was as a traffic manager at McCann-Erickson [advertising agency]. I was quite certain I wouldn't make traffic my life's work, but I thought that at least I'd be able to get some idea of what went on in an ad agency."

Shortly afterward, Gordon was drafted into the army, where again he was drawn to advertising activities. He wrote copy, helped produce some TV commercials and training films and generally made himself available to the army's marketing staff (yes, even the army has one). He came out with a stronger determination than ever to do movie advertising. Then, instinctively again, he did all the right things, the first of which was looking for a job as a job in itself.

"I borrowed money from a credit union to produce this very elaborate resumé. Since my experience had been limited, I decided to do the resumé in a joking way, pretending my 4H Club work raising pigs back home was real good experience for what I wanted to do. The resumé consisted of a five-part mailer with photographs and other visuals. I sent it to about four hundred people, each one identified by name, and not one to the personnel department.

At the public library I researched the names of the people who could hire me and the names of companies I wanted to work for. With the twelve companies I was most interested in, I also found out the name of the secretary to the person I

Gordon Weaver, president, worldwide marketing, Paramount Pictures, with ad for *Flashdance*. *(Raoul Gatchalian)*

mailed the resumé to. I sent each a telegram which in effect said, 'Do me a favor and give my resumé to your boss. You never know, I might end up working here and could be in a position to return the favor some day!' I figured I had to market myself in order to prove I had ability . . . and part of marketing myself was identifying the potential customer."

Gordon did a fine job marketing himself. Two hundred people responded to the four hundred resumés; twenty-two of those offered him a job interview; and eleven offered him a job. One of the final offers was from MGM, in their publicity department.

"During my MGM interview I was asked if I had heard of a book *The Haunting* or of its author, Shirley Jackson. I said I had, and the man interviewing me said, 'Great, because we're making it into a movie and I'm considering you to work on the advertising and publicity for it.' I immediately went out and bought and read a copy of the book and was in fact offered that job. I had never done any of what I was being hired for, but I figured I could do it as well as anybody else. I had jumped right in. Movie companies were different then—more work was done in-house—so I got to do everything: planning, publicity, creating advertisements, producing promotional material. It was wonderful. My first real campaign! I learned as I went along, asking questions and taking it all in. I think the reason I was able to catch on despite my lack of experience was that I had a real instinct for this kind of work."

Perhaps it was just that instinct that showed Gordon how to turn a mistake into a glorious piece of luck.

"We sent out a publicity release with the words *The Haunting* printed on the outside of the envelope. Fine—except the mailroom left out the publicity release, so when people opened it there was nothing inside. Everyone thought it was a terrifically interesting promotional idea, and I wasn't about to say it was a mistake. I said, 'Thank you very much, I'm glad you like it.' Anyway, *The Haunting* campaign was a big success."

And Gordon was on his way. While at MGM he did what any good advertising manager ought to do, whether he's selling tickets to movies or soda pop. He got to know the business he was involved in, particularly the sales network, not only from an advertising point of view but from every point. He learned how and why you book a movie in one theater and not another, how contracts are drawn up, how theater owners operate, and he grew in his capacity to handle responsibility, which is, after all, the "secret" to success. When someone was needed to go down to Mexico and work as a publicist on the John Frankenheimer film *The Extraordinary Seamen,* Gordon was chosen.

"I had never done any publicity work before, but I suddenly found myself in the jungle with a typewriter in front of me. Again, since I wasn't aware of what I couldn't do, I figured I could do anything. Perhaps had I had more formal training or been brought up in New York and been more street-wise I wouldn't have had that attitude. Because I didn't know much, I kept using my hometown as a point of reference. I'd ask myself what would they like to know about this film and its stars back in Farmerville. And that worked. The stories I wrote about Faye Dunaway's beauty secrets or Mickey Rooney's wives were interesting to people around the country. And the editors of the local papers were quite receptive to what I was sending them. So, I learned how to write copy, how to do interviews and deal with stars, and how to operate in a foreign country."

When Frankenheimer needed a senior publicist for his next project, to be shot in Budapest, he asked Gordon, who gladly packed up his wife, daughter and newborn son and moved with the company to Hungary for seven months.

"In Budapest, the situation was different. It was a fairly big-time operation. There was an assistant publicist, two secretaries—one English, one Hungarian—and a lot of visiting press. But I did the same thing—trying to make contacts around the country. I'd write the Dallas *Times Herald* and say, 'Here I am in Budapest; what can I write for you on an exclusive basis?' I wrote personalized stories for newspapers all over the country, always keeping in mind to write things people *really* wanted to read about as opposed to what people in New York at the home office thought people wanted to read about. To this day I always make that distinction. I tell my staff that while we work in New York and Los Angeles, our world is between those two places. I encourage them to take the time, whenever they have an out-of-town appointment, to walk around, stay at a motel, go to the local supermarket, read the local paper and listen to the local TV and radio. This gives you a sense of what real people in this world are doing, which you can't get living and working in New York or Los Angeles."

Gordon enjoyed his European stint so much that he was considering remaining there as the head of European publicity for MGM. But when he was offered a job as head of advertising and publicity for a new film company, Cinema Center Films, that CBS was forming, he said yes. At Cinema Center, Gordon would be responsible for not just one but all their films. And so, it was with this job Gordon learned what was meant by movie marketing, and what it was to head up such a department.

"This was a job where I would really be creating advertising and publicity, where I would be working with a big-time ad agency as a real client. Our first agency was Jack Tinker & Partners; then we went to Ogilvy & Mather. A large part of the job was creating a marketing strategy for whatever films Cinema Center Films was producing, then convincing a producer, or director, or even a star, that my point of view regarding selling his film was correct, and that we, the studio, would do a good job marketing-wise. Its ability to market a film is probably the second most important thing a studio can offer film-makers (the first being money). Therefore, if you want to keep those filmmakers with your studio (creative people work for studios on an independent basis), you have to convince them you can do a good job marketing their film. Many producers and directors approach working with the studios with some apprehension, because suddenly their film—one that they've been working on for years—becomes one of twenty films released that year, part of a release schedule. So what I started to do then, and continue to do today, is work closely with producers, directors and stars in determining how we will handle each film and making them comfortable with the way the marketing department works. Also, something else I found out during that time is that one's personal opinion and one's professional opinion are entirely different things. Whether a marketing director likes a film should have nothing whatsoever to do with his ability to successfully market it."

In 1971 Gordon was approached by Paramount Pictures. They were looking for someone to head up their publicity department. At about the same time Cinema Center moved out to California. He was interviewed at Paramount and was offered the job, at a considerably higher salary than he was getting at CBS. He accepted. A couple of days before he was to move to

Paramount, someone called to say they had some difficulties giving him the salary they had agreed upon. To some, this would appear to be an act of bad faith. Gordon said, "Fine, no problem. However, if I turn out to be as good as I think I'll be, when it comes time to give me an increase, you're going to have to give me much more than you originally said." Obviously Gordon turned out to be as good as he thought he would be, even better. Three years later he was named a vice-president, then he took a detour and became assistant to Paramount's chairman, and eventually he was asked to head up Paramount's marketing department, which encompasses all aspects of marketing: advertising, publicity, promotion and sales. Except for eighteen months in 1978–79 when, with partner Steve Rose, he formed Barrich Productions to produce pictures for Paramount, Gordon has remained their man in charge of marketing. Today, as president in charge of worldwide marketing, his responsibilities have taken on international scope. Answering to him are various vice-presidents in charge of advertising, publicity, promotion, etc., a large internal staff including production people, publicists, and media coordinators, and the staffs of forty-six advertising agencies across the country.

For creative assignments (i.e., print ads, TV commercials, trailers), Gordon uses two primary agencies: Diener-Hauser-Bates, the entertainment advertising subsidiary of Ted Bates, and Spiro & Associates, and various smaller shops—some having five to ten people, others just one or two. (No movie company retains only one agency for all its projects; typically, assignments are given out picture to picture.) Most times, Gordon will give out the same work to more than one agency simultaneously to get as many points of view on a picture as he can.

"Ultimately," he says, "I have to make the decision as to which way to go, but the more information I have, the more input, the more points of view I get from big agencies, small creative shops, and the people working on the TV commercials, the trailers, the more clearly a concept begins to emerge. It may turn out you get copy from one place, a visual from another, a logo design from somewhere else. Creating a campaign is a constant process of communication between me and my staff and the management and staff at the various agencies we deal with. I communicate with everyone, formally at meetings, informally all the time. Also, I'm always in touch with our sales organizations and show them the ads and TV spots. I also work with them in determining where to advertise, which depends on where they've booked the film. And of course, early on, even before a film is made and throughout the process, I meet with the filmmaker—that is, the producer, director and/or star. We often have a fairly well-defined plan, one that's obviously subject to change, two years in advance of a release of a film.

"In the early stages of a campaign I'm not selling tickets. Rather, I'm trying to create an image around the country, getting people interested. You keep adding layers. First is the publicity campaign: people on talk shows, stories in newspapers and magazines, press junkets, screenings, things to get word of mouth going. Then there's the advertising. Advertising brings the product to the attention of the public. What we try to do with it is tell a story in a short, concise, straightforward way, so that the public can understand what the movie is about and why they should go see it. In *An Officer and a Gentleman,* for instance, we told the audience that seeing it would make them feel terrific, give them an "up." Our whole campaign was designed to have people come out of the theater saying, 'That really was a good old-fashioned film that makes you feel good.' Which in fact is what they did say. And when word of mouth reflects our original advertising ideas, it means we have a very successful campaign indeed. When we have enough lead time, we try to first get the attention of that one percent of the population whose opinion everyone respects. Obviously that only works with certain films. With others, our advertising is aimed at particular groups; and with still others we try to bring out whatever in a movie we think will appeal to various groups. Which means we generally develop a number of campaigns for a film, those that are directed at target audiences and those that are planned for various times (preview time, to open a film, to support it and so on). At any rate, there are many, many things to do to propel people into saying, 'Gee, I want to go see that movie.' "

In addition to the New York ad agencies, Gordon retains over forty regional agencies. "For media and publicity, it is important to have a local presence," he explains. "I don't know the most popular talk show in Biloxi, Mississippi, and neither

Ad for *An Officer and a Gentleman* (copyright © 1982 by Paramount Pictures), Gordon Weaver, president, worldwide marketing.

does my New York ad agency. And I don't want to wait until it gets published in some media guide. Using local ad agencies, we can assure local exhibitors that Paramount is supporting the film in an appropriate and immediate way."

Keenly aware of the importance of reaching small-town U.S.A., Gordon is no less aware of the international market. He spends a good portion of his time on and in the international front, addressing foreign sales, marketing, exhibition and publicity people. This he accomplishes in two ways—by traveling abroad and by a kind of international teleconferencing. Every six weeks or so he sends around the world, to the Paramount offices and support agencies, an hour-and-one-half videotape that he appears in. The main purpose of these tapes is a sharing of information. On tape he describes the development of the original campaigns so that his international people can find the particular strategy (ad trailer, or promotion) that would be valid in the marketing of the film in their territory. As the international market is crucial to the success of a movie, so it is important to Gordon Weaver, head of *worldwide* marketing.

Gordon was lucky in that, early on, he knew what he wanted to do. But his finding out how to do it, and then actually doing it, had nothing to do with luck. Gordon succeeded because, yes, he had a clear-cut career goal, but also because he had guts and determination and something very important in this so-called glamour business—a strong sense of reality. Asked how it feels to be where he is, to have realized his dreams, Gordon replies:

"I'm very thankful to be doing what I started out wanting to do. And I'm very much aware how wonderful it is, coming here to this fabulous carnival every day where I have all these marvelous resources at my disposal: ad agencies, creative people, a huge budget, and jetting all over the world, and what have you. But, I am just as aware how important it is not to get carried away with it all. Because once I do, then I start doing advertisements to please the chairman of the board instead of to get the people in Monroe, Louisiana, in to see a Paramount movie."

If he were advising others who are interested in working on the "client side" of movie advertising, Gordon would say if you're interested, make the effort to show it:

"A lot of people approach us for the wrong reasons. They

come because they want to work in a glamorous business. Yes, this is a glamorous business, but only to those who love the work. We're the ones who create the glamour. Behind it is dumb-ass hard work, real hard work. They look at the finished product, not at the three hundred cities, forty-six ad agencies, *x* number of TV stations, magazines, newspapers and local standards we have to deal with in order to create the so-called glamour. Truthfully, I find it difficult to find terrific people, people with a real instinct and love for the work, which to me is more important than if they have an MBA from Harvard. One reason, of course, is that people still think of advertising as only Madison Avenue, which it is not. Most large companies have marketing departments, certainly all the movie studios do. The people who most interest me are those who've bothered to find out who we are, what we've done. I think back on my own experience . . . how I typed those four hundred letters and addressed the envelopes . . . how I researched company structures and the names of those I wanted to work for. I'm impressed when someone does something special like that, something with style to get my attention. I'm not suggesting that everyone go out and do skywriting, just that they do something that demonstrates who they are and what their ability is."

And Gordon has these final words about working in advertising for a movie company:

"First of all, you should be aware that in this business, every day is like living your life on the edge of a razor. Someone once asked me how often my contract came up for renewal. I said every half hour. And that's true. They love a campaign, they hate a campaign; they love one, hate the next. If you're the type of person who melts every time someone doesn't like your work, you will not last. Campaigns can always be redone, and no matter how good one is, it still won't feed hungry children in India, so you must keep things in perspective. I do think, however, that you must have the ability to experience and believe in the magic that this business produces, because that's what we're selling—magic. And if you don't believe in it, well then, you won't be able to sell it."

PART III

AGENCY ADMINISTRATION
AND ACCOUNT SERVICES

The Administrators and Account Service People

Advertising's administrators and account service people manage agencies, guard the client/agency relationship, conceptualize marketing and media strategy, and intercommunicate with everyone involved in the advertising process. They are advertising's organizers, developers and conduits.

9 Agency Administration and Account Service Job Descriptions

Account Management Jobs. Account people do just what their job title indicates—that is, they manage the accounts, acting as liaison between agency and client. Clients look to account management people for marketing and business consultation. Creative people look to the account group for product information, market analysis and time schedules. Agency management holds account management people responsible for account profitability. Account management people write the market plan (the report which recommends how to market and advertise a product or service), coordinate the development of the advertising program, present that program to the client and follow through to see to it that the approved program is implemented. At the small agencies there may only be one or two account service people responsible for these tasks. At the larger agencies, each assignment is handled by an account group, with every member of that group having a counterpart on the client side; the higher up the account person, the higher up his client contact. Typically, an account group consists of a *management supervisor, account supervisor, account executive, assistant account executive, account coordinator* and two or three *account secretary/assistants.* Each title is described below. In addition, at some agencies, at the very top, there is a *management representative* who reports to the president and is responsible for assuring top-quality account management work; for mediating impasse discussions between account management, creative and media personnel; and for representing the agency with senior client management. Some agencies also employ *field account executives,* who travel a geographic territory calling on retail stores to explain the advertising and merchandising programs of their clients. Field A.E.'s and their managers are usually required to have sales promotion, merchandising and/or retail experience. Most agencies look for

MBAs or the equivalent (BS/BA plus experience) from upper-level account people. The agencies want organized, analytical, persuasive and inspirational people who are, in addition, creative, innovative and self-starting. They ask that account people have well-developed interpersonal skills, be self-confident and flexible. They must also have sound management skills and the ability to direct and motivate people, at least for the upper- and middle level jobs. Of course, they must be effective speakers; clear, concise business writers; and good evaluators of advertising solutions. For further information on account management jobs, see the profile of Ken Angel, management supervisor on R. J. Reynolds for BBD&O, in Chapter 10, page 82.

Management Supervisor. A management supervisor handles a number of clients and supervises a number of account groups at the same time. As head of account groups, the management supervisor is responsible for managing them, the resources of the agency (e.g., research and creative) and the clients—in order to produce for his clients the best possible work; to satisfy the clients; and to ensure a profit for his employer, the advertising agency. Managing supervisors are responsible for managing, organizing and controlling all aspects of their accounts and for managing the account personnel involved. They are also responsible for knowing everything that affects their clients' business and for keeping current on trends in advertising. It's the managing supervisor's job to initiate the advertising planning process, to coordinate with client and agency staff the advertising plan, to continuously review and comment on the development of the advertising plan, to direct and contribute to the presentation of that plan to agency management and the client. It's also his responsibility to coordinate with the various department heads on the selection of the best people for specific assignments and projects. The managing supervisor prepares the account group's salary budget and monitors all expenses. He reviews all major work before presentation to clients, communicates to agency staff the needs and problems of his clients and reports the status of accounts to top management. He also manages all personnel problems—that is, he establishes job specifications with his group; evaluates the job performance and provides counseling, training and development opportunities for members of his account group; approves and/or initiates requests for raises and promotions; and takes corrective action whenever necessary. For someone to be hired for or promoted to this job, it's usually required that he have at least five to eight years' experience in account management, brand management (on the client's side), marketing, media or research and an MBA (because his match on the client side—the group brand manager—usually has that degree). Promotion from account supervisor to management supervisor is one of the most difficult jumps in advertising.

Account Supervisor. It's the account supervisor's job to maintain contact with the client, at the assigned level (it's often the account supervisor who is the agency's principal representative to the client), and to coordinate the development and supervise the implementation of the advertising plan. Along with his managing supervisor, the account supervisor develops guidelines for the plan, then prepares a strategy statement. He coordinates staff contributions to the plan and participates in the presentation of that plan to top management. The account supervisor is responsible for giving direction to all account executives reporting to him and for reviewing creative and other staff work before he submits it to his managing supervisor, to ensure that it reflects the plan objectives. He oversees the scheduling and flow of work, participates in presentation to the client, maintains client contact to make sure the agency is aware of client's needs and desires and that the client is aware of what the agency is doing for them. And, he is responsible for informing his managing supervisor of any key developments and for learning about client's product, service, market and competition; also for evaluating the work of his account executives. An account supervisor must have two to five years' experience as an account executive.

Account Executive. It's the account executive's job to maintain contact between the client and agency at his level and, most important, to conduct whatever daily activities are required to implement the advertising plan and ensure timely completion of assignments—as well as the ultimate acceptance of the agency's work by the client. In other words, he is the account group's "legman." With his account supervisor, he reviews the guidelines for developing the plan and gathers pertinent data from the various agency departments and from the client in order to prepare a strategy statement. He prepares a work schedule to coordinate copy, art and production activities, and monitors that schedule with particular attention to the due dates. He keeps agency personnel informed of client interests, participates in meetings and informs client of status of work. He also watches over the budget, supervises client's billings and monitors time sheets. The account exec oversees the activities and development of his assistants and learns about his client's product, business, competition and market. At some agencies, there are senior-level A.E.'s.

Assistant Account Executive.   Assistant account executives assist the A.E. and/or the account supervisor in client contact, staff coordination and account administration. They help by fetching market and research data from appropriate departments, monitoring traffic and production schedules and by keeping the client informed. They are sometimes called on to maintain account records, check media estimates against media plans and obtain client approval of those plans. They are often asked to check invoices (production and media) against estimates and then forward to client. They too are expected to learn about the client's business and competition and to keep abreast of trends in advertising. This is, of course, the ideal entry-level job for anyone interested in a career as an account person; it is also one of the most sought-after. It is often the first job that agencies with account-management trainee programs give to their trainees. Again, an MBA is looked upon with favor.

Account Coordinator.   Very large agencies employ someone who, under supervision, coordinates the flow of work within the agency for a particular account—sort of an internal, one-account traffic manager. He issues work requests, obtains media and production estimates, coordinates and maintains media and production schedules, coordinates network clearances (every TV commercial aired must first be cleared—that is, approved—by the network on which it is to be shown) and legal approvals. He also maintains records of client expenditures, and controls and settles differences over estimates and invoices. He may also be asked to provide administrative assistance and secretarial support to his account group. Account coordinators with real promise might also be asked to serve as backup liaison between agency and client. This too is an excellent entry-level position for anyone interested in account management.

Account Secretary/Assistant. It's the account secretary/assistant's job to answer and screen all telephone calls, meet and greet clients and other visitors, type all correspondence to clients and otherwise do whatever is necessary to help his account management boss build a strong and lasting agency/client relationship. Secretaries working for A.E.'s may be asked to maintain production progress and keep their boss informed; type copy for submission to client; make certain necessary client approvals have been secured; proofread; advise production personnel of any corrections; make sure media schedules and shipping schedules are provided to art and production personnel; and in general, create and maintain the proper environment both with the client and with the entire account service team. This too is considered a viable entry-level job for anyone considering a career in account management or any area of advertising, since all work starts and ends in this department.

Agency Management Jobs (a.k.a. General Management and Administration). Advertising agencies, depending on their size, may be managed by a chief executive officer (CEO), chief operating officer (COO) and chief financial officer (CFO) together with an executive committee; or by partners (perhaps a creative person teamed up with an account person); or by a lone president. Whoever it may be, "management" is responsible for planning, developing and establishing agency policies and objectives. Some top management people become such by starting their own agencies; others, particularly at the supersize conglomerates, work their way up the corporate ladder. As is always the case, responsibilities vary from agency to agency, depending on size, corporate hierarchy and particular requirements. Obviously, for the top management jobs, only those with a broad experience in advertising, generally gained through a series of important positions over many years, will qualify. Typically, every agency has someone whose responsibility it is to conduct the affairs and activities of the corporation to assure growth and profitability with fair and harmonious relationships within the agency. He is responsible for long-range plans for the agency, for approving the employment of key personnel, for being the person to whom all operating division heads (e.g., creative director, head of account management) report, for assisting in new business developments and, in some cases, for serving as management representative on very big accounts. (See the section "Account Management

Jobs," page 61, for further explanation.) Super-size agencies generally employ a CEO, COO, CFO, president and other corporate officers to manage the parent corporation as well as those to manage each of its various subsidiary companies. At larger agencies, the overall management is normally vested in an executive committee, one of whom is principally responsible. Members are generally appointed by the board of directors of the parent company, and usually have other responsibilities in addition to their managerial ones. In addition to the CEO, COO, and president, executive vice-presidents are also considered a part of management.

Electronic Data Processing and Word Processing Jobs.
More and more advertising agencies are utilizing computers and word processors for media planning and buying, traffic, research, accounting and other advertising functions. Jobs in advertising, both in electronic data processing (EDP) and in word processing, from managers to operators, are and will continue to be available. Generally speaking, jobs in electronic data processing and word processing are one-way tickets to other jobs in the field. (Although it is possible for information specialists to go to the very top and even be a part of a management team.) In other words, these jobs won't lead you to another area of advertising. Below are descriptions of some jobs. However, the field is growing so rapidly that each agency must be continuously scrutinized to get an accurate picture of the kinds of word processing and EDP jobs available.

EDP Jobs. EDP jobs in advertising include those in operations and administration. The person in charge of supervising all electronic data operations is called the *EDP manager*. It's this person's responsibility to purchase computer equipment for the agency, hire and assign personnel, confer with other departments and users about proposed projects, review project feasibility studies and establish work standards. The EDP manager decides what can and cannot be done at the agency's computer center. He is expected to be experienced in hardware, systems analysis and programming—and, most important, in the advertising business and applications relating to advertising. Many large agencies also employ a *systems specialist* who is responsible for specifications, cost analysis and design of new systems for clients. Some agencies employ a *data controller* who acts as an interface between traffic and data processing for production billing purposes. There may also be various *EDP supervisors* and their *assistants* in charge of specific areas, e.g., print supervisor, spot broadcasting supervisor. In operations there are the jobs of *EDP programmer, operator* and *tape librarian.* There is also the job of *console room supervisor,* the person who supervises console input and console requests and the console operators.

Word Processing Jobs. There are both operations and administrative word processing jobs in advertising; although there are fewer administrative jobs in word processing than there are in EDP. At the large agencies, where there is a word processing center, a *supervisor* and perhaps an *assistant supervisor* is employed to supervise a staff of operators, maintain work schedules, distribute work assignments to staff, follow up and check completed work; also, to act as liaison between the WP department and all other departments, including management. The various *operators* are essentially typists with word processing skills. It's their job to type on a word processor whatever information is to be stored and printed. At some agencies, operators are also secretaries handling the traditional secretarial duties as well as those of a word processor. There is also a frequent demand for part-time operators, paid at an hourly rate.

Finance and Accounting Jobs. The finance and accounting people at advertising agencies are primarily responsible for collecting money from the agency's clients and paying media and other vendors. At the very top, they are also responsible for financial forecasting and cost controls. And they handle such work as paying salaries and benefits, producing the agency's annual accounts and liaisoning with account groups and clients regarding budgets and expenses. Depending on the size of an agency, the amount of billings and the complexity of its accounts, the job may fall on one to thirty people, with job titles ranging from chief financial officer to bookkeeper. Jobs in financing and accounting are pretty much one-track, leading only to more responsible jobs in finance and accounting—although it should be mentioned that financing people can go very high in the corporate ranks, with a treasurer or financial executive vice-president being a part of an agency's top management team, responsible for strategic planning and other management concerns. Again, job responsibilites vary greatly from agency to agency, depending on the size of the finance and accounting staff and the tasks at hand. Generally, however, the large agencies employ a *chief financial officer*, who may be the *treasurer* or an *executive vice-president* but whose basic objective is to conduct the financial affairs of the corporation in such a manner as to assure a continuous flow of accurate data on which to base short- and long-term plans which will result in continuing growth and profitability for his agency. This person reports to the chief executive officer of the agency, and the *controller* reports to him. For such a job, ten to fifteen years in financial management, perhaps as controller or treasurer of an ad agency, is a minimum requirement. A *controller* is also typically employed by the large agencies. It's his job to supervise the accounting personnel, to manage and supervise the activities of the accounting department—which include general and cost accounting, budgets, payroll and client billing. Also employed may be a number of *senior* and *junior accountants, assistant accountants* and *bookkeepers*. Some agency finance and accounting departments are divided into various sub-departments (i.e., broadcast media accounting, print media accounting, production accounting, client accounting, payables, general accounting), each with its own set of *supervisors, assistants, estimators* and *clerks*. And, at the very large agencies, there are even people employed specifically to disburse petty cash to agency personnel for temporary advancements, travel expense, supper money, etc.; they are called *petty cash cashiers*. For a related job, see the section "Talent Payment Jobs," page 106.

Human Resource Director.   See the section "Personnel Jobs," page 75.

Librarian.   Several of the major agencies maintain a well-stocked library filled with every kind of magazine, book, photograph and annual report, and employ a librarian to manage it and to gather and retrieve and disseminate information for staff and clients. A librarian answers requests for information and assistance; maintains library files; handles subscriptions to magazines and newspapers for library and other agency personnel; orders and catalogs books; stores research reports and outside supplier reports; and circulates periodicals. A librarian might be called on by management to provide data on a company it sees as a potential new client, or be asked to help a copywriter who might be concerned with the accuracy of a particular statement, or be called upon to find a visual reference for an art director. Librarians are well trained, with most having their Master of Library Science (MLS) degree. For librarians interested in a career change, this could be the job they're looking for. Most often, this job falls within the research department, with the librarian answering to an information specialist. See the section "Research Jobs," page 79.

Mailroom "Boy" or "Girl." While agency mailrooms are no longer considered the traditional first step on an advertising career path, for someone still in school, a summertime or part-time job in an agency mailroom could be good experience. Mailroom boys and girls can learn the flow of things, who at the agency is responsible for what, and whether he or she is attracted to and qualified for a long-term career in the ad game. It's also a good way to get a bird's-eye view of the various departments. Since most mailrooms are computerized, the jobs, unfortunately, are few and not easy to come by.

Marketing Specialist. Some large agencies employ individuals with a high degree of special expertise in marketing plans and strategy and/or merchandising and promotion to provide marketing consulting services to the account management groups, carry out special marketing projects for agency clients, develop new product concepts for clients and prospects, suggest new marketing and/or distribution opportunities for clients and help plan complex marketing strategies and promotions. Marketing specialists are normally required to have a minimum of six to ten years' experience in a marketing-related position—on both the client side (in brand management, marketing, sales) and on the agency side (in marketing or account management). At some agencies there are a *marketing services director, associate director* and *assistants*, with the director administrating the media and research departments, which fall under the marketing service department.

Media Jobs. Media are the various means of communication available. Basically, they are newspapers, magazines, TV, radio, outdoor billboards and train and bus cards and posters. By 1985 it's expected that the advertising industry will spend over $83 billion in media, both print and broadcast. It's the media people who spend this money and who are expected to do so effectively and cost-efficiently. Simply put, what media people do is create media plans and buy media space and time

for the agency's clients. This is a lot more complex and complicated then it sounds, and it's not unusual to find rather large
media departments within many agencies, with a great variety
of media jobs. In small agencies there will naturally be smaller
departments with fewer people working on smaller budgets—
and the jobs aren't so well defined. In a large media department, there will be *directors, assistant directors, supervisors, planners, space-buying group heads and space buyers.* Also there are
statisticians, clerks and *checkers.* For some specific job-title descriptions, see below. While these are not the same in every
agency, the jobs below are quite typical of what will be found
at major agencies today. There are also media jobs at independent space- and/or media-buying services, and also at very
large corporations that buy media through their own in-house
agencies. For those jobs, see Parts IV–V of this book.

Media Director. The media director is the head of the media
department and, as such, it's his job to develop his agency's
position on media matters, set internal policies on media planning and buying, hire and encourage his staff of key media
people to grow and think creatively, represent the department
to management, develop new profit opportunities for the
agency and maintain good relations with outside media VIPs.
Always with his agency's reputation and profit in mind. To
qualify for this job, an applicant is expected to have at least
five years' experience in media management and several years'
additional business experience. Media directors are often
awarded an executive vice-president's title and can be part of
an agency's management team. At some agencies there is also
an *associate media director* and/or a *consumer media director*
and an *industrial media director.*

Media Supervisor. The media supervisor reports to the media director. It's the supervisor's job to develop media plans
that will accomplish the client's objectives and to supervise the
execution of those plans. Also, the media supervisor is responsible for presenting media plans to account and client groups
(or, if there is an associate media director, for assisting him in
media presentations)—and for such things as keeping the
agency account groups and clients informed of developments
that might affect the media, for initiating projects and research
which could improve media performance, for ensuring that the

best work is produced by media planners, for working with and developing new talent from the ranks of media planners and assistant planners and for making certain media work is continuing in the proper direction. At some agencies the title for this job is *senior media planner.* The job is given only to those with a minimum of two or three years' experience as media planners or buyers.

Broadcast Media Supervisor. This person is responsible for the daily operation of the broadcast buying department. He supervises broadcast buyers and broadcast assistants, negotiates radio and television buys, develops demographic cost estimates and works closely with the media supervisor to develop proper buying strategies. At some agencies the media supervisor handles these responsibilities.

Media Planner. The media planner is responsible for working with the supervisors in the development of media data and recommendations, for troubleshooting media problems (wrong ads, missed insertions), and for working up and trafficking media schedules. After obtaining guidelines from account group and/or client for annual planning, the planner initiates necessary media research, then produces written plans detailing objectives, strategies, rationale, estimated performance data and scheduling timetables. He secures approvals for media purchases from client, follows up with performance reviews of media activity and maintains accurate budget controls. He is also responsible for participating in presenting plans to the account group and client. Planners must keep up to date in all areas of the changing media by following trade publications, media suppliers and seminars. This is not a media entry-level position, as planners are expected to have one to two years' experience as media trainees, buyers or in media research. Complete knowledge of media measurement services is also required. Most of the large agencies also employ *assistant media planners,* who function more or less as the planner's "legmen," taking care of details to maintain a smooth flow between the agency, the client and the media. This might include updating budgets, gathering information, researching publications that may be of importance in a media plan and maintaining prompt follow-through. Assistant media planners are generally groomed to move up when the opportunity arises to a job as a media planner. This is an excellent entry-level job into media planning for those with some experience as a buyer or media secretary.

Media Buyer. There are a number of jobs in media buying. They range from *buying manager* to *supervisor* of a particular buying area (e.g., spot TV and radio, network TV) to the various types of *buyers* (e.g., spot TV buyer) to *junior buyer*. The buying manager or director oversees the supervisors and buyers and keeps in contact with the media director, planners and account groups. He develops costs for GRPs*, instructs buyers and supervisors, advises planners and account groups, checks buys and coordinates with the EDP and accounting departments for payment. Buying supervisors are responsible for the management, administration and operation of whatever buying group they are employed to supervise (again: spot TV, network radio, etc.). They represent their buying group in planning meetings with other media people and account management groups and client, assume responsibility for the work of the buyers assigned to them, submit time-cost forecasts to media planners for budgeting purposes, assign buyers to markets and evaluate the buyers' finished buy. They sometimes function as buyers in major markets. Media buyers are responsible for the negotiation and purchase of (depending on what kind of buyers they are) local or network TV or radio time. They serve as market experts, assembling pertinent data about their media; maintain contact with station personnel and station representatives; and cultivate good relations. They also assemble data necessary to support or document buys that are made, and periodically review schedules. Junior buyers (also called assistant buyers) assist media buyers, help prepare order specifications, check confirmation of orders—calling any discrepancies to the attention of the buyer—and help the buyer provide media cost information to media planners for budgeting. Junior buyer is an excellent job for anyone interested in a media career. To qualify, one needs to have some experience as a trainee or media estimator, or a year or so experience in traffic and, of course, a facility with numbers.

Media Estimator. Estimators assist buyers, and planners as-

---

*Gross rating points. Rating is the percent of homes in a viewing area tuned to a program. GRP is the sum of all ratings in a media plan.

semble rates/cost data for preliminary and final cost estimates and carry out such tasks as preparation of media paperwork and liaison with other departments in whatever way necessary. Media estimators are also expected to become familiar with media, media procedures, and the techniques of media buying and planning. At many agencies, this job is considered an entry-level media job and those accepted as media estimators are expected to train to accept the responsibilities of a media buyer.

Out-of-Home Media Manager. Out-of-home media managers are assigned to accounts active in outdoor (i.e., billboards) advertising or other unconventional ad vehicles. They maintain contact with account groups, client brand groups and media planning groups on the planning and servicing of out-of-home media. Out-of-home managers travel quite a bit, in order to select and inspect sites for out-of-home advertising. Out-of-home media planners and buyers plan, recommend, buy and implement the purchase of specialty media. They also make on-site inspection of various media forms to determine their effectiveness and to assure that the client is receiving the recommended value.

Media Computer Coordinator. Some large agencies employ individuals to act as liaison between the media and EDP departments. They may be asked to provide media groups with up-to-date computer reports (i.e., computerized buysheets, pre-buy analyses), inform appropriate computer personnel of any changes (such as a new or deleted client or brand) and inform media groups of computer processing procedures. Computer coordinators are expected to have knowledge of both clerical and automated work flow and of keypunch and computer-room operations. It is not considered a traditional media buying or planning trainee job.

Media Clerk. There are a variety of media clerical jobs: *media checkers*, who are responsible for checking insertion orders with incoming publications to confirm that ads have run as specified; *media billers* and *payers*, who prepare client billing and authorize media payments; *media file clerks*, etc. The requirements for these jobs are generally one year of business experience and a high school degree. While they are not officially considered entry-level media jobs—that is, those holding such positions aren't automatically considered on track for more responsible media jobs—they are an excellent first job for anyone with little or no experience who is interested in a media or even account management career. Also, the job of *media secretary* can be a good first job for a recent graduate or for a career-changer with no advertising experience.

New Business Administrator. At some agencies, account, media, research and creative people are responsible for new business functions, while at others—mostly very large agencies—a staff of *new business directors, administrators* and *coordinators* are also employed to go after new business. This group of individuals works only on new business activities and is responsible for administering, supervising and coordinating the preparation of material needed for new business presentations. Some of their duties are to serve as a source of information for agency management, meet with new business prospects, develop procedures to organize the new-business pursuit, oversee the scheduling of new business presentations, maintain up-to-date information about prospect companies (key personnel, ad budgets, past agencies), be available to help prepare new business presentations and read trade journals (*Ad Age, Ad Daily, Gallagher Report*) for news about companies that are looking for a new agency.

Office Management Jobs. Most agencies employ a chief administrator for each of their offices, particularly the headquarters office. This individual, called *administrative manager* or *general manager*, is responsible for assigning offices to employees, the efficiency of the various office management departments (e.g., word processing, mail room), acquisition of real estate for office purposes and other such tasks. Also, most agencies employ an *office manager* and perhaps an *assistant office manager*, who are responsible for hiring and supervising general secretaries; providing agency personnel with the services, equipment and materials necessary for operations; coordinating and maintaining work priorities and work flow, office housekeeping, general filing systems and office security. International agencies, with offices throughout the country and the world, often employ a *regional office manager* or *general manager* at each who is responsible at his office for developing new business, supervising the accounts, controlling expenses, managing personnel and planning and meeting the office's target profit. At smaller and middle-size agencies, office management responsibilities are handled by one or two people; but at large agencies there is often a full staff of executives and assistants to handle the job.

Owner/President, "Boutique Agency." Many creative and account people start their own small agencies after working for a large or middle-size agency. Their reasons range from dissatisfaction with the corporate world to a desire to make more money to not being able to get themselves hired. Generally, the owner/president is responsible for a great many functions other than administering the agency. Chief among them is the pursuit of new business. Depending on his staff and area (art, copy, marketing), he may also do all or some of the following: service clients as an account manager, write marketing plans, write the ads, conceive of and produce TV commercials, decide on the client's appropriate media vehicles.

Personnel (a.k.a. Recruitment, Development of Human Resources, Benefits Executive) Jobs. Ad agency in-house personnel people are responsible for recruiting, training and developing administrative people (but not creative). Jobs vary from senior executives earning six-figure incomes to supervisors in charge of particular personnel functions to clerks and assistants and secretaries. Depending on the size of the agency, personnel (or human resource) staffs may be as large as twenty people. The need for improving productivity has changed many agencies' approach to the personnel function. More and more, jobs and their titles have been upgraded from personnel to human resources, with the chief human resource managers working closely with top management. This is quite a leap forward from the status of the old-fashioned personnel director. The change means a bigger role for human resource experts in advertising and a greater need for trained people to employ, making this a good area for anyone who is interested in advertising but not necessarily in creative, account management, media or research.

Programming Executive. Large agencies often have a division within the media department or a separate syndication subsidiary charged with buying and sometimes developing TV programming either to sell to television stations on a barter basis or for cash, or to be used as a showcase by their clients. The person in charge of this function might be called *director of network broadcasting operations, director of programming, broad-*

cast programmer or some other such title; it's different at every agency or subsidiary. Generally, in addition to a few executives, assistant programmers and, of course, secretaries are also employed, with the latter positions being possible entrées into this highly specialized part of advertising. Also, some agencies employ a "programming information staff." They are responsible for attending screenings of new TV shows, evaluating the network lineup and advising clients and agency personnel on the programming for the upcoming seasons. A working knowledge of TV production and the people who perform this work (producers, directors) is essential; also, a flair for anticipating popular taste in entertainment. Several of the larger agencies are involved in cable TV, developing programming and/or getting clients in as advertisers. Some of those employ one or more persons to explore the possibilities and opportunities for advertising within the cable industry. As this is a new area, the job descriptions of those involved, as well as their titles, vary greatly from agency to agency. Some *cable experts* have responsibilities other than those involving cable, and some—a very few indeed—concentrate completely on the cable industry. Those interested in the area of cable and advertising would do best to contact the agencies most heavily involved. In New York, those are: Backer & Spielvogel; Young & Rubicam; Batten, Barton, Durstine and Osborn; Dancer Fitzgerald Sample.

Public Relations Jobs. Public relations jobs are available with both independent public relations firms and advertising agencies with public relations subsidiaries or departments; also, within large corporations. (For those, see Part V, "Supporting Services.") Small PR firms and ad agencies generally employ PR generalists and call them *account executives,* while large firms employ a *director of PR services, supervisors, general account executives* and maybe some with special expertise—say, *theatrical A.E.'s* or *financial A.E.'s* or someone in charge of *corporate communications.* Also, *writers, publicity/contract people, researchers* and *production people.* Some general job titles are described below, but as always, it must be kept in mind that PR job descriptions vary from agency to agency (and from PR firm to PR firm) depending on the size of the agency, the client roster and the size of the client's budget. Something you should know is that in public relations advancement may not be awarded in the same way as in advertising, where your job title changes with each promotion. Rather, advancement is awarded by the type and number of clients you're expected to handle and, of course, by raises.

Director of PR Services (a.k.a. Public Relations Director). This job exists within ad agencies that keep a public relations arm. It's this person's responsibility to set objectives for the public relations operation, establish policies and budgets, set fees for PR accounts and oversee their management; also, to maintain contact with top-level PR clients, consult with advertising account management for integration of public relations activities into the advertising function, and exercise final authority regarding the employment of public relations staff. This is a top-level job requiring managerial experience, experience in PR techniques, and a knowledge of advertising.

Public Relations Account Supervisor. The PR account supervisor is the primary contact between the client and the company. But he is more than the contact. He is a manager and a coordinator; he is also a salesman, diplomat and a planner. He integrates overall public relations planning with the total marketing effort, he consults with the director of public relations or president to ensure that agreed-upon objectives are reflected in both the plan and the creative product, he manages the accounts budgets and he is responsible for training and supervising account executives. At least two years' experience as a public relations account executive is required for this job. Many PR firms—independents as well as subsidiaries of ad agencies—also employ account supervisors with special knowledge of one or more industries, such as *theatrical PR supervisors, financial PR supervisors* and *community relations PR supervisors*, to handle responsibilities on those accounts. Such supervisors are employed where the nature of the client contacts are such that the client has more confidence in dealing with someone holding the title of supervisor.

Public Relations Account Executive. The account executive helps develop and write PR plans and strategies for his clients; makes arrangements for the implementation of PR programs; selects, directs and evaluates outside suppliers whose products and services are purchased in the course of implementing the client's PR program. Where editorial contacts are involved, the public relations account executive makes and maintains those contacts required to assure his clients of editorial exposure. Also, the A.E. maintains day-to-day client contact, and when the account involves advertising, maintains liaison with advertising account executives. When no writer or contact people are employed, PR account executives may be called on to do their own writing and editorial contacting; also, to plan, implement and attend special events. The job generally requires some training or experience in public relations or journalism.

Public Relations Account Writer. PR writers are called upon to research, write and edit press releases, speeches, stories, scripts, reports, picture captions, product information and technical material, filmstrips, newsletters, annual reports, new business proposals, and/or anything else required in the performance of client service activities. The PR writer assists in the development of concepts and may also be asked to carry out arrangements for client activities as assigned by the account executive. Writers sometimes are responsible for "selling" the media on their story ideas, for assisting the A.E. in making client contacts and for other so-called A.E. functions. The job generally requires writing experience in public relations or for the media.

Publicity Contact.   This person, or the PR account executive or writer doing this task, contacts the press, the media and trade publications editors to interest them in publishing client news. The traditional line here is to get to the right editor of the right publication at the right time. This means, as a contact person, you must have a knowledge of how newspapers and other media operate, be familiar with the interests of individual editors, and have a persuasive personality.

PR Researchers.   Large PR firms sometimes employ researchers to gather material for articles, gather in statistics and other information that will help the account people and writers to prepare presentations, design PR programs and in general to understand and evaluate their client's problems and image. Researchers may gather their information informally through interviews and the reading of written material or by sophisticated research techniques, in which case they will probably supervise the work of outside suppliers.

Production Supervisors.   Large PR firms employ production supervisors et al. to carry out assignments for mailings, printing, photography, graphics and other production work. These individuals maintain contact with production resources (printers, photographers), obtain production estimates and maintain production records on all public relations accounts. Requirements for this job are experience in production and familiarity with public relations techniques.

Public Relations Assistant. Assistants may be called on to perform the traditional assistant/secretarial duties as well as all or some of the following: arrange interviews and special events, contact the media, do research, followup on production, write blurbs and even press releases, work with clients in case the A.E. is not available, hire photographers, maintain files and clippings records, and, in general, serve as assistant to all PR personnel. This is an excellent entry-level job for anyone interested in public relations.

Research Jobs. Research specialists design, execute and interpret research. More and more, with multimillion-dollar marketing and advertising decisions being made on its findings, the advertising industry has come to depend upon research. There are a wide variety of jobs available with advertising agencies, PR firms, marketing research supply firms, and with corporations—that is, on the client side of advertising. The jobs described below are those you'll find at ad agencies; for the others, see Parts V–VI. Small and even middle-size ad agencies often don't employ research people; whatever research is required is "farmed out" to an outside research firm or consultant. Most large agencies, however, do employ several research specialists. The numbers and types vary from agency to agency, with some agencies employing staffs as large as any research firm. The basic jobs are described below; please keep in mind that the titles and responsibilities are rarely the same in every agency. For most jobs in research you will probably need a degree in statistics or psychology.

Research Director. The research director is responsible for all research and research personnel. He plans, budgets and staffs the research department to provide marketing and advertising research services to the agency and its clients. He is responsible for supervising and assigning responsibilities to research personnel, for assuring the quality of the research projects and interpretations, for contracting outside research suppliers' services, for consulting with management supervisors and account supervisors to determine staff requirements for each account and for keeping the department up to date on research problems, techniques and methods. This is a top-level job and requires someone with a broad knowledge of research including a familiarity with suppliers, statistical analysis and decision theory. It is not unusual for a research director to have a minimum of fifteen years' research experience. The director may be part of the agency's new business team, as well. At some large agencies there are also employed various specific directors, who answer to the marketing director or *director of marketing services* (the person responsible for the marketing, media and research departments). For instance, there might be a director of consumer studies—responsible for such areas as attitude studies, concept testing, sales measurement, target-audience profile studies, product- and package- and name-testing, and advertising market-effectiveness studies. There might also be a *director of marketing studies,* a *media research director* and an *associate research director* responsible for specific accounts or, perhaps, new business research, and for collaborating with the research director in formulating research department policies and procedures. Only those well-rounded research professionals with experience and training should consider jobs of this caliber.

Research Supervisor (a.k.a. Senior Analyst). For assigned accounts, it's the research supervisor's job to develop and plan research projects. In order to do this, he reviews previous research and available information about products and markets; advises account group and client on needed research; writes research proposals stating objectives, methodology, time and costs; constructs required questionnaires; obtains bids from and selects research suppliers; oversees research studies from inception through field work, tabulation, and final report and presentation; and reviews and updates the design of continuing studies. He also participates in projects to develop new research techniques and supervises the project directors. Research supervisors must have a thorough background in research techniques and their application.

Project Director. Project directors are responsible for implementing specific research projects as assigned them by the research director or supervisor. They supervise the suppliers and research assistants; they draft research proposals and research questionnaires; they set coding and tabulation specifications;

perform initial analysis and draft reports and handle report and proposal production. In some agencies, there are also *senior project directors*. Some agencies don't specify that experience is required for the job of project director, but preference is given to people with academic backgrounds in research and one or two years' experience with a research supplier. Senior project directors must have five to ten years' experience in either agency or marketing research. Experience should include activities in all related areas: interviewing, questionnaire design, coding, tabulating, analysis and reporting. An academic background in psychology, sociology and statistics is also impressive.

Analyst. Analysts work with senior members of the research department and report to the project director or directly to the research director. They are responsible for analyzing data from research projects; preparing presentations for client and account groups; supervising field work; coding and tabulation of data; maintaining files on research performance; supervising billing and accounting for projects; and for keeping up to date on the latest research techniques. To qualify for such a job, a person is expected to have a statistical background and some work experience.

Statistical Clerk. This individual assists in assembling general statistical research information for broad departmental use and/or for specific projects. This is a good entry-level job for someone with some experience or academic background in the field or in an allied field.

Information Specialist. This individual gathers research material and routes research information to staff members. He classifies incoming material, reads internal and external marketing and research reports, assists the department by doing research for some studies, supervises the librarian and in general is responsible for the efficient operation of the library and/or information center. A degree in information science is often required for this job, as well as some experience in library operations or information retrieval systems.

Secretary. It is possible to find employment as a secretary in just about every area of advertising: account management, agency management, accounting, personnel, media, programming, public relations, research, traffic, creative, etc. Sometimes the job of secretary is good for a more advanced career in advertising. At other times it is a one-way street. There's no cardinal rule here, but generally speaking, *executive secretaries* (those who answer to a president or executive VP and do dictation and heavy typing, screen phone messages and free an executive from as many routine details as possible) are on the one-way street, while creative secretaries, or TV production or media secretaries are in a stepping-stone, entry-level job. So some secretarial jobs are good for getting in the door and learning what goes on behind it, and others are not. At the large agencies, *floaters*—assigned to various departments, filling in for vacationing staff members—are employed. This, particularly, could be a good first job for anyone just out of or even still in school interested enough to learn firsthand what goes on in an ad agency.

10 Profile of a Management Supervisor

Ken Angel, Vice-President and Management Supervisor, Batten, Barton, Durstine & Osborn, Inc.

Ken Angel is an account man at BBD&O, the world's fifth-largest advertising agency. As an account man, it is Ken's job to act as liaison between the client(s) he is assigned and his agency. As a *senior* account man—in fact, top-level management supervisor—it is also Ken's job to manage for his agency a rather large piece of business, the R. J. Reynolds Tobacco account.*

Because account people are involved in the intangible—managing, reviewing and mediating—rather than the tangible—writing, designing and producing—their jobs perhaps are the least understood of all. Ken Angel, who for over ten years has been doing account work on various levels for a number of agencies, describes the job this way: "First of all, it's the account group's job to help run a client's business. In a sense,

---

*At the time this book was published, Mr. Angel had been offered and had accepted the job of director of advertising for Revlon, Inc., taking on the responsibility of managing that company's in-house agency as well as the activities of their outside agencies. In the meantime, R. J. Reynolds has moved the Camel brand from BBD&O to another agency.

we are their marketing partner, giving marketing advice and helping develop strategy for their brands, based on our knowledge, research and advertising know-how. In some cases, we write a marketing plan for the client; in other cases we review the plans the client has written, to provide new insight and direction; other times, we sit down together to write the marketing plan. Once a plan is written and the strategy set, it becomes our job to communicate to the creatives what the client wants to communicate to the public. And, that's not a simple matter. The client and the creatives are often at opposite ends of the world and it's up to the account person to have the language to bring them closer together. You have to know everything about everybody. The account job is probably the hardest job of all, because you are the middleman, the one who must come up with the compromises."

Being a management supervisor is the highest kind of account person one can be, and the most difficult to become. Naturally, Ken didn't start as such, but climbed the account service ladder one step at a time, starting not even at the bottom, but from left field. For Ken's first job in advertising wasn't in account work, but in media.

"I was a marketing major in college, not because I wanted to go into marketing, but because my parents didn't want me studying radio and television, which was my first choice. I was graduated from Syracuse in 1967, and went on to Pace graduate school. When I started looking for work, I figured the best place to go was where I had some connections. A friend arranged an interview for me at Dancer Fitzgerald Sample, where there was a job opening as a media planner on the R. J. Reynolds Tobacco account. I was offered the job and took it. It was the kind of first job that still exists today—one in which the agency underpays you and overworks you, knowing full well that you intend to leave as soon as you get some experience under your belt. I got promoted to media supervisor at the end of the year, which meant I became more involved in media planning than in the implementation of strategies. This was when the government ruled cigarette advertising was no longer allowed on television. Because so much of Reynolds's advertising was out-of-home, they were going to send me out 'riding the boards,' which means driving around the country checking out billboards for location and legibility. At that point

Ken Angel, vice-president and management supervisor, Batten,
Barton, Durstine & Osborn, Inc. *(Merri Milwe).*

I didn't think I ought to be doing that work, so I left and went to BBD&O as a media supervisor. I worked on the Schaefer Beer and the Pillsbury business. Soon after, I was promoted to associate media director, which meant I had planners and supervisors reporting to me. I remained in media at BBD&O for two and a half years."

Because it is the function of the media people to do work for the account people, Ken came in contact with several top account people at BBD&O. One of these men had just been recruited by Wells, Rich, Greene, to work on Westinghouse and General Mills as a management supervisor. He needed someone to act as his account executive and asked Ken if he wanted the job. Ken was most fortunate to be singled out and given the opportunity to make the sidestep into account work, a more prestigious and sought-after (though more risky) area of advertising than media. Many are never invited to move over. And some would just as soon remain where they are, sacrificing higher status and salary for a bit more job security. However, Ken was not one of those. He took the risk, and his first experience as an A.E. was not atypical.

"I went to work at Wells as an account executive on the General Mills business. I was the liaison between the agency and the brand manager. Soon after I got there, General Mills gave the agency ninety days' notice, and I, in effect, was out of a job. Normally, when an account of that size is lost to an agency, the A.E. assigned is fired because that's all he works on—one account, in fact, one brand. Which is what makes the job so risky. (Creatives, media people, and even upper-echelon account people, who work on a number of accounts, aren't so vulnerable.) But when an agency feels an A.E. has real potential and ability—and not just for that one account—they may invite him to stay on. Wells offered me other positions; none, however, that I was interested in. (Certain types of products attract account people on the climb—those that demand more sophisticated marketing and high visibility.) So I left Wells for Grey, because, while they didn't have a great reputation for the way they treated their people, they did have a great one for marketing."

At Grey, Ken was promoted to the next level of account work.

"Within nine months of my coming to Grey to work on the

national launch of Cycle dog food, I was promoted to account
supervisor and became more involved in the thinking of
brands. As you move up the ladder, the job becomes more
strategic than executional. That's true of all jobs in advertising.
On the top levels your energy is put into mental rather than
physical activity. On the entry-level jobs you know more about
what goes on on a day-to-day basis; as you move up, you're
expected to concentrate on long-range objectives."

Ken remained at Grey for a year and a half, until it became
apparent that he had real differences of opinion regarding the
handling of Cycle. (He believed the brand should be marketed
as a concept; management believed each individual type of Cycle should be marketed on its own.) The person who had taken
him to Wells from BBD&O had come back to BBD&O on Gillette, and offered him a job. He didn't like the offer and de-
clined. A few months later BBD&O came back with another
offer, a position as an account supervisor reporting to an executive VP, which meant on that assignment there would be no
management supervisor over him. Ken accepted, and in doing
so, came back to an agency he had already worked for, which is
not uncommon. While there, he eventually worked on a number of accounts in the packaged goods field, which he believes
is a good idea for the career-oriented.

"Packaged goods are the backbone of the industry. While
account people can specialize in one type of goods—and many
do—I believe in general experience, for the simple reason that
if an industry goes bad and that's all you know, it will be difficult for you to find a position. With general packaged goods
experience, you can work in any category. And the more you
know, the more valuable you are to an agency."

Ken was made a vice-president within four months, a com-
paratively short time. He was also given a corporate assignment on an important and troublesome piece of business, the
3M Corporation. The account had problems; there had been
three account supervisors on it in only four or five weeks' time.
The client had related to none.

"I was told to go in and make the problem go away. And I
did. The guy was an intellectual, and I am well-read, so we
were able to converse. In corporate advertising you are dealing
with consumers' perceptions of a company, rather than sales,
so it's particularly important that a client be able to relate to
his account man."

Besides 3M, Ken was assigned a number of accounts.

"At one point I had four assignments with four management supervisors to report to, which is a physical impossibility. You can't report to two people, let alone four, so I didn't report to any of them. No one ever said anything, so I kept on doing that. Then the executive VP for whom I had returned to BBD&O called and asked how long before I could get off my current assignments. I said a month. He said 'too long.' He wanted me to work on Pillsbury because they were planning on repositioning Figurines. And, he wanted *me* to tell my management supervisors I was no longer available to work on their business. That was a difficult position to be put in."

Through negotiations and incredible diplomacy, Ken managed to get out of his assignments and on to the Pillsbury business without stepping on toes or losing anyone's support. He managed to impress everyone by making a sensitive transition come out to his benefit while not causing bad feelings among his co-workers and former clients. Sometimes the ability to play corporate politics is as important to an account man's future as is his ability on the job. As Ken says: "So much of the job is about relationships. Had I not accepted the challenge, I would have lost a supporter for life. The same is true of the clients I work with. I can't afford to lose their support, either. As I move up, they move up. The grouper [group brand manager] of yesterday is the marketing director of tomorrow. One day we are both going to be top management and remember each other when. It's the old-boy network at play."

Ken was on the Pillsbury account for four months when BBD&O was asked to handle domestic advertising for Camel cigarettes, for R. J. Reynolds. Ken was approached.

"They [BBD&O management] knew the type of person I was and the type of people the Camel brand group were. Everyone, including myself, agreed it was a natural for me, so I took the assignment."

The assignment, to "restage" the brand and put a stop to a long market-share decline, turned out to be Ken's golden opportunity to prove what he could do. Over two years, Camel sales were boosted 24 percent, thanks to a masterly tactical move (transferring the parent brand's masculine image to the light brands, and excellent advertising that got people "experientially involved"); changes in media selection, including an increase in use of newspapers and out-of-home media; and the introduction of various promotions. Ken Angel was made management supervisor on the account. (To give you some idea of how difficult this title is to attain, of 900 employees at BBD&O, there are 200 vice-presidents, but only 20 management supervisors.) His client, John Shostak, was promoted from senior brand manager to marketing director for his participation in Camel's triumph in the marketplace.

Ken's accomplishments as an account man came about for a number of reasons, not the least of which is his enthusiasm for and inexhaustible knowledge about each and every product he is assigned to. Whether he is assigned to maintain an account, boost sluggish sales by repositioning a brand, or launch a new brand, Ken's interest in the product his client is selling is limitless.

"Whatever category I am put on, I spend months learning about it. Strengths, weaknesses, product formulations—these are things that never actually appear in the advertising but must be known in order to develop an effective strategy. The first thing I do is read everything that will give me a feel for the category. That includes back research, previous marketing plans, the strategic orientation of previous agencies—anything that will give me insight into what happened and what was done about it. With that information you move forward. You become totally involved, learn about supermarket sales and measurements, about warehouse movement, about consumer buying habits. When I was on Pillsbury I learned all about the diet category and dieting . . . how frequently people dieted, what their expectations were, what they were and weren't willing to give up. On Camel, I went on tours of the plant and learned how cigarettes are made. When I was on anti-perspirant I learned about human anatomy and spent time with chemists trying to understand how anti-perspirants and deodorants work and how they differ. My area of expertise is advertising, not manufacturing, but each time I get a new assignment I learn all I can about that product. How else could I understand what the problems are and communicate intelligently with my client? And how could I possibly come up with a solution to anything without understanding the problems? And as a senior account person, you must have a recommendation for every step along the way. It's my job to help my client solve problems and to convince him my solutions are the proper ones. . . .

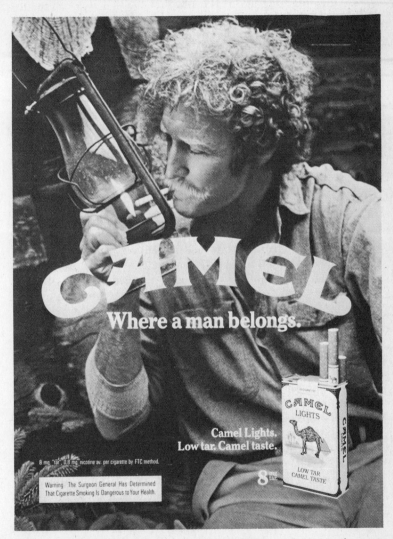

Ad for Camel cigarettes, as created by BBD&O, Ken Angel, management supervisor (copyright © 1981 by R. J. Reynolds Tobacco Company).

The only way I can do that is by speaking his language.

"Besides learning about the product itself, I learn all about the audience the product is to appeal to. The way you approach a marketing problem depends largely on the agency philosophy. But, basically, it's all very logical. First you have to find out who the audience is, who the heavy users of a product are; what they want, what they don't want. If a product exists, you learn what problems that product solves for people and write the marketing plan accordingly. Sometimes you find that a product needs to be modified in order for it to succeed. If the product's a new one, it must be given a clear reason for existing so that people feel there's a benefit in buying that product. Which is the real purpose of advertising, after all."

Another reason for Ken Angel's success as an account person (remember, they are responsible not only for developing what should be said in the advertising but also for coordinating the advertising activities of all concerned) is his knowledge of the process of advertising: from new product development to research, media selection, creative work, through to production.

"At some point in every step along the way, one or another account person is involved. The strategy is written by a combination of people, usually the account supervisor working in association with the client, the management supervisor and the creative team. (At some agencies the creatives are handed a strategy and told to go execute it, which I think is a terrible idea.) The strategy sets forth what it is you want to communicate, what you want the consumers to believe about a product—that it is the best or that it solves a particular problem. Creatives must agree with and understand what you want to happen because they're the ones who are going to execute that belief. It's at the execution stage that the account executive takes over. That's not to say the supervisors go off to live in a dreamworld. They keep very much on top of things and make certain the process is moving along, because if something goes wrong, it's their job on the carpet.

"When the creatives are ready, they review the work with an A.E., get his comments, make appropriate changes and modifications, then do the same with the account supervisor and, finally, with the management supervisor, who may think the work is off-strategy or that it's executed well. If it's the latter, the work is presented to an executive of the agency and then to the client. In the old days only the account group presented to the client; today, the creatives participate as well. At this point—client presentation—anything can happen. This is, after all, not an exact science. I've been to presentations where the client felt the work was totally off-strategy. I've been in situations where the brand manager didn't want to present the work to his superior but the agency did. That can be very sticky. It then becomes the account person's job to come up with a compromise position; a marketing director or executive VP certainly isn't expected to settle disputes between his staff and agency. The process of getting work approved is not a short one, and most of it is on the shoulders of the account group.

"Once the work is approved and ready to be produced, the account executive and supervisor stay on top of the progress. They pass important information on to their managing supervisor. Certainly anything having to do with large sums of a client's money must be approved by an account person in charge. People can get very cavalier with other people's money. With commercials costing as much as $300,000, we keep tight controls. An account supervisor generally attends production meetings and casting sessions and the actual shoot, whenever physically possible. In the case of print, many an evening has been spent by an account person at the printing press, making certain the job is done well. By the time a commercial is completed, the management supervisor comes back into the picture to present it to client top management. Once approval is obtained, the account executive works closely with traffic and legal departments to arrange for necessary network and legal clearance."

Clearly, the job of account person is all-encompassing and far-reaching. In order to succeed at such a job, one must possess some very special traits. Ken has this to say:

"First of all, you have to be willing to give a lot of time. This is a seven-day-a-week, twenty-four-hour-a-day sort of job. There's a joke about an account man that sums it up: One account man says to another, about a third: 'Did you hear Larry died?' 'No kidding,' says his friend. 'What did he have?' 'Oh, Procter & Gamble, the Pillsbury Company . . .' That's this business. Besides total commitment, what makes a good account man is the ability to blend in with a number of different types of people. I've had clients who were intellectuals and others who were street-born. I had to relate to both types. Also, you've got to be a self-starter, because no one is going to hold your hand. And you've got to be comfortable with yourself. Sure of yourself. And have the ability to understand and act quickly—plodders don't make it here. And while I certainly wouldn't say you have to always agree with everyone, you do have to know the art of compromise if you intend getting anything done. Also crucial is an ability to understand the consumer. A lot of that is gut reaction, but in order to have it you must know and have insight into the people you're trying to reach. You must read and travel as often as you can. You can't understand people by sitting in an office somewhere in New York, because that's not real. Besides traveling, I go to the movies and watch TV and try to keep in touch with everything that's happening."

As to starting a career in account work, Ken adds these words:

"First of all, don't lose heart. It's very difficult to get into the field, but once you're in, you can get ahead if you work hard. I'm living proof of that. I would say to take whatever job in advertising you can get, even if it's not directly in this area, because just getting in the door gives you some credibility and the opportunity to meet people and learn of other openings. And in this business, it's much easier to get work from the inside. As far as the job itself is concerned, well, the worst part is that you never rest. The best is that you're not doing the same thing day in and day out. There's always something exciting and new and different . . . and you never know when there will be a fire somewhere you have to put out. In my opinion, this is the most exciting business in the world. And, if you can stand the anxiety, you won't find a more stimulating, exciting environment to work in than advertising."

PART IV

AGENCY CREATIVE
AND PRODUCTION

The Agency Creative and Production People

Creative and production people influence the marketing plan, then express that plan in the print ads, TV and radio commercials, logos, and collateral material they design and produce. They are advertising's imagination and creators.

11 Agency Creative and Production Job Descriptions

Art Director and Art Director–Related Jobs. Art directors are the people who visualize how the print and television advertising should look and then supervise everyone concerned to make certain that the advertising does in fact turn out the way it is supposed to. Art directors need not be fine artists, for it is their job, along with the copywriter, to conceptualize and design an ad, to make sure that all the visual elements communicate the message, not to actually draw it. While they are not responsible for actually doing the artwork, they are responsible for the work of the artists and photographers they choose to produce the ad or commercial. At small agencies there might only be one or two art directors; at large agencies there are many at various levels and with specific responsibilities—for instance, *executive art directors, senior art directors, art directors, junior art directors, assistant art directors* and *art assistants* or *secretaries to the art department.* These job responsibilities, as well as the overall structure of art departments, vary from agency to agency, again, depending on size, billings, the number of employees and the type of work required of the art department (one client may need only print ads; another only TV; another, no artwork at all—as would be the case if the client were a recruitment account). At most large agencies, the higher up the art director is, the more he is likely to be responsible for the supervision of others; and the lower down the scale he is, the more he is likely to be responsible for hands-on work. Those at the very top of the art department answer to the creative director or whoever is head of creative services (which includes art, copy, print and TV production). There is also the job of *mount room specialist,* which, while being a good training job for a junior or assistant art director, is often within the production rather than art department. An *art file custodian* is employed in the print production department of some large agencies.

Executive Art Director.   The executive art director is responsible for the performance of the art directors, graphic artists
and production art personnel, and for providing them with leadership and guidance. He assists art and production departments in solving problems and handles special projects, functioning as an art director on important assignments. He
provides direction and recommendation to graphic artists and
production art department personnel concerning sources of
supply or labor that will aid them in satisfactory completion
of their work. He is very often responsible for the training of
graphic designers and art directors and for keeping his department current and excellent in all typographic matters. And,
most important, he is responsible for bringing in assignments
on time and within budget.

Senior Art Director.   The senior art director consults with account groups, media and marketing staff and anyone else, to
gather information about a product to determine a visual concept and style for his agency's advertising. He works with the
writers at the concept stage to help conceive and develop imaginative and persuasive print and television advertising. He
executes or supervises the execution of layouts (a rough sketch
of what the advertisement will look like, with the headline lettered in) for newspaper, magazine, outdoor media and television storyboards (pictures in a flip-chart style that indicate,
frame by frame, the main action of the commercial and what
the viewer will hear). He supervises the photographer or illustrator and selects and/or approves models and locations. He
specifies and designs typography and supervises retouching
and cropping of finished art. He is responsible for assigning
work flow of art directors within his group and/or supervision.
Senior art directors usually have several years' (six to eight) art
direction experience on consumer, industrial and corporate advertising assignments in both print and broadcast.

Art Director.   The art director works with the senior art director, creative director and writer in the formulation of creative concepts. He develops graphics on his accounts, and submits his work for discussion and approval. He works with
production personnel in preparation of cost estimates relating
to layout, illustration, photography, type, retouching and pasteup. He regulates budgets, costs and expenditures pertaining
to graphics. He purchases and directs the work of illustrators,

photographers and retouchers. He works with production personnel on preparation of ads, and he specifies and designs typography. At times he works on the concept, production and execution of television commercials, but typically this work is handled by a senior art director. Art directors are required to have a few years' experience as an agency junior art director, assistant, or mount room specialist before being hired as such—or to have experience with a commercial design studio. Also, at this stage, they're expected to have knowledge and experience in advertising idea development, and production and mechanical technique. At some agencies, art directors, in order to get hired, must have sufficient art talent to perform "on the board" when necessary.

Junior Art Director.   A junior art director has no responsibility so far as designing or conceptualizing his agency's advertising. Rather, he assists art directors, prepares mechanicals, pasteups, rough layouts and anything else that might be needed. This job is generally considered a training period for an art-director spot. Sometimes those with no experience but with an impressive "book" (a sampling of work—see Part VI, "Finding a Job," for more on that) are hired as junior art directors; other times, agencies look for someone with experience as an assistant or mount room specialist or someone with experience at a commercial design studio.

Assistant Art Director.   The assistant art director's function is to help the senior, junior and art directors in the performance of their duties. This could mean anything from helping to keep the creative department orderly and presentable and maintaining art department equipment to, on occasion, doing layouts and mechanicals. It almost always means acting as the art department "gofer" on the set and in the office. Many senior art directors and creative directors got their start in advertising as an assistant or junior art director. (Sometimes the titles are interchangeable.)

Mount Room Specialist.   This entry-level art/production job is found only in the large agencies employing many people. The mount room specialist assists art directors in assembling finished layouts and storyboards by mounting finished prints, art work and proofs. Also, he stocks art materials necessary for mounting, and may be called on to construct dimensional models, boxes and displays to be used in presentations.

Art File Custodian. This is a low-level job within the print production department of some large ad agencies. It's this person's responsibility to provide pieces of art, mechanicals, plates and proofs to art directors, traffic supervisors, production managers or whomever. The art file custodian files all art, mechanicals and proofs once they've been used; keeps a record of all art on file; sends final proofs of all advertisements to the personnel involved; and ensures that an adequate supply of proofs (typically ten) are kept on permanent file.

Broadcast Business and Operations Jobs. There are various types of jobs within ad agencies that involve handling the administrative details connected with broadcast operations. Broadcast business and operations people are concerned with the step-by-step growth of a commercial from the time it has been created through to its delivery to the station for airing. They handle such things as broadcast traffic and clearance, making sure the commercials are completed on time and with the required approvals. (The person handling this job is often called the *broadcast coordinator*.) Even before a commercial is produced, they keep track of and coordinate the bids made by the various film-production houses, scrutinizing each as it comes in, comparing price quality and quantity of services offered—and for those bids accepted, making certain that final costs and overages are consistent with the original bid. (The title given to the person doing this job is often *production bidder*; at some agencies the job evolved as a safeguard against "payola," the practice of TV production houses' paying off or bribing agency producers to secure a job.) They establish and maintain uniform and efficient methods, procedures and policies for the handling of broadcast business affairs; they negotiate with the various unions (e.g., SAG, AFTRA); they order film elements, tapes and prints; they ship approved spots to the networks or stations in time to make air dates; they pay talent for their first performance in a commercial and every time that commercial is used. (See the section "Talent Payment Jobs," page 106.) At a small agency, a producer might handle all of the above, with the help of outside supply firms (e.g., a talent payment company). But at the fairly large agencies, large staffs are employed to handle these functions. Job titles here vary widely from agency to agency depending on structure, size and needs.

Casting Director.   Casting directors and their assistants are employed by ad agencies and sometimes by TV production companies to screen and audition talent used in television and radio commercials and to maintain up-to-date files on available talent. Casting directors consult with creative staff to determine the type of actor required for a specific assignment. They then review casting department files and canvass talent agents to assemble suitable talent to prescreen. They advise agency staff (producer, creative director) and client on the talent most likely to do the best job, and book the approved talent for the filming sessions. Casting directors also constantly search out new talent by attending plays and motion pictures, and through frequent contact with talent agents. They periodically review audio and video tapes to keep promising talent in mind and keep current on the availability of celebrities and their approximate fees. At times, casting directors are called on to participate in new business presentations in the form of suggesting possible "names" to be identified with product campaigns. Casting directors also negotiate the contracts for each booking in cooperation with the agencies' broadcast business administrators. Many small agencies have no on-staff casting director, but the medium and large agencies usually have more than one. The entry-level position is *casting assistant*. Casting assistants coordinate and run the casting sessions; book talent; type talent casting reports and scripts and all correspondence for the department.

Copywriters.   Copywriters are the poets of advertising. It's their job to turn the research data, marketing plan and endless client/agency conversations into a concentrated, imaginative, powerful arrangement of words—known as "copy"—that talks directly to the consumer and triggers an appropriate response. In developing an approach for an advertisement, copywriters work with the art director. In some agencies they are teamed together on all assignments; in others they get a new art-director partner for each assignment. Some copywriters specialize in particular kinds of copy—for instance, direct mail copywriters, pharmaceutical copywriters, recruitment copywriters and catalog copywriters. A small agency may employ only one copywriter, but the large agencies typically have many, at different levels and with varying responsibilities. Generally speaking, the higher in status the copywriter is, the more important his assignments—meaning, those at the very top of their profession get to write TV commercials and high-visibility print ads for the big "important" clients while the newcomers work on low-budget assignments and trade ads directed at limited audiences. Also, high-level copywriters are often responsible for conceptualizing an ad—that is, generating an idea—while lower-level writers are given the job of actually writing the advertisement. Below are descriptions of the various kinds of copywriter jobs to be found at the large ad agencies. However, it should be kept in mind that there are opportunities for a copywriter with small agencies, where the job is less defined; with in-house agencies at large corporations; with promotion departments of publishing companies and magazines; with retail operations. Also, many copywriters, particularly the specialists in direct response writing, work free-lance. See also the description for direct mail copywriter.

Copy Director.   Most of the large agencies employ someone to head up the copywriting division of the creative department. This someone is the copy director, also called copy supervisor or manager or copy "chief." It's this person's job to maintain high standards of writing within his department and to help develop and guide creative ideas. The copy director attends meetings with agency and client personnel to gather facts on products, services and direction. He supervises senior writers and writers, and chairs creative "sessions" with them. He is responsible for assignment schedules and, in general, works with the art directors, creative director, account executive and client on concepts, campaigns and all assignments involving copy services. This is a top-level job and requires five to ten years' writing experience on a broad range of assignments.

Senior Writers.   Senior writers are responsible for working (in concert with senior art directors) to create TV and print advertising for their agency's big-budget, high-visibility accounts, and for guiding the work of the copywriters and junior writers assigned to them. Senior writers attend agency and client meetings, become acquainted with the marketing approach and problems of the clients for whom they work, determine a communications problem and then boil that problem down to its essence. Senior writers, along with senior art directors, originate the concepts, words and images that will serve as vehicles for the client's message. They organize and guide "idea sessions" with assigned copywriters, review copywriters' work and make presentations of the group's work to the supervisor or copy chief. They are also responsible for training and developing all copy people under them. Senior writers have anywhere from three to ten years' writing experience.

Copywriter. Copywriters consult with supervisors and senior writers to obtain information about products or services and to discuss style and length of advertising copy, considering concept, budget and media. They write original copy for newspapers, magazines, billboards and transportation advertising, and sometimes write TV and radio commercials. They work with an art director, to achieve total concept. At times they are called on to write themes for campaigns and ideas for individual ads. Copywriters, in order to gain employment, must have a portfolio demonstrating their ability to present ideas, words and visuals that would interest consumers and trigger them to buy or use the product or service being advertised. Some agencies, if impressed enough by a writer's portfolio, will hire them without previous copywriting experience. Most agencies, however, require a year or two as a junior writer or copy trainee.

Junior Copywriter. Junior copywriters, or copy "trainees," may be called on to perform a multitude of tasks, some having to do with writing, others not. They might be asked to write body copy for ads whose headlines have already been written, submit ideas for new ads, write sample catalog copy or a trade ad. On the other hand, they might be asked to type a copywriter's copy and in general help the writers to do their job in any way they can. Some of the large agencies have copywriting trainee programs and in those cases (see Part VI, "Finding a Job," and Appendix C for details) junior writers or trainees are formally and informally educated in the art of copywriting.

Creative Department Secretary. For those not fortunate enough to get into a copywriting trainee program, this could be a good entry-level writing job. Creative department secretaries handle all typing of correspondence and copy, handle phone calls, maintain the creative department files and generally keep track of all affairs of the creative department. Occasionally they are called on to perform copywriting tasks. For those with no experience, it's a perfect job for learning the creative side of the business and beginning to put together a portfolio.

Creative Director.   There are various titles given to the person or persons responsible for an agency's creative output. The most common is *creative director*. But at the very large agencies, there is someone even higher up the creative ladder, a member of the agency's management team who is responsible not only for the creative department (that is, art and copy) but also for print production and TV commercial production and administering operating budgets. Often, that person is called a *senior vice-president, creative services*. And, the *creative director, associate creative directors* and *creative group supervisors* report to him. The creative director is responsible for supervising all levels of art directors and writers in the creation of advertising. In fact, in most cases the creative director is responsible for an agency's creative product. In addition to working with art directors and writers—giving them advice, guidance, and constantly reviewing their work—he works with management, account supervisors and clients on the development of account strategy. On important accounts he generates campaign ideas, headlines and themes, and organizes and guides idea-generating sessions. He helps with media development, works with production people, attends client presentations. He is ultimately responsible for selecting a creative staff (with the help, at some agencies, of a *creative personnel manager*, whose job it is to review portfolios and conduct initial interviews). He assigns work to writers and art directors and determines priorities. Also, he ensures that the advertising created can be produced within a client's budget. Associate creative directors work with the creative director and help him carry out his responsibilities—at times, managing a creative group. Some agencies also award the title "creative group supervisor" to the key writer or art director within a creative group. It's his job to develop creative strategies and to serve as the key link between his team of writers and art directors on the one hand, and management, account services and the creative directors on the other. Both jobs—associate creative director and creative group supervisor—are good ones for a creative person interested in becoming a creative director. Both require much writing or art directing experience as well as knowledge of all advertising-related functions. Creative directors are expected to have at least five to ten years' experience in creating advertising, either as writers or as art directors, with a strong sense for both words and images. Directors of creative services are usually well-versed in all areas of advertising—marketing, research, media and account services as well as art, copy and production—and have at least ten to fifteen years under their belts in the creative sector of advertising. There are many who consider the creative manager's job the most important and sought-after of all in advertising. For further information, see the profile of Amil Gargano, creative head of Ally & Gargano, in Chapter 12, page 110.

Direct Mail Copywriter. Direct mail copywriters write direct mail pieces: letters, brochures, flyers, catalogs. They work for direct marketing advertising agencies, sales promotion agencies, mail-order companies, mail-order divisions of retail stores; also, publishing companies, charitable organizations, manufacturing companies, insurance companies and even banks. Also, many of them work free-lance for all of the above. Direct mail copywriters need to communicate clearly, believably and, most important, persuasively, because it's their job to cause a direct response from the consumer. In order to do that, they must know about the people who will read their words and about the business they are writing about. Direct marketing advertising is growing so rapidly that there is a real shortage of direct mail copywriters. The best way to get started is to work for a company that uses direct mail in its advertising. Mail-order companies are excellent training grounds. Many cities (twenty-two, to be exact) have local direct marketing clubs, some with job placement divisions to bring job-seekers together with prospective employers. To get more information on this lucrative career, contact your local direct marketing club and/or write the Direct Mail/Marketing Educational Foundation, Inc. See Appendix B, page 223, for details.

Layout/Mechanical Artist. Most every agency, no matter how small, employs someone to "layout" their ads and prepare camera-ready mechanicals. In the larger agencies, several people are employed, and the job is divided: one artist prepares the layouts (a rough sketch of what an advertisement will look like, with the headline lettered in) and comps, or comprehensive layouts (done after a layout is approved); another prepares the mechanicals (the first assembly of the headline and the body-copy type and the artwork—from which the printing plate is made). Layout artists (a.k.a. bull-pen artists) are often would-be illustrators. They must be skilled artists able to translate an art director's instructions into visual reality. Early layouts are very rough and done primarily for internal communications—that is, so that everyone knows what everyone else is talking about. The best of those are shown to a client so that the agency can learn whether they're going in the right direction on a particular ad. As the ad gets closer to approval and, ultimately, production, the layout artist's work becomes more and more specific, until finally it looks pretty much the way the actual ad will look. Once final approval is obtained, an illustrator or photographer uses the comp for guidance; an art director "specs" the type (specifies the type style and spacing); and the comp is on its way to becoming an ad. When the type is set and the artwork completed, the mechanical artist actually pastes up the elements, creating an exact and accurate guide for the position and size of all elements in the ad. Both these jobs are traditional entry-level art jobs within the advertising industry, and can be found almost anywhere advertising is created, from ad agencies to art studios to retail stores. It is quite common for mechanical artists to moonlight and do freelance mechanical work in addition to working on staff at an ad agency. Mechanical work is often tedious and demands extreme meticulousness. While it can be—in some agencies—a good way to break in, it isn't necessarily a way to become an art director. Layout work, also, can be dead-end rather than a way to an illustrator's career, so watch out that you don't get pigeonholed as a layout or mechanical artist.

Print Production Manager. The print production manager and his staff are responsible for the quality control of all printed matter, including advertisements and collateral material. Print production managers are employed by most advertising agencies, graphic studios, in-house retail stores and corporate advertising departments—and anywhere else printed material is reproduced. At large companies you will find more than one print manager, with perhaps each one handling a specific function such as four-color printing, black-and-white printing, color separation, typography and mechanical preparation; or with each assigned to particular accounts. In those cases where there are more than one, the print production managers would answer to a director of print production services. In all cases, the print production manager works closely with the traffic people, the art department and the other departments in scheduling, coordinating and expediting advertising materials. They establish working schedules for all advertising production projects; monitor all production jobs to assure their on-time completion; liaison with printers, typographers, engravers, retouchers and media to make sure that all work is technically correct and on time. They assign and work with bull-pen artists in mechanical preparation, process photography and/or illustrations, and maintain budget control for the print production department. Print production managers are required to have from two to five years' experience in print production, as an assistant production manager at another agency, or in working for a printer or art studio. Print production managers are expected to be experienced in all areas of graphic arts, have knowledge of the advantages and limitations of the various types of printing and engraving, and have a critical eye for color and a knowledge of art techniques. Good entry-level jobs for this area are assistant production manager, print production assistant, proofreader and secretary to the print production department. Those interested in learning about the field should read *Pocket Pal, A Graphic Arts Production Handbook,* available through International Paper Company. (See Appendix B, page 218, for details.)

Production Assistant. This traditional entry-level job is sought after by most people who are aiming at a career in TV commercials production, either as a producer or director. The job is found at production houses and advertising agencies, though anyone interested in directing would do better to work at the former, as that's where production activities happen. Those interested in producing would get more useful experience at an ad agency. At production houses, production assistants are generally responsible to the producer; they assist the director, assistant director and production manager when assigned by the producer to do so. Some of their responsibilities are to take notes during casting sessions; take production notes and timings; transcribe all notes; keep the client (i.e., the agency) informed of production status; arrange appointments for meetings and lunches—and reservations for dinner, travel and lodging when necessary. P.A.'s are an important part of the crew and help everyone concerned in the coordination and efficient operation of the TV-commercial production. At ad agencies, production assistants assist producers in all phases of production, including arrangements prior to shooting commercials through to talent payments. Depending on their status and experience, they may be called "production secretary," "production coordinator" or "production assistant," and might be given many and various jobs . . . from follow-through of TV commercials from pre-production to post-production, paperwork, casting, purchasing props for shootings and demos—including wardrobe, art and products—to attending screenings with account group and client. Production assistants need to have some TV production background, familiarity with casting procedures and film techniques, typing skills and be detail-oriented.

Sales Promotion Manager.   Some of the large agencies employ one or a few individuals to plan, direct and coordinate promotions and exhibits for clients. They are responsible for determining the form an exhibit and/or promotion should take; for presenting their idea to the client; and for guiding the day-to-day development of promotion and exhibit material—supervising and selecting outside promotional and exhibition companies. Those hired for such jobs generally have some experience creating promotions and exhibits for specialized firms, and for corporations—and know sales as well as the creative field.

Talent Payment Jobs.   Talent payment jobs, of various responsibility, can be found with medium- and large-size ad agencies and with firms that specialize in this function—that is, talent payment firms. Within ad agencies, job titles range from *director of talent payment* to *talent payment supervisor, talent payment assistant* and *talent payment clerk,* with the last two obviously being entry-level jobs. Basically, the job entails processing payments to performers who have appeared in an agency's radio or television commercials, and assisting in the negotiation and preparation of contracts relating to this area. In addition, talent payment people are responsible for knowing and interpreting, for the agency personnel, union contracts (SAG, AFTRA, AF of M); for preparing estimates for creative, account management and production departments; and for consulting with producers about the cost of session fees, rehearsals, overtime, travel and any special circumstances that might arise when producing a commercial. Upper-level talent people work with an agency's legal counsel in the preparation of contracts—for instance, for over-scale talent, sports figures, music rights—and negotiate contracts with talent agents. Lower-level people are more concerned with maintaining records and with details of accounting. For the entry-level jobs, most agencies ask only for payroll experience or an aptitude for figures. For middle- and upper-level jobs, you must have knowledge of talent-union contracts, and background in estimating talent costs from initial storyboard to session fee through final use and reuse periods. You also must have practice in dealing with union officials. The very top people in talent payment have at least four to five years' experience in the field. Contrary to what many neophytes believe, this area does not lead to a job in television commercial production. However, it can lead to a more responsible job in broadcast business administration.

Television Producer. TV commercial producers work for ad agencies and for TV production houses. (For the latter job description, see Chapter 13, "Supporting Service Job Descriptions," page 129.) Those employed by ad agencies are responsible for producing radio and TV commercials for their agencies, as well as any sales force presentation, customer presentations or any other audio or visual communications needed by a client. TV producers are specialists who coordinate the many production details, liaisoning with the account, creative, legal, casting, talent payment and broadcast operations departments as well as outside production suppliers. They are involved with a project from its inception, discussing with copywriters and art directors the objectives and themes of assignments and contributing visual and technical ideas so that workable storyboards are produced. Following client approval of the storyboard, the producer selects—from bids—the production house he believes is best qualified to handle the project at hand. He submits cost estimates to clients for approval and controls the approved budget through all phases of production. Producers direct the logistical flow of production through pre-production meetings, casting sessions, shooting, recording, editing, scoring, opticals, color correction and client approval. At all times, TV producers are responsible for keeping current on developments in film and tape technology, for soliciting and viewing sample reels from directors, production houses, talent and music-scoring companies; and for keeping members of the creative department informed. For radio commercials, producers are responsible for reviewing copy with copywriters and for making technical as well as creative suggestions and talent recommendations; also, for submitting cost estimates, selecting and contracting talent and recording studios and sometimes taking on the responsibilities of a director. Producers are responsible for running the entire TV production department, including supervising *assistant producers, casting people, production assistants* and *projectionists* (those employed to run the audiovisual equipment). Assistant producers help producers in any way they can—for instance, in obtaining releases from people whose faces or voices or, in some cases, personal property have been used in a commercial; in preparing production estimates; keeping the broadcast library in order; providing the creative department with sample reels; and at times actually producing commercials. TV producers are expected to have a working knowledge of all facets of film and videotape production, including casting, sound recording techniques, scoring, animation, location and studio, creative and technical personnel, set design, special effects, post-production, unions, costs and budgeting. Most have had at least three to five years' solid experience either with a production house, a TV station or another agency, before they apply. The best entry-level jobs are, of course, assistant producer, production assistant, assistant to a producer at a production house, or a casting job.

   Type Director.   The type director is a member of the print production department, and is responsible for working closely with the art director in determining which typeface to use for a particular ad, and which outside type shop should be hired to actually set the type. He consults with the creative department on all questions of type design; estimates cost of typography in advance of work; checks accuracy of typography layouts for fit and mechanical requirements; makes recommendations to improve appearance, cost and use of typography; evaluates performance of type shops; and approves all typography billing. In small and in some medium-size agencies, this work is done by the art director, so the job can only be found at larger agencies with full print production departments. Three to five years' experience in typography is normally required for the job; the experience can be gained by working for a typographer or as a *type department assistant.* Type department assistants do such things as maintain a log of type orders and deliveries, obtain costs from type shops, call in minor corrections or additional instructions to type shops and other chores delegated by the type director. Some agencies maintain typesetting equipment and employ a *typesetter* to operate the machine. He also may be asked to design and lay out in-house material (invitations, questionnaires, forms) and do pasteup work, making it a good first job for someone interested in the art/production area. Some also employ a *proofreader* to read type proofs, check for errors in the type and/or misspellings. In many agencies, the type director, typesetter and proofreader are the same person.

Traffic Jobs. The traffic department is responsible for scheduling, overseeing and controlling the flow of work through an agency, and for ensuring that the work gets done as specified, on schedule, and that it ends up where it is supposed to. Traffic jobs, of varying responsibility and status, are available with most ad agencies, even the very small ones, and with corporations with in-house agencies. The number and titles of the traffic personnel depend on whether the function is structured as an autonomous department or is integrated into other agency departments—such as account services, print and broadcast production, media, accounting, etc—also, the size of the agency and the kind and amount of work it produces. Consequently, traffic job titles vary greatly from one agency to another. Basically, however, there are heads of traffic departments, traffic supervisors and traffic assistants. Descriptions for these categories follow. Because traffic work intersects most advertising disciplines, it is an excellent area in which to begin one's career.

Traffic Manager. The traffic manager is responsible for the overall performance of the traffic department (although he may answer to a director of production/traffic services). He supervises the planning and execution of all traffic controls, serves as mediator between traffic staff, creative and account groups, improves interdepartmental procedures, assigns traffic personnel to assignments or accounts, oversees the traffic supervisors and the training of the traffic assistants and remains in contact with other group heads and managers. The requirements for this job are three to five years' agency traffic experience.

Traffic Supervisor (a.k.a. Traffic Coordinator). The traffic supervisor coordinates the flow of work from its inception to completion. Work in an ad agency, on any given project, begins with a request from an account person, called a "job order. The job order details all pertinent information relating to that job: the publication or network, scheduling instructions, size, length, color, issue, closing date, creative due dates and instructions. To this request, a traffic supervisor assigns a "job number," a permanent billing code number. From then on, all material pertaining to the creation of that job is ordered under this number. Supervisors also open a "job jacket," a master control file that holds all items pertaining to the job (stat of layouts, copy, type, estimates, proofs) and keeps it up to date. The progress of the job is continuously checked by the supervisor. He distributes instructions to the appropriate departments, schedules work loads for production and creative staff, follows up and adjusts schedules and makes sure that publication and network closing dates are met. He also prepares preliminary budgets and secures internal corrections and approvals, as well as certain client and legal approvals. He might also be responsible for supervising and training traffic underlings, such as planners or assistants.

Traffic Planner/Assistant. Most larger agencies employ one or both of these to help see that all timetables and schedules are met. Both are excellent entry-level jobs. A traffic planner might be asked to open job jackets, assign job numbers, establish time plans, compile production cost estimates, issue purchase orders, etc. Little experience is required for either job.

12 Profile of a Creative Director

Amil Gargano, President, Creative Director and Chief Executive Officer, Ally & Gargano, Inc.

Amil Gargano is creative director of one of the most creatively outstanding advertising agencies in New York, Ally & Gargano.

It's an agency he helped start, some twenty years ago, with one client, two partners and a secretary. Today, the agency's client list includes MCI, Federal Express, the Travelers, Saab, Calvin Klein, Commodore Computers, Time, Inc., Dunkin Donuts and many other major corporations. And it's no wonder.

Think about Ally & Gargano advertising. The funny, true-to-office-life Federal Express spots. The hilarious parody of the Bell Telephone commercial where the woman is crying, not because her son called to say he loved her but because her telephone bill is so high. The youthful vibrancy and beauty of the Calvin Klein Activewear commercials. That it's advertising that works creatively is obvious. What's not so apparent, however—and what makes it truly great advertising and Amil Gargano a great creative director—is what each campaign did for its client's business! The fact is, when Federal Express started with Ally & Gargano in 1974 it carried 9,800 packages per night; at last count the number averaged 254,000. MCI had annual revenues of $95 million in 1979 when Ally & Gargano was hired. Three and one-half year later, MCI's revenues are $1 billion. Calvin Klein Activewear was successfully introduced during a difficult retail year.

That's great advertising. It's why *Advertising Age* named Ally & Gargano Agency of the Year in 1982. And why Amil Gargano was inducted in 1982 into the Art Directors Hall of Fame. And why he is considered one of the most talented, undeceptive, clear-sighted and innovative advertising men in the business—a combination of qualities not often attributed to advertising people in general, and particularly not to "creatives," who are often thought of as impractical, shortsighted and egocentric. What's interesting is that some twenty-five years ago, Amil Gargano, too, thought negatively about advertising people. "How could anyone with brains and talent work in advertising permanently?" is what he asked himself after he took what he thought would be a temporary job in the bull pen of Campbell-Ewald, an agency with home offices in his hometown of Detroit.

Amil had been studying music and art since he was a child. He decided he'd like to pursue a career in art, so he attended Cass Tech, an arts-oriented high school, and then went to Wayne University. As he grew older, it became clear to him what he wanted to be: a commercial artist who earned a living as an illustrator. He was definitely *not* interested in a career in advertising. Coming out of Cass Tech, a serious school with good teachers, Amil soon realized Wayne University would not advance his art education the way he had hoped. He left there for a nonaccredited art school, a school Uncle Sam did not deem worthy of deferment. After sixteen weeks of basic training, Amil was sent to Korea as a combat infantryman.

After fighting in the front lines, Amil Gargano returned to Detroit and enrolled at the Cranbrook Academy of Art. Again, he felt it wasn't the right place for him and had the guts to follow his instincts. "I found myself at odds with my teachers and unable to cope with the cultural shock of being in this lovely little school, after Korea. Working nights and weekends, and with the help of the GI Bill, here I was with all these comfortable rich kids who were making pretentious declarations and talking in abstractions. Restless and impatient, I left with the idea of getting a job as an illustrator in Detroit. By then I had a portfolio of my work to show: drawings, paintings and designs. I knocked on the door of every art studio in Detroit. Mostly what I got for it was criticism, criticism that was narrow and ridiculous and showed little understanding. They did what people still do today: try to pigeonhole individuals so they can define and better handle them. My work couldn't be pigeonholed so it was considered unacceptable."

Amil had heard that Chrysler Corporation was recruiting designers, so he tried there. And, he was offered a job designing lettering that would eventually appear somewhere on Chrysler-made automobiles. The job paid $100 a week, a lot of money for a first job in 1955, yet he declined. His would-be employer was infuriated. "The guy at Chrysler couldn't believe I wasn't going to take the offer. He started lecturing me, saying he had learned from *every* job he ever had and so would I. But I didn't feel the job was challenging, and certainly didn't warrant the fifteen years I had spent studying art. I understood the guy's taking offense, but I couldn't help but weigh my options. I had been offered another job with a small design studio; and while the pay was lower, after much thought I decided to take it."

Unfortunately or not, Amil took too long weighing his options and the design job was given to another artist. Disappointed, he took the before-mentioned "temporary" job in the bull pen at Campbell-Ewald, for many years and still today *the*

Amil Gargano, president, creative director and chief executive officer, Ally & Gargano, Inc.

agency in Detroit, because it handled a large part of the automobile industry.

Amil's job in the bull pen was not unlike many others. He got paid very little ($55 a week), and worked hard at rendering layouts and doing mechanicals. After six months he decided to quit advertising and again go after his dream job. "I disliked the idea of not executing the finished artwork myself, and so in the evening I worked on my portfolio, determined to find a job as an illustrator. When I told my boss what I planned to do, he said, "I was going to make you an assistant art director, and would urge you to reconsider. . . . You'll find as an illustrator you'll have even less control over the work because ideas are handed to you. Would you rather work in a business where you can create ideas or in a business where ideas are created for you?" It was the best advice I ever got because it allowed me to remain in advertising and discover what indeed went on there. From the bull pen I was getting a rather limited perspective on advertising."

Campbell-Ewald moved Amil along quickly. After less than a year he was made a full-fledged art director; and after two years, a group art director responsible for five small accounts. While some art directors then (and many even today) took on trade assignments resentfully—nobody wants to spend a lot of time doing technical ads that will only be seen by a small population—Amil saw an opportunity to make them visually interesting. He was so captivated with the idea of seeing his design ideas evolve into approved ads, he didn't care what he was working on or to whom he was communicating.

Actually, caring more about the design of an ad than whether it's communicating the message was typical of art directors in those days. It worked well for Amil back then, but eventually he learned that that for an ad to be successful, it must be more than visually interesting. And, in the meantime, he was exploring his style and developing a fresh, new visual approach, committed to doing things the way he believed they should be done rather than the way they always had been. He recalls those early, formative days of his career this way:

"My accounts weren't very large or important. But I was doing things I found fascinating. I was looking at the work purely as a design—How can I take these elements and make them interesting on the page? I was experimenting, trying to make four-color ads out of two-color ads, using much of my art background, a lot of design influence from my education. I look at those ads now and see they make absolutely no advertising sense. I was getting great satisfaction practicing design, but I didn't understand advertising. Fortunately, it didn't take too long before I began to understand that this was a business of communications, and that design is only one aspect of that—an important aspect, but not the critical one."

Amil was captivated by a new phenomenon in advertising, largely attributed to Doyle Dane Bernbach. This was to give the art director authority equal to the copywriter's. Doyle Dane was the first to create the art director/copywriter team. Prior to that there was a hierarchy: the account person, who controlled the business, would tell a copywriter what was needed; the copywriter, being the creative leader, would write an ad and *then* give it to an art director to render. As Amil describes the way he remembers it: "The art director was not permitted to have much input. He was considered a necessary evil who had to be tolerated and controlled lest he take the copywriter's words and ideas and destroy them. I would not have remained in advertising had there not been a major shift in attitude that took place largely because of the influence of Doyle Dane and Bernbach. They were creating advertising that piqued everybody's interest. The whole industry took notice. Actually, what had happened was that Bill Bernbach had brought the art director in as a full partner in the creative process. And that became a system of doing advertising: the copywriter/art director team that prevails today."

Amil had always wanted to come to New York, so after four years in the Detroit office he asked his supervisor to transfer him. As it happened, an account man he had worked with in Detroit had been transferred to the New York office to work on the Swissair account and to develop new business. The account man, Carl Ally, felt new creative people were needed in New York, and when he heard Amil was interested, he was more than happy to get him. Amil, along with Jim Durfee, a copywriter, were transferred and began working on Swissair in New York.

The three made a good team. They liked each other, respected each other's talent, worked well together and had the same attitudes about advertising and the ways in which it could be radically improved, attitudes Campbell-Ewald management did not share. Eventually, push came to shove and the three left Campbell-Ewald and went off in their own directions. But before they did, they vowed that at some point they would work together again, preferably in their own agency. It is not uncommon for advertising people, when facing a conflict with management, to make this vow. It is less common, however, for them to follow it through, especially not as successfully as those three did.

The circumstances—Carl Ally's approaching Volvo after hearing that they were looking for a new agency—aren't nearly so important to the story as the commitment the three had. Amil recalls what it was like: "The three of us worked on the presentation together in the late evenings after our regular jobs and on weekends. Volvo looked at a number of agencies, but we got the business—based on our knowledge of the automotive industry, our positioning of the product and the ads we prepared for them. They had the courage to hire three guys who didn't have a business or an office. But they liked our work. And our commitment. And they were right in that regard, because in us they got a desire to succeed that they could not have gotten elsewhere."

The Volvo campaign in 1962, one of the first to use direct comparisons with the competition, created quite a stir when it first appeared. Thanks to smart positioning and potent advertising, Volvo became hugely successful, courtesy of the very young Carl Ally, Inc., as the agency was then called.

"We started with the three of us and a secretary and took space in the Seagram Building, fourteen hundred square feet. We thought if we're going to be serious, we'd better look serious. We never wanted to be a little creative boutique; we always wanted to be a full-service agency; so we started from the very beginning to establish ourselves as exactly that."

As Volvo succeeded, so did Carl Ally, Inc. They added another secretary, a traffic person and a production person. (Incidentally, the traffic and production people are still with them.) As the client list grew, so did the staff.

Though both had worked on storyboards, neither Amil nor Jim Durfee had ever executed a TV commercial, so they were thrilled with the idea of actually producing their first one, for Volvo. This made it worse when the experience turned sour.

Back in those days, agencies produced commercials by handing an approved storyboard over to a producer who would then hire the director and crew and get it done—pretty much leaving the art director, the person who visualized and designed the spot, out in the cold. So Amil again found himself in the forefront of a movement that gave art directors more power, this time over the way in which commercials are produced. This movement ultimately led to the art director/producer function, giving art directors the same power over TV production they had gained over print production. But Amil wasn't motivated by a desire to be a part of that movement. In fact, he wasn't even aware it was happening. His motives were the same as always: to do things the way he believed they could and should be done rather than the way they always had been; to deal with substance and plausibility rather than superlatives and hype. It was what he believed in school and at Campbell-Ewald and what he continued to believe—despite strong opposition while he was producing those early Volvo TV spots.

He remembers well that time of his career: "We hired a freelance producer to help us through the first commercial. He told us the first thing to do was send out the storyboard to the few houses that were then established and he would choose one of them. So that's what we did. I tried to work with the producer and the company he picked and kept asking questions such as 'Why must we shoot at midday with harsh light? Why can't we shoot at dusk or dawn?' The producer would answer, 'It can't be captured on film that way,' or some other lame reason why we couldn't do what I wanted. And I wasn't permitted to talk to the director. All my questions had to be put through this producer. I went through our first three commercials with minimum participation and enormous frustration, having every suggestion I made dismissed with some snide remark about naive art directors. A good example is what happened just before I finally said, 'That's it.' The print ads we were doing for Volvo were photo-journalistic, as opposed to the typical kind of fantasy presentation cars had traditionally been given. We showed dirty cars that looked as though they had been worn and used. The headlines read 'You Can Hurt a Volvo, but You Can't Hurt It Much.' And, 'This Is a Car for People Who Don't Like Cars.' And, 'Drive It Like You Hate It.' My idea of art direction for Volvo was to show the car in a very

realistic way so as not to look like an ad! I wanted to do something people could identify with, not only in terms of the
words, but visually too. I wanted people to look and say, 'Yeah,
this ad is real; this car is real.' I thought that was an unusual
and interesting way of dealing with cars and I wanted that to
come across in our TV spots as well. The car we were using was
a brand-new one, just out of the showroom, so I asked that they
get it dirty. My idea was to drive the car around in the mud for
fifteen minutes or so. Their idea was to splash cocoa and flour
on the car and try to convince me it looked like mud. I asked if
they knew what a car that had been driven through mud
looked like. I explained that it took on a pattern; that there's a
motion created by the mud splattering on a car; and that I
wanted that motion—that pattern—to come across. The producer said it was unnecessary and that I would be pleased
when I finally saw it on film. I wasn't. At that point I decided to
change things. I realized by then, that to do something revolu-
tionary in this business, you can't go with the existing system.
And if you're unhappy with something or someone, you have
to make the changes yourself. So I did, and I hired the photographer who had done the print ad for us and had an interest in
film but had never shot a commercial before. I said to him,
'You know how I want this to look, and I know you don't know
how to use the equipment too well, but I think you'll be able to
do it.' He rented the equipment for a weekend, and to get
familiar with it, the two of us went up to the Catskills for three
days and shot. We came back with all this film which I went
through over the next weekend on a rented Moviola. I marked
off each segment I wanted to use and took the film to an editor
and told him I would like to work with him, together, editing
the commercial. Previously, I had been completely elim-
inated from the editing process by the free-lance producer and
director.

"I had a distinct idea of how I wanted to see the pieces of
film put together. I was amazed at the opportunities the editor
presented me with. Working with this editor was a wonderful
learning experience. We spent too long putting the commercial together, but when we finished, we had three spots instead
of one. They were rough and crude, but they had what I was
looking for: a freshness, an authenticity. So I learned I could

get what I wanted. It was a matter of exercising control. Although I had a long way yet to go."

Amil had had another option. He could have sat back and said, "I know nothing about film," and let it be done the way it always had been. That's what most people would have done. But he wanted something that pleased him, and he used his head and realized there must be talented people working in film other than the few established "hacks" who controlled the TV commercial production business back in the early days. He jumped in where others would not. He used common sense, had the courage of his convictions, wasn't afraid to explore new ways of doing things, and finally, he got what he was after. Perhaps it's these qualities which make him, even today, stand out in an industry plagued by fear and conformity.

In 1978, as recognition of his contribution to the agency he helped found—Carl Ally, Inc.—the agency name was changed to Ally & Gargano, Inc. Today, Ally & Gargano employs 226 people and bills $209 million. Jim Durfee has gone off to start his own agency; Carl Ally is chairman; and Amil Gargano, in addition to being creative director, is president and chief executive officer: in other words, management, an unusual position for a "creative" to be in. But then again, Amil Gargano is an unusual "creative."

Amil's days are divided between managing the agency, meeting with clients, arranging new business activities, and managing the creative output. Now and then—that is, every three or four years—he manages to art-direct a commercial, the last one being the Calvin Klein Activewear campaign. His involvement with those was from the very beginning:

"Calvin Klein had gone through some award annuals and decided that our work warranted further exploration. He called the agency, and because new business is an important part of my job, I took the call personally. He came to our office and spent about three hours talking to us. We talked about what he was then doing with Brooke Shields and how successful it was. I said, in effect, 'Well then, you shouldn't change agencies, but I hope that sometime you'll have something for us.' When he did, he called back. It was for a new product called Activewear, and he simply said, 'You're assigned the business.' I decided I wanted to work Activewear myself."

Commercials as art-directed by Amil Gargano for Calvin Klein Activewear (copyright © 1982 by Calvin Klein Co.) and Volvo (copyright © 1962 by Volvo Inc.)

**You can hurt a Volvo,
but you can't hurt it much.**

This Volvo was bought new in Ann Arbor, Michigan, in 1956. Its owner paid $2345 for it, complete. He has raced it, pulled a camping trailer halfway across the country with it, his kids climb all over it, and it's seldom under cover. It has 80,261 miles on it. The head has never been off, the brakes have never been relined, the original tires lasted 55,000 miles, the clutch hasn't been touched, the valves have never been adjusted (much less ground), and it will still top 95 mph. Total cost of repairs exclusive of normal maintenance: One hood latch, $4.50. One suspension rod, $40.00. Not all Volvos will do this. But Volvos have a pretty good average. One enthusiastic owner in Wyoming wrote us that he has driven his Volvo over 300,000 miles without major repair. We think he's exaggerating. It's probably closer to 200,000 miles.

VOLVO

Volvo 122S compact. Like the Volvo above, it runs away from other popular-priced compacts in every speed range, gets over 25 miles to the gallon like the little economy imports, is virtually indestructible.

One would think "work" for Amil Gargano wouldn't have to mean nights and weekends any longer, what with Ally & Gargano being considered one of the best agencies in town. But it does.

"My day is filled dealing with the affairs of the company: dealing with clients, dealing with our staff and interpersonal relationships—that is, whether they're having difficulty with either an advertising problem or other people. So I was only able to work on the Calvin Klein advertising in the evening. The writer I worked with, Ron Berger [a group copy head], and I spent time with Calvin Klein talking about his viewpoints on fashion, on this particular collection, and about how he worked. He gave us articles to read—which we did—to find out more about him personally and his work philosophy, to make sure we understood what we were writing about. The last thing you do in the creative process is sit down and write an ad. That's the tip of the iceberg. But underneath is where the hard work is, digging out the information, gathering data about the product—performance, market, competition. You have to understand the client's goals. It's a real team effort among the account people, media, research, and the creatives. Anyway, after doing research we made some conclusions and started working. What we decided to work with was the Calvin Klein mystique, the Calvin Klein phenomenon."

The result of their work, the Calvin Klein Activewear campaign, was another outstanding, award-winning (the campaign won Amil a gold award from the Art Directors Club), trend-setting, creative achievement. Asked to comment on the consistently excellent work that comes out of his shop, Amil replied:

"At Ally & Gargano, the creative process is collaborative. While there are art/copy teams, they are not rigid—as is the case in some agencies—but fluid, so that people get to move around and work with others. Today, the difference between a good art director and a good copywriter isn't that big. It was once the art director's job to visualize a copywriter's words—so copywriters thought only about what was being said, and art directors only on how the ad looked. Today, however, creative people are coming to realize that an advertisement, print or broadcast, is a piece of communications, and they are all thinking in advertising terms. Perhaps Ally & Gargano advertising is effective because it evokes a human response from the audience. We try to touch people in a variety of ways: with humor, with stark reality—but always with the truth. We never talk down to them, or strain their credulity or sensibilities as so much advertising does. If Ally & Gargano has a creative formula, it is: 'Find the one piece of information that, if communicated to your audience in a memorable way, would cause them to respond exactly the way you intended them to.' A good example is the campaign we did for Pan Am in the nineteen-seventies. 'Every American has two heritages; we'd like to help you discover the other one.' The advertising dealt with a much larger issue. It was the quintessential airline campaign. It had a profound humanity. It touched people at the core of their emotions and made them feel good about the product. It was an accurate statement of what Pan Am was all about. And we did it without making any preposterous claims or unbelievable promises. We try to express in our work these things that are common to all of us; the things that never change; the things that people have always felt from the early development of the species. That's a more solid place to be. Trendy advertising is not for Ally & Gargano."

Another important factor in the creation of great advertising, according to Amil, and a good piece of advice for future creatives, is: "Conviction makes good work. It's the same with any kind of communications activity. If *you* believe something, you can go out there and convince others. If you don't believe it . . . well, then, you probably won't do a good job of convincing anyone else. That's why so much work out there is eminently forgettable. It's just out there, filling time and space. In order to write or visualize with conviction and authority about a product, you have to learn everything there is to know about the product. Knowledge is a weapon. To do a really effective job for a client, you must provide some new insight. Before you can do that, you have to get to know that client, what they're about and what they're trying to accomplish, and what the consumer thinks."

Another reason, perhaps *the most important* reason Ally & Gargano produces consistently exceptional, creative work, is the kind of creative director Amil is. He creates a good, comfortable environment in which people can function with some sense of freedom and contribution, a place where they feel their voices can be heard. This is not any easy task in the advertising business.

"Any kind of corporate structure has some threatening characteristics. It's my job, as creative director, to minimize those, to try to create a place where people say, 'I like what I am doing. And most important, where they can say, 'I trust the people here. I believe in the place!' It's remarkably simple, but abused so often. How can people do good work when other people are conspiring around or systematically undermining their confidence? Part of my job is to eliminate that kind of thing and encourage good relations and create the right environment for good work to flourish—to encourage good work by commenting on work in a constructive way, to preserve often-times fragile egos so people will come back with the job well done, so they can identify clearly their efforts and their contributions. To get them to look at an ad as an accurate representation of the product and the world in which it exists. Every once in a while, I like to do some of the work myself and hope it turns out successful. I believe, if you respect the work of the people you're working for, there's a good chance you'll better be able to accept their criticism."

A large part of being a creative director is making certain the right people are hired for the agency's creative jobs:

"A good or even brilliant portfolio isn't enough. I look for people who are a good fit for the agency, people who make the rest of us feel good about working with them. The chemistry has to be right. I want people who give of themselves and feel good about what they're doing. Creative snobs who are not willing to do anything unless it's completely on their terms are unacceptable, no matter how talented they are."

For would-be creatives Amil has this to say: "I wouldn't encourage or discourage someone I cared about who was thinking of getting involved in this business. I would suggest they learn as much about the business as possible so they could reach their own conclusions. I think, however, that it's important to understand that even competency doesn't come easy and that it requires an inordinate amount of hard work; to understand that it takes time to learn all one needs to know to produce good work. It's a slow process. I've been doing TV commercials for years, and it's only in the past few that I really know how to make things happen, how to get what was in my mind onto the screen. I would urge getting as much training as possible, to learn your craft and not to expect to do TV or major campaigns right away. And, understand, one needs perseverance and resiliency as much as talent. Because rejection is often the rule—you get rejected, your work gets rejected, your ideas get rejected. You've got to be able to come back. You must not be too soft, but you must not be too harsh or become obdurate. And you have to be able to fight off excessive cynicism and continue to maintain your conviction. If you become apathetic, you will become dull, and that is the worst curse in this business."

PART V

SUPPORTING SERVICES

The Supporting Service People

Supporting service people are specialists who supply the others with goods and services needed to get the job done. They are advertising's facilitators.

13 Supporting Service Job Descriptions

Accountant. All agencies require some outside accounting counsel, some more than others. Depending on the in-house financial staff, this counsel can be quite important to and greatly influence the profits of the agency. Accountants interested in servicing ad agency clients must have special knowledge of and understanding about the specific problems facing agencies. For instance, cash flow, media commissions and production charges are typically troublesome areas, as everyone must get paid on time in order for an agency to qualify for any discounts due them; however, most clients never pay on time. Advertising accountants work as independent consultants (sometimes also as a business-affairs consultant to an agency or production company) and for large accounting firms. For related jobs, see the section "Finance and Accounting Jobs," page 67.

Animator. There are several "animation houses" specializing in the creation of animated commercials. There are also, lately, computer animation houses or individuals who specialize in the art of computer animation for commercials. Animators work on animated commercials and/or parts of live-action commercials where animation is required. They also work on corporate logos, network identifications, industrials and even feature films. The jobs are varied, and most require technical and/or artistic training. For many, you must belong to a union (IATSE or NABET; see Appendix B for details) to qualify for employment. Some of the jobs available in the field are: *animation cameraman, animation designer, animation director, animation editor, background artist, checker, in-betweener, inker, matte artist, opaquer, computer artist.* For related jobs, see the sections "TV Commercial Crew," page 145, and "Video Technician," page 148.

Color Lab Jobs. Color labs do all work that is necessary on color photographs and artwork, including color correction, color enlargements and color retouching. Jobs run from the *sales rep*, who is responsible for contacting and servicing agency production people, to in-house *production managers*, to technicians such as *strippers, color separators* and *color film processors*. Many would-be photographers are attracted to color lab houses as a way of earning a living and improving their knowledge of film processing while trying to build up careers in photography.

Commercial Artist (a.k.a. Illustrator). Illustrators create the "artwork" (the term refers to charts, diagrams, pen-and-ink sketches, paintings) for advertisements, posters, displays, packages, collateral material, book covers, record albums and magazine articles. Generally, commercial artists work on a free-lance basis and secure work through an artists' "rep," whose job it is to show the artist's work to art directors. (For more on the relationship between an artist and his "rep," see the section "Photographers' and Artists' Rep," page 140.) Once an artist has been commissioned by an art director to illustrate an ad or other material, the two meet and discuss such things as what is to be conveyed by the artwork, the style the art director is after (although most times the artist is hired because of his style), the various mediums and materials which might be used, the size of the work and where it will be shown. The artist is usually shown a rough layout or preliminary design and the type style (or typeface) to be used. The illustrator then creates the artwork, always keeping in mind the art director's vision and instructions. Depending on the clout of an artist and/or his relationship with the art director, he may venture to formulate a new concept or alter an original idea, or he may create his artwork strictly to the art director's specifications without deviating. Commercial artists, unlike noncommercial artists, always strive to create work which is not only artistically excellent but which will attract the attention of consumers and stimulate their interest in whatever product or service is being advertised. The work requires enormous talent and skill. Most commercial artists are able to draw, sketch, paint, letter, retouch; and make charts, maps, architectural renderings, logos, etc. In the beginning of their careers, many commercial artists do all of those, in order to earn a living and to get their work seen. However, once an artist is established, he tends to specialize in a particular area and therefore be identified by the advertising community accordingly. He might be known for a particular style: realistic, abstract, cartoon; or for a medium: paint, acrylics, drawing; or for subject matter: sports, portraits, real estate.

Commercial artists may also design graph[...]
trademarks and logos, but mostly that wor[...]
designer. Building a successful career as a [...]
long and often difficult process. Most art[...]
careers by going to a good school such as [...]
Parsons, and work as a "bull-pen" artist [...]
graphics studio before venturing out on t[...] own. However,
there are some artists, just out of school, who go right out and
show their work to art directors and artists' reps in an attempt
to get work and convince someone to represent them. In any
case, a commercial artist must put together a portfolio of his
best work which most represents his style.

Conference and Exhibition Jobs.   Some time ago, ad agencies handled everything to do with the mounting of conferences and exhibitions for clients. Today, more and more, people with expertise in this area are being hired as independent
consultants and as employees of companies which specialize in
both or one of these fields. Jobs vary from *sales* to *conference
planners* to *artists* specializing in the creation of exhibitions.
For the names and addresses of possible places of employment,
look through the *Advertising and Communications Yellow Pages*,
under "Convention Services and Facilities."

Executive Search Placement Manager.   People who have
this title work for employment agencies such as Jerry Fields
Associates, the Judy Wald Agency and others that specialize in
placing people in jobs in the advertising/communications field.
Most often, placement managers such as these concentrate in
the particular area of advertising they have experience in. For
instance, a placement manager in the copy division will most
likely be a former copywriter. In addition to knowing their
field of interest, placement managers must also be skilled salesmen, as much of their job involves selling: persuading agencies
to hire them to recruit people, persuading people to leave
their jobs and take the new ones they are offering. This is a
good area for those with some experience in advertising and/or
a related field (marketing, merchandising, promotions), or for
those very skilled in recruitment and sales techniques.

Food Stylist.   Food stylists work free-lance for TV production companies and print photographers, and on the staff of
large corporations that produce packaged foods. It's their job
to make "camera ready" any food used on a shoot, whether the

the actual product or a prop for another product. Food
ists prepare the food, garnish it, treat it for special effects
d in general solve any on-camera food problems for the photographer. They know ways to keep food looking wonderful
under the intense lights needed to photograph a commercial or
print ad; they are capable of cooking in portable ovens at
makeshift locations and of others things related to the preparation and presentation of food to be used in photography. Most
food stylists are educated as home economists and have had
some experience with professional food before they venture
out on their own. One way of starting a career in this field is to
work as an assistant to a food stylist or food photographer, or as
a home economist for a company which manufactures packaged foods. Also, there are several universities which offer a
course in home economics.

Industrial (a.k.a. Business) Filmmaker. Industrial filmmakers create business films, mostly directly for the client; occasionally in conjunction with an ad agency. They work for
companies that specialize in the industrial film (as opposed to
the TV commercial). Often, these are companies that they
themselves have started—there are many entrepreneurs in this
field. Many industrial filmmakers are one-man operations, in
that they go after new business, write proposals, prepare budgets, write the film script, produce and sometimes direct the
business film. However, there do exist large industrial film production companies who employ writers, producers and salesmen with expertise in elements of industrial filmmaking. The
industrial film serves the client in a wide variety of purposes,
from public relations to selling tools to internal training. The
films range in length from a few minutes to over an hour. For
those interested in the field, a good entry-level job is that of
secretary/receptionist to an industrial filmmaker or to the
audiovisual department of a large corporation that makes, or
has made for it, business films on a regular basis.

Jingle Writer. Since radio was invented, the advertising industry has been using musical tunes as an immediately identifi-
able slogan for their clients—musical logos, so to speak. In the
past few years, advertising has increased its use of music, perhaps because studies have shown that music aids awareness
better than visuals or voice-overs. (Or perhaps it's because, as
David Ogilvy, a founder of Ogilvy & Mather, is reputed to have

said, "When you don't have anything to say, sing it.") Whatever the reason jingles are so widely used, those who write
them are highly talented musicians with a knack for the commercial. They must know how to write music *and* how to create
effective advertising. Most jingle writers work independently,
on a free-lance basis, project to project. Some work on-staff for
jingle-composing firms such as Michlin and Company, New
York, and HEA Productions, Inc., one of the city's most prestigious suppliers of music. In a very few cases, a music person is
employed by an advertising agency full-time. For example, for
many years, McCann-Erickson, a major New York–based ad
agency, has employed Billy Davis as a music director. Jingle
writing can be a very lucrative career once the writers are
established. Not only do they get paid handsomely for writing
jingles, they have the added opportunity of perhaps having
that jingle turn into a royalty-producing single hit—as with
"I'd Like To Teach the World to Sing," which began as an
advertising theme for Coca-Cola.

List Manager and Broker. List managers market other people's mailing lists. For instance, a large publishing company
might have a list of subscribers they wish to rent out, but they
have neither the staff nor the expertise to do the job themselves. They would hire a list manager. List brokers offer professional list consultation and services to ad agencies and/or
clients wishing to zero in on a particular market through the
mails. Brokers make recommendations as to which lists to rent,
and arrange for the actual mailing—that is, arrange for proper
postage, make sure the mailing piece is up to standard, and
even help prepare the direct mail piece itself. Jobs with list
managers and brokers range from entry-level *clerical* jobs to
computer-related jobs to *sales* jobs. (In this field, salesmen are
frequently called account executives.) For anyone interested in
this field, the Direct Marketing Association in New York runs
an educational foundation and has literature available. See Appendix B for details.

Media Sales. Media sales, the selling of time and space to
ad agencies, has come a long way since advertising's begin-
nings. There are media sales jobs available with newspapers,
magazines, radio and TV stations, and with independent media-
buying companies. The job of selling "time" is different from
the job of selling "space," and is therefore being handled sep-

arately (below). One similarity is that good media salesmen are depended on for much more than just taking orders. Media buyers depend on them for information about the reading or viewing habits of the audience they want to reach. They must have a broad knowledge of advertising, of their own medium and of their audience. Another similarity is that both time and space salesmen rely on creative and promotional staff members to help them do their jobs. Almost every newspaper, magazine and radio or TV station maintains a staff to prepare collateral material—media kits, presentation material, slides, filmstrips—anything that will support an advertising effort. Also, some media maintain a staff to help produce advertisements for the advertiser who doesn't have an agency or an in-house advertising department, making the media a good place for all advertising hopefuls to look toward for employment.

Print Sales.   Ninety-five percent of national magazines could not survive without the revenue they receive from their advertising pages. The same is true of most newspapers. The burden of earning this revenue is on the *advertising director, ad manager* and the staff of *space salesmen.* It's the ad director's job to oversee, for the publishers, the publication's entire advertising effort, from promotion to sales. It's the ad manager's job to supervise the sales staff, functioning like a sales manager at a corporation. Space salesmen call on ad agency, media and account people, via the telephone and in person, to present their publication and generate interest in the advertising pages for sale. Their tools are demographics that allow them to pinpoint just who the readers are, where they live, and what they earn. Space salesmen must be extremely well-versed, be persuasive about their medium and, in the case of trade publications, know about the business of their readers. (For instance, salesmen on the staff of *Meetings & Conventions Magazine* should know all there is to know about the convention business.) They must know and communicate at a moment's notice everything about their publication: editorial content, circulation, total readership, the quality and socioeconomics of the audience, publication rates and reader demographics. Space salesmen must be self-starters who can handle rejection, be able to deal with data and have a feel for figures. This is an interesting and lucrative area of employment, not often thought of when considering a career in advertising. One of its major benefits is instant responsibility, in that one starts out on a high level. Also, because the job is frequently on a commission basis, it is possible to earn a lot of money soon. From time to time, the large publishers (Hearst, Time & Life) run training programs for people interested in advertising sales. One publisher, Ziff-Davis, puts prospects through a four-hour written exam before interviewing them for the job of space salesman. A good book on the topic is *Selling Smart: How Magazine Pros Sell Advertising*, by Ira Ellenthal, published by Folio Publishing Corporation, of New Canaan, CT.

Time Sales. Time salesmen work for the networks and for independent TV and radio stations and for advertising-supported cable stations. It's their job to sell advertising time to advertising agencies and their clients—the advertisers. As commercial television, and some cable television, is dependent on advertising for existence, this is clearly an important function. It's no surprise then that the television industry spends millions of dollars and manpower hours to service the ad agencies, in an attempt to get a piece of the pie. There are several people involved in this complicated task, on all levels and of varying responsibilities. First of all, there are the top-level people, typically titled VP or director of whatever division of sales they are answerable for. For instance, *director of network news,* or *vice-president in charge of prime-time sales,* or, lower down the corporate ladder, *manager* of news sales. These are the people responsible for securing the greatest dollar revenue from their station's programs; also, for keeping the scheduling of programming in the hands of the media rather than those of the ad agencies—a condition that prevailed in radio in the 1920s and is always dangerously close to recurrence. Some of the responsibilities of top-level television sales people are: to recommend the pricing to management on all properties produced by their station (this is usually done by estimating the dollars in the marketplace each quarter versus program availability); to advise network management and the sales department of competitive situations on other networks (this is done by frequent contact with ad agencies and clients); to recommend the budget needed to run the department; to approve all sales of programs made by the sales personnel; to assist in developing sales aids produced by the promotion and advertising departments. Top-level sales jobs are complex and difficult and require a great

deal of skill, good judgment and diplomacy. Many top-level
people have come up through the ranks from sales jobs or from
media departments at major ad agencies. It's the job of the
salesman to respond to agencies, advertisers and reps as to
availability of time and pricing of programming. He may also
decide what programs may go into a sales plan, what information on sales should be sent to agencies and/or advertisers, and
when additional sales aids such as brochures or media studies
are needed. These tasks may be assigned to a sales manager.
The job of media sales is a difficult one requiring knowledge of
the pricing of all programming and the workings of the major
agencies throughout the country, as well as the ability to sell
and service advertisers and agencies. Top sales executives are
responsible for securing major advertisers as clients to ensure a
steady stream of money and profits. A strong background in
agency media is a good background for this type of sales job.
Also, a competitive spirit is essential, as sales representatives
must contend with competition from all three networks and
cable and independent stations, many of which run programs
simultaneously geared for the same target audience. The job of
sales representative and/or executive is also available with
radio stations. An interesting fact here is that radio sales is
apparently becoming a good field for women. According to the
Radio Advertising Bureau, 85 percent of radio stations employ
at least one saleswoman.

Media Representatives and Independent Media Buyers.   In addition to media sales jobs with print and broadcast media, there
are jobs available with independent firms that represent a
number of stations or publications. The large firms, such as
Katz in broadcasting and Story and Kelly-Smith in newspapers,
employ quite a few reps. Other firms are made up of just a few
persons, representing a small number of publications or independent stations. Magazine reps are generally paid 20 percent
of the net page rate, while TV reps are mostly paid on salary,
with a few earning a commission as well. In any case, reps must
be excellent salesmen, as they not only have to sell agencies on
their media, but also have to sell the media on themselves—
that is, on retaining their company to represent them. There
also exist media-buying jobs with independent media-buying
companies who service small ad agencies without a media department.

Merchandising and Sales Promotion Jobs. Merchandising and promotion are forms of advertising used to give a sales boost to a particular product. For example, giveaways, display and merchandising material, matchboxes and prize competitions are typical of this kind of advertising. Increasingly, the planning, coordination and execution of sales promotions are being handled by specialist companies—with the guidance of an agency *sales promotion coordinator*. This coordinator selects, negotiates terms with and supervises the work of outside suppliers. Jobs with suppliers and specialist companies run the gamut from sales to administrative to creative. These jobs exist with a multitude of merchandising and promotions companies: contest and sweepstakes creators, display and point-of-purchase giveaway manufacturers and marketing consultants. (For a list of specific companies, look in the *Advertising and Communications Yellow Pages*, your local Yellow Pages and *The Creative Black Book*; also, look for the Premium and Incentive Show at the New York Coliseum.) Often, ad agencies will require suppliers to come up with new and innovative merchandise and promotions to service their clients; other times, they hire them merely to implement an idea thought of by the agency or client. This is a sixteen-billion-dollar industry, with companies charging administrative fees of approximately $5,000 to, for instance, run a sweepstakes. So, unless you have real experience in the field, don't expect an upper-level job. But for those willing to start at the bottom, this is an interesting and lucrative and, at times, creative supporting service.

Model and Talent Agent. Models used in print ads and actors used in TV commercials are represented, in the first instance, by a model's agent (such as Eileen Ford); and in the second instance, by a talent agent. Generally speaking, model agent and talent agent are two separate careers, with each demanding particular talents and taking place in different working environments. Talent agents work for talent agencies that may or may not handle commercial actors exclusively. The probability is that the smaller agencies will be specialized, while the larger ones—like William Morris—will have a commercial department. J. Michael Bloom and Jacobson-Wilder are two which specialize in talent for commercials. Model agents work for model agencies, the four largest (known collectively as the Big Four) being: Ford Models, Inc., Elite Model

Management, Wilhelmina Models, Inc. and Zoli. These four agencies are quite powerful in the business and have managed to increase model fees some 400 percent in the past few years (with top models earning $2,500 per hour). Recently, a number of new agencies have sprung up in New York, providing alternate places for would-be agents to look for work. Among them: Charney Model Management, Legends and L'Image. More than six hundred agencies can be found throughout the country, with several in Los Angeles. Many powerful agents began as secretaries to a seasoned agent, working their way up to an *assistant agent* or *booker,* and ultimately to full-fledged agent. And some of those went on to start their own agencies. For example, Sue Charney headed Ford's women division before forming her own agency. Both talent agents and model agents are often called on to do a lot more than find work for their actors and models. First of all, they often scout potential models and actors in an attempt to find new faces and fresh talent, which gives them a big part in deciding who will or who won't work in the advertising industry. Model agents must often act as surrogate parent, accountant and psychiatrist, for many models are in their teens or early twenties when they leave their hometowns for modeling careers. And talent agents are relied on by ad agencies and production companies—when they haven't a specific actor in mind—to make casting suggestions based on a storyboard or even on a sketchy verbal description. The large agencies have formal training programs for would-be agents, highly competitive, although the TV commercial area is not so bad as the feature film or theatrical divisions. One usually starts out as a secretary, so it's a good idea to brush up on typing skills and phone manners if you're interested in either of these jobs. An interesting variation on the job is that of *animal agent.* That's right, an agent representing animals that appear in TV commercials and print advertising. For those interested, there are a few agencies—Animal Talent Scouts and All-Tame Animals, in New York—specializing in the field.

New Product Development Jobs. There now exist about a half dozen new-product companies which develop new products for packaged goods manufacturers. These companies, typically owned and run by former advertising agency employees, specialize in the conception of new product ideas and in repositioning existing products. For example, putting Arm & Hammer baking soda in refrigerators is an example of a product repositioning that sent sales soaring. This is a rather new and unexplored area with few job openings. However, it might be a good area for those with experience in research, for much of professional new-product development involves research. Also, this area opens up a new sphere of work for those who've worked in new-product development or marketing on the client and agency side. Gerald Schoenfeld, Inc., is a new-product development company located in New York.

Outdoor Advertising. Outdoor advertising (billboards) is big business—with millions of dollars spent each year by agencies on behalf of their clients. People who manage this industry are responsible for obtaining, from property owners, leases to sites for erection of billboard signs, for negotiating prices and for selling billboard space to ad agencies. As many major advertising agencies assign outdoor advertising accounts to junior account executives, this could be a good place for would-be account executives to get some early experience and be one-up on the competition. Most towns in the country have billboards, so they also have outdoor advertising agencies. A related job is that of *sign painter*. An apprenticeship with a seasoned sign painter might be a good first or part-time job for would-be advertising artists, prop makers, etc.

Photographer. Commercial photographers work on their own, free-lance, for ad agencies, graphic studios, corporations and retail stores. Also, some work on-staff for large ad agencies, photographic studios, graphic arts studios, retail stores and corporations. In any case, it's the photographer's job to provide photographs to illustrate print advertisements and collateral material (brochures, annual reports, point-of-purchase material). In most cases, *on-staff photographers* are called on to do internal assignments—that is, house newsletters, public relations news releases, new business presentations, etc., while free-lancers are employed to shoot major photographs that will be used in print ads and various other pieces of material. Photographers, like commercial artists, find work through a representative, who shows the photographer's work to many different art directors. When an art director believes a photographer, based on his style, experience and price, is correct for a particular job, he is retained. Then, his relationship with the art director evolves into one that is similar to the art director's with the commercial artist. That is, it becomes the photographer's job to implement the art director's vision. The photographer is shown a layout of the ad, discusses concept, size, and style with the art director—and only then takes his pictures. He's responsible for selecting and assembling the equipment, according to subject and desired effect; for planning composition; finding a location; altering or measuring light level; directing the action of the models and the activities of the other workers (food stylists, stylists, assistants); and for making sure that the quality of the prints delivered to an art director is superb. Again, depending on a photographer's clout and/or relationship with the art director, he may be given a great deal of freedom or he may be told to deliver exactly what the layout calls for, right down to the camera angle. Many advertising photographers specialize in a particular area, such as *food, fashion, product* or *aerial* photography. And most—although there are a few exceptions to this rule—concentrate in either advertising or editorial photography. When a photograph is indicated, most times that photograph is crucial to the success of an ad; this makes the photographer's job important. Competition for work is intense, and those who make it are usually more than a little talented and skilled. One way of breaking into the field is to work as an assistant or stylist for an established photographer. (Look through *The Creative Black Book* for a listing.) Those interested in the job must prepare a portfolio of their work which indicates the type of photography they do and the degree of their skill.

Photographers' and Artists' Rep. It's the job of these unique "salesmen" to discover artists and/or photographers who are salable, commercial and reliable; and to get them work within the advertising industry. Most reps market either the work of photographers or illustrators; a few represent both. Reps accomplish this difficult and highly competitive job by calling on thousands of art directors and/or art buyers at advertising agencies throughout the country, in person, by phone and through the mails via "mailers," which are scaled-down samples of an artist's work. They show artists' portfolios, discuss upcoming jobs with art directors and make suggestions as to appropriate artists. Reps come from all fields of work, including those related and not related to advertising. One of the most prominent illustrators' reps, Darwin Bahm, was a magazine publisher, copywriter, motel owner and scrap-metal broker before, at age 35, he started his career. Artists' rep can be a highly lucrative career, with reps earning 25 percent commission on their artists' work. However, it can take years before one develops a reputation strong enough to gain entry into the major agencies and attract successful artists. One way is to discover new talent (established artists like to be represented by established reps) and go outside of New York to find work for them.

Printing Sales Rep.   There are several types of jobs available with large and small printing companies servicing the advertising industry. However, most are highly technical (for instance: pressmen, quality control people, foremen) and have little to do with the rest of the advertising industry. Yet there is the job of printing sales representative, which is an interface-type job. Printing sales reps are crucial to the advertising industry, as they are the liaisons between the industry and the printing trade. As such, they must know about the business of both. It's their job to visit advertising agency production departments to solicit business; to provide formal and informal cost estimates; to explain, to agency staff members, technical choices such as the various methods of reproduction, types and weights of paper, shades and types of ink; and to follow through on quality control. (It's not unusual for a printer to stay with a job into the middle of the night . . . when that job is important to one of his important ad agency clients.) Some salesmen branch out on their own, becoming *brokers*. Top sales representatives at big printing companies usually work on commission, and can earn very large amounts. Large printing firms employ a great many people, including an art staff, proofreaders, estimators, production managers and purchasing personnel (e.g., to buy paper)—making it feasible for someone to learn the printing business from within and work his way up to sales rep or into an agency production department.

Property Maker and Handler.   Props are all physical adjuncts necessary to the creation of a TV commercial except for lighting, scenery and wardrobe. The people who make props and models in wood, plastic, metal, glass, fabric, clay or in any combination of materials for use in print ads, TV commercials, promotions and/or presentations, are known as *propmakers*.

They are employed by one of several property companies which specialize in building props and models (e.g., the Prop Shop), turning an art director's concept (e.g., a ten-foot hamburger) into a working reality. In addition to the job of propmaker, there are several free-lance union (NABET) jobs dealing with the handling of props. These are *property master*, the person on the set responsible for the entire property department, *property assistant*, and the *outside property person*, the individual responsible for locating and arranging for the rental or purchase of properties to be used in a TV commercial. The technician who dresses the properties on the set, under the supervision of the art director or stylist, is called the *set dresser*. Not all ads or commercials require the same number of prop people; sometimes only one person is needed.

Research Jobs.   In addition to the research jobs within advertising agencies and the advertisers, which have been described in other parts of the book, there are also jobs available with independent research companies, generally referred to by agency people as "the vendors" or "the suppliers." Such firms are employed by ad agencies of all sizes for a variety of reasons. Small agencies with no research departments of their own completely rely on suppliers for all research programs. Large agencies use them to supplement their own internal staff and to perform the field work. Upper- and middle-level research jobs with independent suppliers are pretty similar to those with agencies or advertisers; however, here is where you will find the entry-level research jobs. More specifically, *junior analysts*, *field operators* and *telephone solicitors* are all entry-level research jobs requiring little or no experience, which can be found at outside research supply firms servicing the advertising agencies.

Retoucher.   While this job is within the print-production area, retouchers are rarely employed by ad agencies. They either work free-lance or for companies that specialize in this service. Such companies are few. Retouchers are artists; they can make magical changes on a photograph, whether they're changing the color of a beverage, adding a desirable feature or minimizing an unattractive one. Retouchers use pencils or watercolors to accentuate lights and shadows and to produce clear and attractive photos. There are also artists known as *airbrush artists*, who are expert at mixing and spraying paint, and who concentrate in the retouching craft. The job of retouching is highly skilled, and requires a great deal of patience and knowledge. Most of the art schools offer courses in retouching, and it sometimes is possible to find a job as an apprentice to a seasoned retoucher. Once you are established, you can go out and contact ad agency production managers and art directors, show them your work and tell them you're available for free-lance assignments.

Script Person. The script person or script clerk is an important member of the TV production crew. It's this person's job to maintain the shooting script for the director. This entails keeping a detailed, accurate, up-to-date script by recording all details: changes in dialogue and action, camera placement and movement, actor and prop positions, actor distance from the camera, prop and set dressing locations, costume conditions and placement. The script supervisor is also responsible for maintaining continuity and timing. He keeps a detailed record of everything that happens during a take so that juxtaposed scenes may be matched. He records satisfactory "takes" as dictated by the director. And he organizes all script notes, scene changes and modifications to be delivered to the director and film editor at the end of production. The accurate final script that the script clerk prepares during production is crucial to the successful editing and timing of a commercial. Script clerks are members of one of the two craft unions, and the only way to get trained as such is by apprenticing to an established clerk.

Set Designer. The set designer builds the set for the commercial director. Together they plan what a set will look like, but the set designer is responsible for supervising the actual construction of the set. It's his responsibility to visualize the director's concept. Set designers are members of the union and generally work on a free-lance basis for TV production houses.

Stock Photo and Stock Music Company Jobs. Not all advertisers can afford original photography; and in some cases, even when the budget allows for it, something else stands in the way, such as the subject being dead or a shot being out of bounds to anyone but an astronaut. In such cases, stock photo people are called on to look through their files for suitable stock photographs: photographs that are owned by and available for rental from a stock photo company. If one of their photographs is chosen by the ad agency, the photo company charges a rental fee, the amount depending on where and how many times the photo will be used. Stock music companies offer agencies the opportunity to score their commercials with something other than expensive original music. Such firms maintain a library of tapes and records which they rent out for a fee. To work for either of these types of rental companies, one needs some knowledge of their respective disciplines as well as an understanding of where and how music or photography can influence a TV commercial or print ad. While neither of these jobs will lead directly to a career as a jingle writer or photographer, both can be excellent first jobs for someone interested in those professions. Working for these types of "storage places," even as a clerk, could put one in contact with the industry and provide an interesting education. For a list of stock music companies and stock photo companies, see *The Creative Black Book.*

Stylist.   Stylists are responsible for dressing and accessorizing the actors and models employed for use in TV commercials or print ads, and at times for dressing the properties on a set under the supervision of the art director and/or director. Most stylists work free-lance, are union (NABET) members and get chosen for projects by the director—in the case of TV commercials—and by the photographer for print work. Some stylists work on-staff for big production houses and/or photographic studios. It's the stylist's job—after studying a storyboard and conferring with the director, photographer and art director—to determine what "look" they are going after and, after meeting with the actors or at least studying their pictures, to go out and shop for all clothing accessories, fabrics, and sometimes props, needed for accurately reflecting the tone and style of the advertisement and the characters being portrayed. In addition to a flair for style and a good eye for fashion, stylists need to be skilled in determining which clothing and accessories will yield optimum photographic realization. Much of their time is spent buying and returning items and, when period costumes are required, supervising the execution of costumes—all at the direction and subject to the approval of the art director, director, and/or photographer. Good stylists tend to work repeatedly for the same directors. For those interested in this job, contact NABET for further information.

Talent Payment Firms.   There do exist talent payment companies that perform a variety of jobs for their clients, the advertising agencies. For the small agencies that have no talent-payment staff, these firms function as a radio and television broadcast business department, servicing all their needs from pre-production through broadcast use and reuse of commercials. For the larger agencies, such firms might only be required to make periodic payments to actors and maintain accurate records on the life cycle of each commercial. At any rate, jobs within such firms range from administrative to accounting, and are only one-way streets to other jobs within talent payment. But, for someone unable to find such a job within an agency, this could be the place to seek entry-level employment. For related jobs, see the section "Talent Payment Jobs," page 106.

TV Commercial Crew. There are several jobs involved in the actual making of TV commercials—on the set at the time of photography and in post-production work such as editing. Many of those jobs have been described in this chapter. The others, mostly technical, are: *cameraman, carpenter, cartoonist, costumer, editor, electrician, grip, laboratory technician, makeup artist* and *hairstylist;* also, *scenic artist, set painter, sound technician, special effects man,* et al. Depending on the type of commercial, the size of the production house shooting the spot, the budget and where it's shot, the technician staff will be union or not, skeleton or full, all free-lancers or some on-staff people. Generally, crew members belong to one of the entertainment unions, such as the Directors Guild of America (with offices in New York, Los Angeles and Chicago); NABET—National Association of Broadcast Employees and Technicans (also with offices in those three cities); and IATSE—International Alliance of Theatrical Stage Employees and Moving Picture Machine Operators of the United States and Canada (with offices throughout both countries). And, they are hired by production houses rather than by agencies. Specific admissions information must be sought from the union locals, but generally speaking, exams are given, and those who pass are placed on an apprentice list and must work enough hours within a three-year period to gain experience. It is not easy to get into a union, and some say it is nearly impossible, but some do manage. (For further information on unions, see Appendix B.) For job descriptions of these technical jobs, see *The Business of*

Show Business: A Guide to Career Opportunities Behind the Scenes in Theatre and Film, a Harper & Row book by this author. In addition to TV commercial crew jobs, there are some technical film and video jobs available within the ad agencies that own studio facilities (some large agencies have studios that are equal to broadcasting stations) where they screen commercials in various stages of completion for agency people and their clients, and where they screen sample reels, conduct casting sessions, look at slides and all other audiovisual material. The equipment includes film projectors; videotape players and monitors; audio tape players; slide projectors; and sometimes cameras, lights and other equipment needed in a television studio for recording pictures and sound. The people employed to handle the equipment are a union *projectionist*, a union *stagehand* and sometimes—to supervise everyone involved and arrange bookings for the screening rooms—an *audiovisual manager*. (For further information on TV commercial technical jobs, see, in this part of the book, descriptions of the following jobs: animator, casting director, food stylist, industrial filmmaker, jingle writer, property maker and handler, production manager, stylist, television director, producer, set designer, script clerk, video technician and production assistant.) For in-house audiovisual jobs, it's required that applicants have some sort of technical or vocational school training and on-the-job experience. For free-lance crew jobs, applicants must also have experience in the field and be trained in their particular craft. Neophytes traditionally start out as production assistants and then try to convince someone in the business to train them in whatever discipline (makeup, camerawork, sound) they are interested in. For further information, see the profile of Jeanne Harrison in Chapter 14.

   TV Commercial Director.   TV commercial directors are specialists with an expertise in the creation of TV commercials as opposed to theatrical films. (Although many commercial directors do ultimately direct features after gaining experience in this area.) It's the director's job to "shoot the storyboard," that is, to turn a piece of paper into a thirty- (:30) or sixty- (:60) second effective TV commercial. He is responsible to the agency producer and for directing the production activities of cast and crew. In order to "tell" the storyboard cinematically (and that's just what he is hired to do—he can add to the storyboard but never subtract), he surveys locations; plots the camera angles; blocks and directs the action of the actors; supervises the action of the crew; oversees the film editing, sound recording, voice-over, music scoring and the mix (where all sound elements are mixed together on the track). He is knowledgeable in all areas of production: photography, lighting, sound, set design, music, editing, quality control and, finally, in coaxing good performances from actors. Many are expert in the techniques of videotape. While a few of the very large agencies employ full-time TV commercial directors, most do not. Generally, directors work for production houses (where they are the main attraction), but some head up their own firms (where they may be the only director on the staff). On projects where the director requires assistance, a *first assistant director,* and sometimes a *second assistant director,* is hired. This is a highly competitive area that is difficult to break into. The traditional entry-level job for director or for any job in TV production is that of production assistant; But any job in a production house would be a good first one for someone considering a career as a TV commercial director. For further information, see the profile of Jeanne Harrison, TV commercial director, in Chapter 14, page 149.

TV Commercial Production Assistant.   See the section "Production Assistant," page 105.

TV Commercial Production Manager.   Production managers work either free-lance, on a project-to-project basis for several production houses, or on-staff, full-time, for one production house. They are directly responsible to the production house producer and/or director and are, in fact, the producer's representative on the set. Production managers are responsible for arranging and scheduling all TV production elements. Their duties consist of budgeting, preparing a sequence breakdown and shooting schedule, determining the need for and then hiring the appropriate number of union technicians and selecting and organizing permits for location shooting and studio facilities. And, most important, production managers authorize all orders and expenditures and disburse company funds. At some production companies, the person handling these responsibilities is given the title of "producer," and has the added responsibility of dealing with the client (the agency) on a daily basis. Production managers are members of the Directors Guild of

America (DGA). The best way to train for this job is, first, as a production assistant, then as an assistant to a production manager. For further information, contact the DGA for information on their intern program.

TV Production-Company On-Staff Jobs.   Television production companies range in size from very large (e.g., Steve Horn with about thirty full-time employees) to boutiques. In the first case, producers, directors, production managers, production assistants, casting directors, secretaries and sometimes even location scouts, stylists and some technicians are employed full-time. In the second, more usual, case, only one or two people will be on staff full-time; the others are called upon from a regular pool of talent on an as-needed basis. Many of these jobs have already been described in this part of the book. The one job that does differ somewhat in this situation is that of *production-company producer*. While it's the job of an agency producer to liaison with the production company, it's the job of the production-company to take care of business for the production-company director. This entails such things as preparing competitive bids based on storyboards sent from the agency to at least three production companies, and after a job is awarded his company, maintaining a good rapport with the agency producer and/or client, keeping track of all expenses, supervising the production manager. Some production companies employ the services of a *production-company rep*, whose job it is to solicit work for the company director(s) by approaching agency producers and getting them to see a reel of the best and/or most significant work of the director. The traditional entry-level job at any production company is gofer, the low man on the totem pole responsible for doing everything no one else wants to do—like getting coffee and running other errands. For further information on TV production jobs, see the profile of Jeanne Harrison in Chapter 14.

Video Technician.   In the past few years, TV commercials have been made on videotape as well as film. This fact, coupled with the "electronic revolution," causes a need for people trained in videotape production. And since video equipment is different from film, technicians are not interchangeable: engineers, technical directors, video operators and even video directors must be specially trained in the art of videotape. Yet this training is not easily available—no school could afford to keep equipment up to professional standards because of state-of-the-art changes every week. Those interested in the field would do best to look for work with a video production and/or rental house, even as a messenger, to learn the needed skills and about the equipment. For a list of such companies, see *The Creative Black Book*. One video company in New York is Modern Telecommunications, Inc.

Miscellany. There are many more supportive service jobs than there is room to mention. Just to name a few, there are jobs with *typographers*, which produce the type the art director chooses: *art supply and equipment companies; photostat companies*, which duplicate, enlarge and/or reduce printed material; *advertising agency associations and service organizations; advertising award organizations*, such as the Clios; *advertising schools, advertising personnel offices; recording studios; film equipment rental companies*, a traditional first job for would-be camera operators. There are law offices that specialize in handling advertising agency clients, particularly the merging of agencies. Hall, Dickler, Lawler, Kent & Friedman is such a firm. There are services and companies that never existed before someone identified a need and started them. For example, in St. Louis a company provides telephone information to customers and, right in the middle, zaps them with a commercial. In New York a company was formed which flashes ads at customers while they stand in supermarket checkout lines. Another creates electronics ads at airports. An enterprising American was the first person to open a Yellow Pages agency in England and Italy. So, if the mainstream isn't for you, scrutinize *The Creative Black Book*, the *Advertising and Communications Yellow Pages* and other directories and look for supporting service organizations that interest you. Or if you believe you can offer a service which doesn't yet exist . . . perhaps involving the new electronic media . . . start something yourself.

14 Profile of a TV Commercial Director

Jeanne Harrison, TV Commercial
Producer/Director, Harrison Productions

Jeanne Harrison is a TV commercial producer and director, working out of her own production shop which she began in 1970. It's the job of a production company, and therefore

Jeanne's job, to turn the agency's storyboard into a film or videotape commercial. In Jeanne's own words, "What I do is take the storyboard and interpret it for the agency and the client. I start out with a piece of paper and a set of pictures with dialogue. I end up with a thirty- or sixty-second story on film or tape. I make it come alive for the agency. And when I'm doing that, I never forget for a moment why. I'm doing it to move the goods off the shelf for the advertiser."

Some of the products Jeanne has helped "move off the shelf" are Anacin, Dristan, Quaker Oats, Listerine, Mazola Corn Oil, Dermassage, Arrow Shirts, Stove Top Stuffing, Oleg Cassini Clothing, Arm & Hammer products, Ocean Spray Cranberries, Good Humor, Pond's Cold Cream, Jif Peanut Butter, Bloomingdale's fashions, cosmetics and appliances; and many, many more. As an independent producer/director she has created over two thousand spots and won several industry awards, including several Clios and Andys. Before becoming a director, Jeanne was an advertising agency producer and worked on the client side, although she laughingly remarks, "I've really always been a director."

Jeanne Harrison is a remarkable lady, with a career that defies every rule in the ad-game book. First of all, she's managed to succeed at an occupation, TV commercial director, more sought-after and harder to attain than any other in advertising. Second, and most astounding, she is a woman director who ventured out on her own at a time when the only other women found on a set were actresses, or perhaps makeup artists. As she herself readily admits, "Lady directors are still very strange beings to some people; even today I'm considered somewhat of a freak." Lastly, and again uniquely, because she has worked in every environment—for an ad agency, for an advertiser, in commercial production and even for the media— she knows well all facets of advertising, not only her particular discipline. Jeanne is proof that, providing you have belief in yourself, guts, determination and ability, you can do the work you want, via the route most fitting for you, even in a business overrun by convention and pigeonholing.

Jeanne's entry into the business of advertising was interesting. She began as what many commercial directors aspire toward becoming, a director of full-length films. But she found the challenge of directing "little pieces of theater, a new one every week" much more enjoyable.

"I started my career in radio. Before that I went to college, Temple University, from which I was never graduated. My mother, who was quite unusual for her time, was a radio program director, so radio was a natural place for me to look for work. I started as a secretary to a producer/director at a radio production company, Ziv. After I'd been working there one year, my boss phoned in sick one day and said, 'Today, Jeanne, you're going to have to direct the radio show.' Which I did. I guess I had been learning through osmosis. At any rate, eventually I made a producer/director out of myself. Because the company went from producing radio entertainment to television entertainment, I moved along in the same direction, becoming a television director in the process and directing such shows as *Boston Blackie* and *The Cisco Kid*. Again, I learned by watching other people do it and by asking questions. Asking questions is something I've never been afraid to do. It always seems ridiculous to me to try to bluff your way through—it's so much easier and smarter to simply ask an expert how. Ziv moved out West and I chose to remain in New York. I was married then [Jeanne is the mother of two grown daughters— one a producer with an advertising agency, the other an actress], and I felt this was my home."

That was in the early sixties, and Jeanne's knowledge of TV production landed her a job with J. Walter Thompson as one of the first women producers in the advertising industry. She remained with J. Walter for seven years, doing what agency producers do: liaisoning between the agency and the production house and making certain her commercials were brought in on time, within budget and creatively on target. Her accounts were Lever Brothers, Standard Brands and Warner-Lambert. And she was good at her job—so good, in fact, that American Home Products (an advertiser) approached her to handle their commercial production at Ted Bates Advertising, then American Home's agency. It was an enviable position to be in, having the client on your side, recruiting for their advertising agency. Jeanne accepted the invitation and left J. Walter Thompson. However, while off on a holiday in Mexico, Jeanne learned Bates had resigned the account and she was out of a job. But, not to fear, American Home valued Jeanne too much to leave her in the lurch. They wanted her to handle their radio and TV

Jeanne Harrison, TV commercial producer/director, Harrison Productions. *(Bill Bragdon)*

production, one way or another. The way they found was for Jeanne to help turn their small, print-only, in-house agency into a full-service shop complete with its own TV production division, and with Jeanne at the helm of the division. So she moved over to the client side, serving for three years as senior vice-president and creative director, producing and directing spots for all of American Home's products.

Working at American Home taught Jeanne many things and made her privy to the behind-the-scenes goings-on of a large corporation. Even though her job was in TV production, this was an in-house situation that put her much closer to the marketing decisions, the sales force, etc. Jeanne became even more aware that it's the ultimate job of a commercial to sell products. Also, she gained greater insight into the corporate mentality and learned what the concerns of a client are and why production, for them, is sometimes such a nerve-racking process. It's where the buck stops. Where the marketing strategy, creative plan and endless meetings come to fruition. After maybe six months of talking, designing and planning, the commercial is finally being realized. And all that talk, strategy and design must be squeezed into thirty or sixty seconds. So, working on the client side was excellent exposure for Jeanne. But after three years, she was satiated with the corporate environment and ready to go off on her own "to make some money for myself." She decided to open her own boutique production company with her as the star director; this despite the odds against success. (Being accepted as a "new" independent director is never easy in a field *always* glutted with talent. And her being a woman made it twice as hard—this was 1970, a time when women were not exactly greeted with open arms: not by agencies, by clients, or by hurly-burly technicians unaccustomed to taking orders from a woman.)

"I had a small contract for some work from American Home and belief in myself as a director. In spite of everything, I just knew it would happen for me. And I was right, it did. But not immediately. The first few years were very, very tough. My production manager, who has been with me for many years, was with me then; and at one point we had so much time on our hands that we wrote a handicraft book (a charming how-to providing instructions for needlepoint dolls). It really was touch-and-go there for a while. I tried using a producer's rep, but that didn't work either."

Slowly, work started coming Jeanne's way—mostly, she says, "because of excellent word-of-mouth. Every time I did a spot I was given another to do. Repeats, even today, is what gets me work." Eventually Jeanne built up her little boutique into a four-million-dollar a year business. The first contract with American Home had provided her with grist for the mill, a chance to prove she could do it. That was only half of it. The other half was getting out there and meeting people and convincing them she could deliver exactly what they wanted and needed. Advertising people are a cautious breed, and unless a director has on his reel a commercial that exactly reflects the quality they are looking for, an agency won't even bid a production house for a job. It was a challenge for Jeanne to demonstrate she could produce all kinds of commercials: comedy, hidden-camera, food, fashion, health-product spots, when many producers would only hire her to do what she already had done. (Scores of directors never overcome this barrier, and spend their entire professional lives directing one type of product in one medium and in one directing style.) Yet, Jeanne, while she is primarily known for her slice-of-life campaigns and for cost-efficient spots, has managed to direct a wide variety of film and tape, including a series of seventeen industrial shows with Bob and Ray for Alcoa, spots with "Elsie the Cow" and glamour spots with Cristina Ferrare. Quite a few years ago she directed her first videotape commercial, a medium Jeanne and many others believe has revolutionized the industry.

"I first started working in video because, in its infancy, it had some definite cost advantages over film that it doesn't always enjoy today. A few adventurous agency producers decided to give me and it a try, so I decided to jump in. Before I jumped in, though, I picked the brains of everyone I knew who knew anything about tape (again relying on asking questions rather than bluffing her way through). The early days of videotape were both exciting and frustrating. The equipment was horrendously large, with cameras as big as vans; and there were more things you couldn't do than things you could. Still, it was amazing to play back a shot almost instantaneously, get client approval and get on with the editing. No dailies, work prints, rough cuts. Of course, videotape editing in those days was a problem, taking hours longer than today's computerized luxury. Hardly a day went by, in the beginning, without a new development—just as today almost every twenty-four hours brings another new piece of equipment, a new technique to broaden the capabilities of tape. With the incredible equipment available, I don't think there's going to be anything you can't do in videotape—video is certainly where it's all going to be in the future, and I would encourage anyone interested in commercial production to learn all they can about it."

Today, Jeanne works in both film and tape, but prefers tape "because it's more satisfying and faster to work with, and because certain products respond better to tape than to film. . . . It gives you that urgent 'now' look that I'm so often after," she says. Whatever the medium, Jeanne loves what she does.

After trying all sides of the business, she finally found her niche. Now, her days as a director are divided three ways: into pre-production, production and post-production.

"Working as I do as a producer/director [with a full-time staff of four and a pool of the best technicians available], I get involved with a commercial from the time an agency producer sends us a bid request and remain with the spot until it is 'in the can.' Agencies are supposed to send out bids to at least three different production companies, a practice instituted some years back by agency management to discourage payola from influencing a producer's choice of production house. Either my production manager or my assistant will go over to the agency to what is called a bid session—at which time the storyboard is gone over and we find out approximately how much time we would be given to shoot, whether the spot is to be on film or tape, and what the philosophy behind the spot is. Sometimes they tell us if the spot will be shown nationally or if it is regional or if it is to be a test; sometimes even they don't know. Then I study the storyboard and break it down to production elements: how long it would actually take me to shoot, how many in crew I would need, what kind of studio will be rented (very few production shops have their own studios), how much I intend to spend on the set, whether I am responsible for casting or the agency is. We do an A.I.C.P. form, which is a printed form including every production category, leaving room for our price. We send it and the total price back to the agency and either get the job or not. Sometimes an agency will choose the lowest bidder for the job; other times not. They may be more concerned with who the director is, or how much money he intends to spend on the set, or whatever.

"Once I'm awarded a job and the estimate is signed, we have a pre-pro [pre-production meeting] with the client, agency and my key staff. If we agree on everything, a date is set and we spin wheels. My production manager and I gather the crew. I work with the same crew [union—NABET and/or IA] every time. Knowing and choosing excellent technical people is an important part of my job as a director. The first person I usually hire is the set designer. Together we plan what the set will look like. That's the most fun part of my job and very crucial to the success of a commercial. The set, the furnishings, the props, reflect so much: who the characters in the spot are, and whether the target audience can relate. Also, the set is crucial to the visual feeling I want to bring to the job. The set is built a day or more before shooting—or more days if something intricate has to be constructed, which it often does. For instance, I've had a yacht built in a studio for some Bloomingdale's spots, and once on a location in Arizona, I had a dude ranch reconstructed. The set designer and production manager oversee the building of the set, with everything subject to my approval. I also meet with the stylist to say what kinds of clothing I want the actors to wear and what kinds of accessories they should have. She then buys them, or if the budget doesn't call for that, helps the actors choose from their personal wardrobes. If special effects or special props are needed, they too must be bought or built during pre-production. Most times the agency does the casting, but when we are retained, we do so as early on as we can. A crucial member of the crew is the script clerk; and I try to get the same one on all my shoots, because a bad one can easily ruin a commercial by timing something wrong or by not paying attention to continuity. A good script clerk should really function as a troubleshooter, keeping a director out of trouble.

"Once everything is built and everyone hired, we are ready for production. On production day you walk into a studio or on location, and there everyone is—client, agency producer, creative director, copywriter, art director—eating your Danish and drinking your coffee. [It's been said when bidding for a job, 'It's not the reel, it's the meal,' referring to the lavish breakfasts and lunches that production companies are expected to and often do provide for their agency clients.] Everyone is

Jeanne Harrison directing a Dristan commercial. *(Photo by Harrison Productions)*

very nervous and has his own particular point of view and list of things he's responsible for. The client is concerned with the way the product looks, the copywriter with his words, the art director with his pictures, the creative director with every- thing. Then there are the legal matters to worry about: Has this or that word that the SCC or networks demanded be omitted been omitted? If the agency producer is good, he keeps every- one calm and in control and, as much as possible, away from the director, crew and actors, who of course have plenty to concentrate on."

As director, it's Jeanne's job to keep her client—and their client, the advertiser—calm and rational. But more important, it's her job to direct the actors, block out their action, and make sure their intonations are correct, their timing is good, that they're in view of the camera and being picked up by sound. Also, it's her job to guide the crew and make sure the lighting is enhancing, the camera is correctly focused, and the product is translating correctly to film. She must know when she's covered something and when another take must be done; which take will cut; which won't. ("When an agency person asks for another 'take' of a scene," Jeanne says, "I do it. It's smarter than arguing. After all, there's only one way to doing a scene—and that's two ways. It usually becomes apparent, dur- ing the editing, which is right!")

There's a myriad of things the director is responsible for . . . often with much money at stake. (Although Jeanne rarely di- rects very expensive commercials, other directors have been known to charge as much as a half million dollars for a spot.) Also, production can be extremely tedious and emotionally draining; yet the director, throughout, must remain in control, optimistic, encouraging, and supportive of everyone's (and particularly the actor's) ego.

After overseeing the editing (which, with video, can be done almost immediately), the mix, and sometimes the music (though most often the agency handles that), Jeanne puts the thirty or sixty seconds in the can or cassette, sends it off and starts all over again.

Obviously, some very special qualities are required of a di- rector, not to mention technical proficiency and talent. Jeanne believes that sensitivity, a sense of humor and a love of what she does are what most enable her to succeed in this highly competitive, venturesome field. She adds:

"I love this business. I have a good time doing what I do, maybe because I like the people I work with. And when I don't like them, I don't have to work with them again. That's an advantage to working in the commercial area—you're always working with new people on new projects in new locations. I've gone all over the world to shoot: France, Mexico, Spain, and throughout this country as well. Also, I'm not like so many commercial directors who are dying to direct features. I already have, and I found it more gratifying to do commercials. What a challenge to have to establish a character in a few opening seconds on a commercial and make that character believable to a viewer in just thirty seconds."

As advice to would-be directors, Jeanne adds these thoughtful, honest words:

"If you want to produce and/or direct badly enough, then you must be willing to hang in there for as long as it takes. And you must be willing to start at the bottom; be a gofer who gets coffee if that's the only job you can get with a production company. The problem is, so many people who come out of film school or college aren't willing to do that. There are no shortcuts. And you must be able to sell yourself, convince people you're worth hiring. One of my assistants I found while I was on a shoot in Boston. He was a production assistant on the crew, but he stood out like a jewel, doing more than his job called for and so obviously willing to work hard. I invited him to come to New York and work for me.

"Before you begin, I would say to face the truth about how impossible it is to get into production. Each year there are more and more people coming out of film school and so very few jobs for them. Then, if you still want it, find a way—find *your* way—and keep at it until you make it."

PART VI

FINDING A JOB

The secret of success is constancy of purpose.
—BENJAMIN DISRAELI

15 General Advice

It's difficult to find a first job in advertising, but not impossible. And once you get one, your chances for promotion through the ranks are good. That's why it's so important that you take the time and effort to find the right job for you, in an area you can thrive in. Be prepared for long hours, hard work and some disappointments. Finding your first job, whether you're a novice to the work world or a career-changer, won't be accomplished in one fell swoop, but arduously, one task at a time. What follows should be of some help.

Focus Inward

By now you know what jobs exist in advertising, marketing and some related areas. Congratulations. You've completed the first phase of finding a job. Now your task is to look inward; take inventory of your interests, talents, aptitudes and expertise. According to career expert John C. Crystal, head of the Crystal Center, a career-development organization, there are two key questions you need to ask yourself: "What do I have?" and "What do I enjoy?" If you need help assessing your skills and talent, get hold of *What Color Is My Parachute?* or *Where Do I Go from Here with My Life?*—the first written by Richard Bolles, the second co-authored with John C. Crystal. But all that's really necessary for you to do is sit down with some legal pads and list everything you've done professionally, in school, and as part of a hobby and then translate your accomplishments into skills and talents. Be honest and accurate. You may want to go for a career as a creative director when in fact you'd be more suited to be head of research or media. Face that early on, and chances are you will be happier and more successful in your work. This self-assessment step can take weeks, even months, if done thoroughly . . . so don't rush it.

Finding a Suitable First Job

Advertising is a "pigeonholing" profession, which means for the most part, that to do well in it, one must remain in one area and become an expert in that area. While it's fine for beginners to move around, say, from traffic to media to account management, at some point—and the sooner the better you will have to decide where you belong: account management, ad ministration, public relations, corporate marketing, media, research, creative, production, talent management, etc.

Narrow down the area as best you can. Then figure out which entry-level jobs will do you the most good—that is, give you an opportunity to learn some skill you'll need for your ultimate goal or put you in proximity to those doing what you want to do. (Appendix A will help you in this task.) If you can't think of any appropriate entry-level jobs, then consider an overview-type job: one in traffic, or secretary to someone in top management. Or consider a job as a "floater" secretary—which job will allow you to touch base with all the departments. If all else fails, while you're thinking and researching, register with a temp agency which handles advertising accounts. You'll learn about a variety of agencies firsthand and get to meet many people, all potential contacts for future employment. Those of you still in school might consider a summer job or internship, and, by the way, November is not too soon to start lining up summer job prospects.

For Would-Be Creatives

If you're interested in working on the creative side of advertising, you *must* put together a sampling of your work. Such a sampling is known as a "spec book," or "portfolio," or just "book." No creative manager (the person at an ad agency responsible for screening creatives), creative director or recruitment specialist will talk to you if you don't have one. There's no getting away from it—you have to first present your work and ideas, gathered together in your book, before you can get an interview with *anyone*. There are certain basic things to be included and a format to follow. Below are some general ideas on how to prepare and organize your book; but, truthfully, anyone interested should get a hold of *How To Put Your Book Together and Get a Job in Advertising*, by Maxine Paetro (listed in Appendix B of this book). Also, scour the pages of Appendix B for clubs and professional associations willing to help would-be creatives put together a good, solid portfolio (for instance, the One Club). There are several short-term courses offered on this very topic, and you'll find those too listed in the appendix. For now, here is some general advice:

The main purpose of your book is to show off your advertising talent—show that you can conceptualize, come up with ideas, and create campaigns that will reflect those ideas and solve advertising problems.

Even if you have no experience, make sure your book looks professional. If you are a copywriter, get an artist to visualize your copy; include headlines and body copy in your advertising. If you are an art director, include headlines. Today, art directors and copywriters have not only to understand each other's work, they almost have to do it. Present your work neatly, mounted, and make sure it's clean—nothing is so bad a turnoff as sloppily presented work.

Don't put too much or too little into your portfolio. Three or four campaigns (each including three or four ads and/or storyboards) and a couple of single ads and storyboards will do. And make sure the best are presented first.

Put a name tag on your book, because you will have to leave it behind for at least a couple of days. If you want to prevent an agency from keeping your book too long, give them a date and time at which you'll pick it up . . . and keep to it.

As far as what kind of book to use, copy books are usually of the soft, loose-leaf variety, and art director's are of the hard type. Ask at your local art supply store, they'll know.

Training Programs . . . Do They Exist, and If So, What Are They?

If you haven't been able to get a straight answer to your question "Do training programs exist, and if so, what are they?" it's probably because no definitive answer exists. Some agencies have formal training programs one year and not the next; others change their programs from an educational format to on-the-job training. Some have them in account-management departments, others in creative. It's truly a mixed bag. The only way to find out is to persist, and to frame your question as

specifically as you would want your reply to be. Don't ask,
"What training programs do you have?" Ask, "Do you have a
training program in *copywriting*? What must I do to apply?
What form does it take?" In most cases, training and recruitment are handled by the human resources (a.k.a. personnel)
department and are only for junior people already working
inside the agency. So, once again, it's best to get in the door
first. Most agencies announce plans for upcoming training pro
grams in the trades, so read them daily to keep abreast. Several
schools, including NYU, offer courses similar to formal training
programs found at the agencies. It could be worth your while
to take one of these at the same time you're working as an
agency secretary or traffic person. And, by all means, tell your
employer you're doing this. You might be reimbursed, and at
the very least, you'll indicate your seriousness.

MBAs

Whether you must have an MBA (and this applies mostly to
account-management people; no one cares if a "creative" has
this degree) is another one of those unanswerable questions.
Some agencies won't look at you without one, others are not so
concerned. To understand, realize why the MBA became a
prerequisite for account people in the first place. Corporations, for a while, were hiring only MBAs as brand and product
managers. The most important quality a would-be account person can have is the ability to get along well and communicate
with the client. So, if the client has an MBA, so must the account person. Soon MBAs were getting such bad press (it was
said they asked too much money; they inflated other salaries;
they lacked common sense), no one wanted to hire them. Then
the tables turned and they were in great demand. What tomorrow will bring is anybody's guess. As a rule of thumb, though,
for those interested in a career in marketing—that is, on the
client side—an MBA will probably always be in order.

Women in Advertising

There is no doubt about it—women have done remarkably
well in advertising and will continue to do so. Whereas in the

sixties there were few women account executives or producers, today there are many. According to *Adweek*, women make up 50 to 60 percent of account executive groups at many advertising agencies. While there are still few women in top management jobs (i.e., CEOs or presidents), there are many in executive and copywriting positions. The good news is, advertising is one of the best fields a woman can enter, on all accounts: women are welcome at an entry level and are given room to advance.

Contacts

Since time began, the best way to find a job was through someone you knew, someone who knew you and what you were capable of doing. In other words, through contacts. What most job-seekers don't realize is that contacts are *made*, not inherited. Part of your job, in looking for a job, is to make them. You can do this in any manner of ways. Call friends, friends of friends, relatives. Exploit (in a courteous way) every relationship. Seek out advice. Ask to see people even if they don't know of a job opening. And most important: *Tell everyone you can what job you are looking for*. Be specific, show them you know enough about advertising to know what you want to do. They'll be impressed that you've done your research, and you'll make it easier for them to help. And make known all you have to offer. Also, seek out people who are doing what you want to do and ask them for advice and for the names of other people to talk to. Get on the mailing lists of all the professional associations you are interested in or that are related to what you want to do. That way, you'll learn of seminars, workshops, conferences. Go to them and mingle with the professionals and other job-seekers; you're bound to learn from both groups. Needless to say, keep up the contacts you've made. Advertising is an incestuous industry, and chances are your paths will cross again.

Letters, Resumés and Interviews

The first thing to consider here is whom to send your letter and resumé to. In selecting your target, always try for the on-line person who would be most likely to hire you. For creatives, you could approach a group head, or at the smaller agencies, the creative director. Some of the larger agencies employ a creative manager. For account people, try for the account supervisor, management supervisor or head of account-management services. As a rule of thumb, go for the heads of departments: the directors of research, media, traffic, production, And it's always a good idea to send a resumé and a different covering letter to the appropriate personnel person.

In writing your covering letter, keep in mind that the way to get someone to show interest in you is to show interest in him. Your letter should be hand-typed and addressed and directed to a person (the person your research led you to), not a title. It should be short and to the point and tailored for the circumstance. And it should be good; it's your opportunity to charm whomever you're contacting into making room in his day for you. Make it self-assured, straightforward, lucid and informative. If you're a copywriter, make sure the letter is well-written, for it is the first sample of your work anyone will see.

Your resumé, too, must be clear and designed to meet the job specifications. If necessary, prepare more than one. Always stress the link between your skills and the work that needs to be done. Potential employers are interested in what you can do for them, how you can help solve their problems. And for those of you just starting out, remember that all experience counts. No one expects a 21-year-old to have a long, full career. What you have to do is show that what you've done—in school, at camp, in extracurricular activities—has given you an idea of how the business world works and has provided you with capabilities and skills. Have your resumé reflect your skills and accomplishments and what you can offer. Putting together a good resumé with little work experience can be an excellent opportunity to show your ingenuity and creativity. Many books have been written on how to write a resumé. If you need help, two good ones are Richard Lathrop's *Who's Hiring Who* and Edward Rogers's *Getting Hired, Everything You Need To Know About Resumés, Interviews and Job-Hunting Strategies*.

Regarding the interview, the most important thing to keep in mind is: Be prepared. Before you go, research the organization thoroughly, find out who the people are, who the clients are, what the agency philosophy is. This kind of research will accomplish two things. It will show your enthusiasm for the organization and it will allow you to relax and speak freely, knowing you're too well informed to put your foot in your mouth. Be yourself; be honest; but don't minimize what you've done—and stress the benefits the employer will gain by hiring you. Follow up your interview with a thank-you note.

Changing Jobs

It's a fact of advertising life. Professionals in advertising move around, from one agency to another, back to the one they already worked at, sometimes to the client side. There's no stigma attached—in fact, getting out of a job that doesn't give you what you want is admired in advertising circles. The thing to remember is, leave graciously, make no enemies on your way out—chances are you'll be working with the same people at future agencies. And find a way to cope, emotionally, with moving around.

Keeping Up with the Trends

Advertising is a fast-moving, fast-changing industry. The best way to keep up with what's happening is, of course, to be a member of the professional community. But for those of you who are not, read the trades, the *New York Times,* the new books. Join professional associations, take continuing education courses taught by professionals, talk to friends in the industry. Appendix B should help.

16 Advice from the Experts

What follows is more good advice on finding a job. It comes from two of the most well-respected recruitment specialists in the business, and from a personnel director at the Interpublic Group of Companies, Inc., the world's largest advertising conglomerate. Some of the advice is reiterated. Good. That means it's correct, on target and important for you to hear again and again.

Jerry Fields, President,
Jerry Fields Associates, Inc.

Jerry Fields is president of Jerry Fields Associates, one of the
largest executive search firms specializing in recruiting advertising talent. He started the firm in 1947, making it the first
employment agency to cater to the advertising and communications community. In his own words, "If all the advertising
people we placed throughout the years got together, we could
fill every seat in Madison Square Garden."

On Getting in.   "Getting that first job [in advertising] is so
difficult, especially when times are tough and competition stiff.
It's harder for us to place a person in an entry-level job than to
recruit the president of an advertising agency. Today there is
no casual hiring. . . . Every hiring is what we call a 'considered
purchase.' Agencies don't have the time to train entry-level
people, and they are too busy to hand responsibility to someone with no experience.

"However, it is possible to get in, and I have a theory on how
to do it. I call it the 'Trojan Horse' theory because it's based on
getting in under any circumstance, any pretext; then, once
you're in, trying for what you really want. No one is going to
hire someone right out of school as a producer or copywriter or
art director. But if you can type or are willing to be a gofer in
an art department and go after *those* jobs, you might get hired.
If you're any good, the next thing you know you'll be the
assistant to a producer or art director or a junior copywriter.
Young men often don't have this opportunity, and any woman
who won't take advantage of it—because she thinks it demean-
ing, or whatever—is foolish. Because the important thing for
an entry-level person is to get in."

On Starting to Search.   "The first thing to know is that looking for a job is a full-time job in itself. You're in the sales
business, and you're selling a very important product, yourself.
You must be prepared to stay at it. And you must give yourself
maximum exposure. I say this with a tear in my eye, but three
out of five jobs are filled by word-of-mouth, not through recruiters or employment agencies or ads. Which means you
have to call all your friends, all your friends' friends, everybody you know who might have a job or know someone who
has. Call it 'networking' or getting on the phone, but do it and

stay at it for a good amount of time.

"Even before you do that, have some idea of what field you want to get into—creative, marketing, account work, media research. You'll be one step ahead of the rest if you do. While deciding what job you want, keep in mind that the semantics of job titles changes from agency to agency. An associate creative director in one agency is called creative supervisor in another. Also, there are jobs which are unique to certain types of agencies, say, for instance, to a direct response agency or a pharmaceutical agency. There are a few fortunate people, usually creatives, who know right from the start what they want to do, but for the rest of us, much effort and time is required."

For Would-Be Creatives. "If you decide on a creative job path, you cannot start looking unless you have a spec book. Four out of five people who come in here looking for a creative job never come back once I tell them that. Sitting down in front of a blank piece of paper can be a terrifying experience. But it must be done. Of the few who do come back with a book, some are quite good, and occasionally we do send them to our clients (the ad agencies) and place them in entry-level creative positions.

"Many would-be creatives ask, 'How am I going to get a book of samples together when I don't have experience?' What they don't realize is that you can put together a good book of ads and commercials based on your ideas. The samples don't have to be actual ads that have been produced for a client. You can even create ads for nonexisting products or come up with original campaign ideas for existing products. If you're a writer, spend a little money on artwork and make the book look as professional as possible—then show it around, to agencies and recruiters.

"Because the creative end is the highest-paying end of the business, many people choose it—which makes creative jobs much sought after. To get one presupposes a certain amount of talent. And training and skill. Artists can get good training at various schools: the School of Visual Arts, the New School, NYU, Cooper Union, the Art Center School in California. It's not so easy for copywriters to get training. And today, copywriters are in the greatest demand. This is a business that constantly calls for new concepts, new ideas; and copywriters are the ones who must supply them. With such a parity of products today, copywriters must be able to come up with what is called the U.S.P.—unique selling proposition—the thing that sets one brand apart from another when there really is no difference. That's no easy matter. Still, except for very few situations, would-be copywriters are offered no training. The only thing they can do is try to put together a good book and try for one of those few entry-level creative jobs. Otherwise, they too should try the Trojan Horse method.

For Would-Be Account Executives.   "Today, the whole concept of an account executive has changed; and for the most part, they are much more qualified than they used to be. A.E.'s are no longer errand boys, marionettes with little to offer except a good set of teeth and a big smile; they're usually MBAs with expertise in marketing, and more.

"Many young A.E.'s are concerned with whether they should specialize in one type of goods or service. In my opinion, it's good but not necessary. What's more important is to become expert in a certain type of distribution channel. In other words, if you've worked on a detergent which is sold through supermarkets, there's no reason why you couldn't switch over to a dog food account, also sold through supermarkets. As far as job-hunting is concerned, having a great depth of experience in one product can work for you and against you. Let's assume an A.E. has been working on an automotive account for a number of years. The ABC Agency has just picked up a big piece of business from Chrysler. They need a good strong account marketing person. Whom are they going to hire? Not someone out of the drugstore business. They'll go after another automotive guy. So in that case, it would be good to have product specialization. But what happens when your area of specialization is doing very badly and there aren't a lot of jobs around? You're locked in. In that case, someone with general packaged goods experience is better off, because he has a broad spectrum of jobs to go after."

For Career-Changers.   "The higher up you are in terms of salary, the harder it is to change from media to account work or from research to media. It's best to make those changes early in your career. As for coming into advertising from another industry or switching from an agency to corporate, it is possible. But you must have a product specialization to offer. It's a key factor. If, for instance, you've worked for a large manufacturer of stereo equipment, it's very possible you could get a job as an A.E. at an ad agency handling a rival stereo account. Or, if you've worked on a number of camera accounts at various ad agencies, you could move over to the client side as a product or ad manager. If your background is right, it is possible to make career changes."

The Interview. "The first thing you should do is your homework. You don't come into an interview asking, 'Hey, what do you guys do around here?' You arrive knowing what they do.

"Also, bring an extra copy of your resumé, because chances are the person has already lost it. Talk about what kind of contribution you could make to the company, not what the company could do for you. Never discuss salary initially. If someone asks you how much money you want, say, 'My salary is negotiable. Let's talk about the job and what I can offer you.'

"Be very positive, show enthusiasm for the job and project your personality. Also, you should come into an interview neatly clothed, holding your resumé and nothing else. Leave the umbrella, raincoat, shopping bags and dog on a leash outside. It's a sad commentary on our society, but first impressions are crucial. What a person looks like, how they talk, how they are dressed—all are important. Someone once said, 'You never get a second chance to make a great first impression,' and I agree.

"The most important parts of the interview are the last two things you do. One . . . before you leave, ask the interviewer who's to take the next action: will he get in touch with you, or should you call him? And, if it's the latter, when? Two . . . before the sun sets on the day of the interview, send a short thank-you note: 'Dear So and So, Thank you for taking time out of your busy schedule to talk with me about the account job with your agency. I look forward to another meeting with your associates.' That's all. You'll accomplish two things: you'll show you have good business manners, and you'll get your name in front of that person's eyes for a second time. It could make the difference between your getting the job or not.

"Expect to get called back for another interview, and don't be surprised if you're called back and back again—three, four, even five times. A hiring decision is about 60 percent cerebral and 40 percent visceral. Often our clients can't make up their minds. They look to the sky and hope the finger of God will appear and guarantee that so-and-so is perfect for the job. But there are no guarantees. Until an applicant is actually working in a job, you never know for sure. So understand your potential employer's point of view and realize why he may call you back so many times."

On Working in the Ad Game in General. "Advertising is not a business for somebody who wants to look forward to eventual retirement. It's definitely a young person's business. I once did an article on what happens to old art directors and A.E.'s and found they do a variety of things. They become consultants, they get jobs at lesser agencies or out of town, they set up their own businesses; the creatives free-lance. Then there are some tragic people who are finished at fifty with no place to go.

"Also, fear dominates the business. Fear of the client, fear of the supervisor, fear that you'll lose business despite your doing a great job for the client. And that happens frequently. The huge MacDonald's advertising account shifted to Leo Burnett even though Needham, Harper and Steers had done a terrific job for them for many years. A new marketing director came to MacDonald's and he wanted his own team: new people, new ideas. So it's a business of change, a business of insecurity.

"But it's also a business that pays big dividends and one that can be very rewarding early on. I don't think there's any business where you can make as much money in as short a time as in advertising. We have people under thirty whom we place in six-figure incomes. Mostly they are creatives, because creatives are the highest paid.

"Since the late seventies, the business has become much more serious. It's not as much fun-and-games as it was back in the sixties, during the so-called creative revolution. Today, it's a tough, hard, competitive business. More agencies are folding, and more new agencies are starting up, making it very difficult to go out and pick up an account.

"Still, all things considered, I would say, next to Hollywood, advertising is the most interesting and colorful business there is. But everyone has to decide for themselves if it's a business for them."

Judy Wald, Chairman of the Board, Judy Wald Agency, Inc.

Judy Wald is the undisputed doyenne of the advertising place-ment field. Her phenomenal success in the business of recruit-ment is a lesson in itself for those considering going into their own business as well as those embarking on a job search. Belief in herself, commitment to advertising and talent enabled her, nineteen years ago, to parlay a $3,000 bank loan into a thriving business with offices in New York, Los Angeles, Chicago, Lon-don and Paris, with affiliates in Sydney and Toronto, and earned her a reputation as *the* most perceptive scouter of ad-vertising talent in the business and an innovator in the execu-tive recruitment industry. (Besides being one of the first in the field to have long-range, thoroughgoing involvement in candi-dates' careers and agencies' changing employment needs, it was she who first instituted the practice of having agencies, rather than job applicants, pay a fee for the job search.) While Ms. Wald is more than capable of addressing all aspects of ad-vertising careers, because of her special expertise in the cre-ative area, her comments here embrace those functions. As her company rarely represents beginners, most of the wisdom which follows is intended for middle- and senior-level creative people, and for juniors, to be kept in mind for future endeav-ors.

On Working with Recruiters. "Since the seventies, lots of people have gone into the advertising recruitment field. Some are qualified, others not; but the point is, it has become very confusing to the poor souls out there looking for jobs as well as to the agencies with job orders to fill. My advice to job appli-cants is to register with no more than two search firms at a given time. Actually, I think it's best to work exclusively with one firm—that is, of course, unless or until they let you down. But working with more than two will possibly do you more harm than good. The reason is, it tends to dilute your value. What you want from a placement operation is for them to help you think in terms of your total career, of the long term as well as the short. When you work exclusively with one recruitment firm, it enables them to establish a rapport with you, to have more than just a passing interest in you and the fee they will gain from placing you in a job. Also, registering with many firms could possibly get you into the middle of a sticky situation regarding fee-claim disputes.

"In choosing a recruitment agency, make certain it is the type that does a thorough, committed job, both for you and for the agency; that it considers several possibilities and takes a long range view. That it is concerned with putting together a good deal from everyone's point of view . . . yours, the agency's and the industry as a whole. Unfortunately, there are very few operations like that. Most seem to care only about making a fee.

"If you can get a reputable firm interested in you, however, you will be better off than going out there on your own. For one thing, we are better able to determine the parameters of a job. For another, we know what the competition is and whether a candidate really has a chance of getting the job. Also, a good recruiter can help someone who is clearly at an impasse as to their next career step. There's a time in many people's careers when they need advice. For example, maybe someone has a combination of agency and corporate experience and he wants to know where he will have the most value next. And, last, we take over the difficult task of negotiating packages rather than straight salaries, which are beneficial to you, tax-wise, as you go up the ladder."

On Presenting Yourself and Your Work to a Recruiter. "A lot of candidates make the mistake of telling me how wonderful they are instead of telling me what they could bring to a job. That only makes me think they're more interested in selling themselves than in the job opening. My criteria for handling a creative person are: First, does he or she have good work? Two, has he an outstanding personality? And, three, does he have the energy and commitment it takes to get the job done?

The worst thing applicants can do is to waste the recruiter's time by not doing their homework. Too often, someone comes in here with thirty-five or forty samples and just hands me the whole thing. You can't expect a recruiter to do all your screening for you. I don't mind if someone wants to eliminate one or two ads, and asks which—in my opinion—they should be. That tells me they've at least thought about what they are showing me. But to just dump everything without first doing their homework makes a very unfavorable impression on me. What many creative people don't understand is that it's *their* judgment and taste that we want to show an employer, and if the recruiter screens the work first, it's the recruiter's taste and judgment that is being presented, not the applicant's.

"As far as the work itself, it should be a carefully screened, representative sampling of campaigns he has worked on, enough to whet an employer's appetite. Twelve to fifteen sample commercials on a reel are enough; and, again, a representational sampling in the print book. And the part played by the applicant in the creation of each campaign should be explained. In other words, did he initiate the idea or just follow through on somebody else's ideas—which, by the way, is certainly valid to include in your sampling as long as that's stated. What I've sometimes recommended that candidates do is put a voice-over on their reel explaining their contributions. It's best to do this on videotape because it's less expensive than film and therefore you can have more than one reel. Candidates should also have a recent, updated resumé. A good resumé should be concise—one page is best, but never more than two. Current experience should be first, and stick to what's significant. Also avoid gimmickry. Very few agencies react favorably to the offbeat resumé. Use a good paper stock and have it printed rather than photocopied."

On Job-Hoppers. "The question of how long a creative person should stay at one agency has no pat answer. If you've stayed too long at one place, some people will consider you stodgy; if you move around, you're classified as a job-hopper. So, somewhere in between is a healthy balance: three to four years in one place, maybe seven at another, and then your final destination. Of course there are exceptions to every rule. Some of the very creative agencies don't really mind creatives who tend to move around frequently—that is, if they're brilliantly talented—because they believe they'll get good ideas from them the year or so they will remain. Others avoid job-hoppers entirely. I would say, though, if you have this tendency, ask yourself why, and make the reasons clear on your resumé. I know some brilliant people who were disastrous job-hoppers who now have their own ad agencies and are doing beautifully. In some cases, it was being unable to work for a boss. Whatever it is, it will do you well to sit back and figure it out."

On Advertising Being a Young Person's Business. "That's changing. In the past few years, there have been more key people in their fifties in creative positions than have been put out to pasture. I think, perhaps, it's because the population in general is getting older.''

On Working in the Creative Area in General.   "Like everything else, it has its good points and bad. It's always desirable to be in the agency that's right for you, doing what you do best. That's not always an easy matter, since so many creatives tend to be individualistic. They tend to prefer operating at their own speed and not to be very good managers, which upper-level creatives are often called upon to be. Of course there are exceptions. Amil Gargano is as good as you can get, and yet he is an excellent manager. But of course, he has his own agency.

"Advertising creatives, like creative people in any field, have to deal with a lot of rejection, and that's difficult for them to handle. Many need much hand-holding and soothing to get by.

"Also, it's a field where you must be willing to get very involved in your work and make it an important part of your life. All in all, I would sum it up in the positive. As Jerry Della Femina says in his book: 'It's the most fun you can have with your clothes on.' ''

Peter Tafti, Manager of Recruitment Services, the Interpublic Group of Companies

Peter Tafti is responsible for account service, creative, and international recruiting. Manpower planning and management development are also part of his position, working with McCann-Erickson Worldwide, SSC&B:LINTAS, Marschalk Campbell-Ewald, and Dailey & Associates. Because of his vast experience in interviewing people at all levels for a number of ad agencies, he was asked to comment on that experience.

The Interview.   "Whether I'm interviewing a $19,000 a year assistant account executive or a $90,000 senior V.P., what I'm looking for is someone with the same overall objective, and that has to be to sell their client's product or service. I am looking for people who are appropriate for my agency, my agency's clients, and for the job at hand. The standards of judging people in the advertising industry haven't really changed through the years: they are excellence, talent, and an understanding of people and what makes them put their hands into their pockets and buy something. The interviewer in advertising is geared to wanting to see someone come in who is high-spirited, highly intelligent and highly motivated.

"Advertising is a competitive field in every sense, in terms of your job search as well as the work you will do. Be aware that you are one of many, and the demand for advertising positions at the entry level far outweighs the supply. While I would like to have a job for every qualified person who comes through my door, I don't; and so I must carefully screen each candidate, and—while it might sound brutal—conduct an interview on a demerit basis. What this means is, when a candidate comes into my office, I assume he is perfect; then, as the interview progresses and the interplay continues, my thinking changes to why I don't want to hire him. Roughly, there are eight areas of evaluation. I'm interested in the person's overall appearance: how well he is groomed and styled; what are his professional polish and demeanor? Next, his presentation skills: how well does he sell himself, what is his command of the language—is he witty, conversant, inspired. Then, there are what we call interpersonal skills. How well does he listen? How does he handle questions, inquiries about past positions and stressful situations? Then you get to other issues such as energy level, assertiveness, motivation, intelligence. The last thing I rate is his potential, so that even if in all the other categories a person is average, if I believe that with a little honing he could be terrific, I will give him a high potential rating. On the other hand, someone could rate high in all categories but not have a high potential. There are, unfortunately, many people like that in advertising. Though they are in their thirties or forties, they will never make it, for example, beyond the account supervisor level onto the management supervisor level—which for account people is the job title that suggests you have management potential.

"All the while I'm interviewing someone, I have in the back of my mind, 'If I were the client, what would I think of this person?' And also, 'Does this person have the characteristics to fit in with this company?' Each company in advertising has its own personality, tone and style; and what makes someone right for Wells Rich Greene will exactly make them wrong for McCann-Erickson. There are things the applicant can do to

make the interview successful. First, it should go without saying, you never walk into an interview without knowing everything there is to know about the organization, its clients, its
philosophy. Also, do what you can to unearth facts about the
person who will be doing the interviewing—what they like and
dislike, where they worked before; if it's a line person, what
they work on. Next—and this will really set you apart from
other entry level people—come to an interview with clearly
thought-out personal goals. Decide how much of yourself you
are willing to give to this business—and it had better be a
lot—and make all that clear to the interviewer. And, last, let
every interview effectively lead you to another interview.
Everyone calls it networking; I call it pyramiding. You start
with one name, which leads you to two names, which lead you
to four, etcetera.

"One mistake many people make is not to distinguish
between the various types of interview situations. It's impera-
tive for you to do this because you need a different approach in
each circumstance. At an interview where there's a job to be
filled, you must sell yourself, say what you have to bring to the
job. But if you're talking with a person who was willing to see
you even though he said there were no job openings, the worst
thing you can do is force your candidacy on him. Rather
than being pushy and aggressive, use the opportunity as an
information-gathering process. If someone who could lead you
to other people is willing to be a resource, why confuse the
issue by treating him as a potential employer?

"As far as whom to get an interview with, I always suggest
sending your letter and resumé to more than one person, including the appropriate personnel manager and the line person
you want to work for. You never know when your cover letter
or resumé may tickle the fancy of a management supervisor, a
media director, or a creative manager, especially if you've
been crafty enough to learn all about that person and say why
you're writing *him* in particular. Personnel people receive hundreds and thousands of letters and resumés, and ninety-nine
percent of the time they'll simply write back saying, 'Thank
you, but we have nothing at the moment.' You increase your
chances, just a bit, by taking the time to write to a line manager
as well. He just might pass the letter on to personnel or, better,
interview you himself.

"Commitment is the key to finding a first job in advertising; entry-level people should be seeking a career, not just a job. So be prepared to make sacrifices and contributions along the way. Your first title is not as important as your responsibility, and the salary you will earn is not as important as the respect and confidence you gain. To find a job, you have to be resourceful and analytical; and whatever happens during the process, don't neutralize your actions by personalizing any rejections."

Appendix A: Jobs in Advertising

Job	Where to Apply for Job and/or Information	Related Middle- and Entry-Level Jobs
Client Marketing Jobs		
Advertising Assistant	Large corporations; retail stores; package-goods manufacturers; movie companies; service organizations (e.g., airlines, insurance companies, banks); any organization utilizing advertising and/or an advertising agency; specialized employment agencies (see Appendix B).	This is an entry-level position.
Advertising Manager	Same as above. Contact: marketing director, personnel.	Product manager, brand manager, assistant brand manager, advertising assistant; also most jobs within an advertising agency, particularly in account service.
Brand Manager	Same as above.	Assistant brand manager.
Consultant	Same as above. Contact: marketing director.	This is a job only for those with expertise in one or another advertising discipline, e.g., media marketing, research, creative production.
Corporate Media Manager	Same as above.	Assistant corporate media manager; also most any media job within an advertising agency, media buying service or media sales department.

183

Job	Where to Apply for Job and/or Information	Related Middle- and Entry-Level Jobs
Corporate Production Manager	Same as above.	Any production job at a corporation, ad agency, art studio, printer, etc.
Corporate Public Relations Director	Same as above, providing they have an in-house public relations dept. Contact: marketing director, advertising manager.	PR writer, PR assistant, any PR job with an ad agency or PR firm, preferably with similar types of accounts. Also, any PR job with a similar corporation.
Corporate Research Director	Same as above. Contact: marketing director.	Marketing analyst; marketing trainee; entry-level job with research firm or ad agency.
Creative Scientist	Major advertisers which manufacture cosmetics, some health-care products, some packaged goods; and some advertising agencies (e.g., Ted Bates) which service such accounts. Contact: marketing director.	Any experience as a biochemist; assistant to scientist employed as such by an advertiser or agency.
In-house Agency Jobs	Advertisers with a fully staffed in-house agency (e.g., Revlon). Contact: advertising manager, personnel.	Assistant or secretary to person in job you aspire to.
Marketing Director	Large corporations; retail stores; package-goods manufacturers; movie companies; service organizations; any advertiser utilizing the services of an ad agency or advertising; specialized employment agencies. Contact: president.	Advertising manager/director, product manager; assistant product manager; advertising agency executive, management supervisor, etc.

New Product Development Manager	Major package-goods advertisers; major ad agencies; new product development firms. Contact: marketing manager.	New product development assistant; sales or distribution job with advertiser.
Package Design Manager	Package-goods manufacturers; graphic studios which specialize in this art; sales promotion companies. Contact: advertising manager, creative director.	Package designer; package design research expert.
Retail Store Jobs	Large retail stores (e.g., Macy's) with in-house agencies. Contact: head of appropriate department, personnel.	There are various kinds of entry-level jobs within advertising departments of large retail stores. Which is for you depends on your area of interest.
Sales Promotion Manager	Large corporations; retail stores; package-goods manufacturers; service organizations; any company utilizing sales promotions. Contact: marketing director.	Display manager; promotion supervisor; promotions assistant.

Agency Administration and Account Services Jobs

Account Management Jobs, Executive Level	Advertising agencies; specialized employment agencies (Judd-Falk, Jerry Fields). Contact: head of account services, high-level personnel representative.	Account supervisor, account executive, assistant account executive, account coordinator, account assistant, secretary to account department.
Agency Management Jobs	Same as above.	Management supervisor, creative director, head of human resources, any job within an ad agency, providing one can grow and advance from said position.

Job	Where to Apply for Job and/or Information	Related Middle- and Entry-Level Jobs
Electronic Data Processing and Word Processing Jobs	Same as above, providing agency is large enough to utilize computers, especially direct mail agencies. Contact: head of EDP department, office service department.	EDP manager, systems specialist, data controller, EDP supervisor, assistant programmer, operator, tape librarian, word processors
Financial Officer, Executive Level	Ad agencies; specialized employment agencies.	Controller, accountant, assistant accountant, bookkeeper, talent payment coordinator.
Librarian	Ad agencies; trade organizations; large corporations. Contact: information specialist, research department, personnel.	Must have MLS degree and work experience with some library.
Mailroom Boy or Girl	Ad agencies; corporations; trade organizations. Contact: personnel.	This is a traditional entry-level job.
Marketing Specialist	Ad agencies; specialized employment agencies. Contact: head of account services.	Marketing assistant; brand management jobs on the client side.
Media Director	Ad agencies; corporations with in-house media departments; media buying companies. Contact: agency management; high-level personnel representative.	Assistant media director, media supervisor, media planner, media buyer, media statistician media-check secretary to media department, media estimator, media clerk.
New Business Administrator	Major ad agencies. Contact: head of account services; high-level personnel representative.	New business director, new business coordinator, account management jobs.

Office Manager, Executive Level	Major ad agencies; employment agencies. Contact: high-level personnel representative.	Office manager, assistant office manager.
Owner/President, "Boutique Agency"	Start your own agency. There are some courses on just this activity offered by continuing education programs and trade organizations (see Appendix B).	Most presidents of small ad agencies or art studios are former creative directors or management supervisors and have at least one client to start their agency with.
Personnel VP	Major ad agencies. Contact: high-level personnel representative.	Personnel director, personnel representative, personnel clerk and secretary. Many upper-echelon personnel VPs today are trained as such; others got started hiring clerks and secretaries and working their way up to being executive recruiters.
Production Assistant	Ad agencies with TV departments; TV production companies. Contact: producers, TV directors.	This is a traditional entry-level job; however, to get it one needs some knowledge and/or experience in TV production, casting, etc. Some gain this by being a secretary to a creative department or casting assistant.
Programming Executives	Major ad agencies with programming divisions and/or subsidiaries (e.g., Doyle Dane Bernbach's DDB/Storyteller). Contact: other programming executives.	Assistant programmers; secretary to programming executive; network experience.

Job	Where to Apply for Job and/or Information	Related Middle- and Entry-Level Jobs
Public Relations A.E.'s	Advertising agencies with a public relations arm; public relations firms; appropriate employment agencies. Contact: head of department.	PR writer, publicity/contact job, PR researcher, corporate communications, PR assistant.
Research Director	Large ad agencies with research departments; appropriate employment agencies; PR firms; advertisers with research departments; research suppliers. Contact: head of marketing services.	Associate research director, research supervisor, project director, analyst, statistical clerk, information specialist, research secretary.
Secretary	Ad agencies, PR firms, suppliers, production companies, etc.—wherever you wish to ultimately work. Contact: *person* you want to work for; appropriate personnel representative.	Receptionist, floater.
Agency Creative and Production Jobs		
Art Director, Executive Level	Ad agencies, graphic design studios, retail stores, in-house corporate advertising departments; appropriate specialized employment agencies; Art Directors Club; the One Club (see Appendix B). Contact: creative director.	Senior art director, art director, junior art director, assistant art director, art assistant, mount room specialist, secretary to art department, bull-pen artist, mechanical "man," lettering "man," pasteup "man," file custodian.
Broadcast Business Executive	Major ad agencies. Contact: head of department.	Broadcast coordinator, production bidder, talent payment coordinator.

Title	Where to Find Work	Stepping-Stone Jobs
Casting Director	Major ad agencies and large production companies. Contact: agency producers.	Assistant casting director, casting assistant, production secretary.
Copy Director	Ad agencies, appropriate employment agencies; the One Club. Contact: creative director.	Senior writer, copywriter, junior copywriter, creative department secretary.
Creative Manager (Creative Director)	Ad agencies; appropriate employment agencies. Contact: agency management; the top person at employment agencies.	Associate creative director, creative group head, copy director, executive art director.
Direct Mail Copywriter	Direct mail ad agencies; general ad agencies with "direct mail" clients; sales promotion companies; PR agencies with "direct mail" clients; charitable organizations; mail-order companies; retail stores;* appropriate employment agencies; Direct Mail/Marketing Education Foundation (see Appendix B). Contact: copy chief.	Any copywriting experience; secretary to direct mail copywriter.
Layout/Mechanical Artist	Ad agencies; art studios; in-house corporate agencies; PR firms; retail stores; Society of Illustrators (see Appendix B). Contact: production manager, art directors.	Pasteup "man."
Print Production Manager	Ad agencies; printers; art studios; in-house corporate agencies; PR firms; retail stores. Contact: creative director, head of print production services.	Assistant print production manager; traffic jobs; proofreader.

* Also, many manage to earn a living on a free-lance basis working for all the above.

Job	Where to Apply for Job and/or Information	Related Middle- and Entry-Level Jobs
Sales Promotion Manager	Sales promotion companies; corporations; ad agencies; specialty advertising companies. Contact: head of marketing services.	Any job dealing with sales promotion within a corporation.
Talent Payment Director	Ad agencies; talent payment firms. Contact: head of broadcast business administration.	Talent payment supervisor; talent payment clerk; secretary to talent payment director.
Television Producer	Same as above and appropriate employment agencies. Contact: head(s) of creative services, TV production department.	Assistant producer; casting director; production and/or casting assistant.
Type Director	Ad agencies; art studios. Contact: print production manager.	Type department assistant; typesetter; proofreader.
Traffic Manager, Executive Level	Ad agencies; in-house agencies; retail stores; appropriate employment agencies. Contact: head of production, head of traffic department.	Traffic supervisor; traffic assistant/planner; secretary to traffic manager.
Supporting Service Jobs		
Accountant	Ad agencies; accounting firms servicing ad agencies. Contact: head of financial department.	Bookkeeper.
Animator	Animation houses; computer animation and graphics companies. Contact: creative chief.	Background artist; checker; in-betweener; opaquer; computer artist.
Color Lab Workers	Color lab houses. Contact: head of operations.	This is an attractive entry-level field for would-be photographers.

Commercial Artist (Illustrator)	Free-lance through artist rep. Society of Illustrators (see Appendix B).	Bull-pen artist; sketch man; assistant art director; any art-related job.
Conference and Exhibition Jobs	Conference and exhibition specialists; corporations which handle their own and ad agencies which arrange such events for their clients. Contact: head of firm.	Conference planner; assistant and/or secretary to conference planner.
Executive Search Placement Managers	Executive search firms. Contact: head of firm, office management.	Most such managers have expertise in the area they specialize placing people in—for instance, ex-copywriters place copywriters.
Food Stylist	Free-lance for production companies and still photographers. On-staff some large food package companies. Contact: photographers.	Assistant to food stylist; assistant to food photographer; job within large manufacturer of packaged foods, perhaps in research and development.
Industrial Filmmaker	Industrial film companies.	Any job in TV production is good.
Jingle Writer	Free-lance for agency producers; jingle composing firms; a few ad agencies with music department. Contact: producers, head of jingle firms.	On-staff of jingle firm (e.g., HEA Productions, Inc.).
List Managers & Brokers	List managing and brokerage firms; Direct Marketing Association Educational Foundation. Contact: head of firm.	Secretary to list manager and broker; clerical job within such firms.

Job	Where to Apply for Job and/or Information	Related Middle- and Entry-Level Jobs
Media Sales	Newspapers; magazines; radio and TV stations; independent media companies; appropriate department of employment agencies. Contact: advertising manager, head of sales.	Secretary to media salesperson. Media planner with ad agency, or any media-related job.
Merchandising & Sales Promotion Jobs	Sales promotion companies; sales promotion suppliers; some ad agencies. Contact: head of firm, head of department (agency).	Any job with supplier (premium and incentive manufacturers).
Model & Talent Agent	Model agencies; talent agencies within commercial department. Contact: head of firm.	Secretary/assistant to agent; booker; assistant casting director with ad agency.
New Product Development Expert	The few new product development firms which recently exist.	Any job in new product development and/or marketing with ad agency or advertiser.
Outdoor Advertising	Outdoor advertising companies; ad agencies; Institute of Outdoor Advertising (see Appendix B). Contact: head of firm, media director (agency).	Depending on area of interest: out-of-home media jobs; sales jobs; etc.
Photographer	Free-lance for ad agencies, PR firms, advertisers. On-staff for retail stores and some agencies and corporations. Contact: senior art directors.	Stylist; assistant to photographer; lab worker.
Photographers' & Artists' Representative	Self-employed. Find some up-and-coming photographers and illustrators to rep!	Assistant to "rep" is the traditional way to get started.

Printing Sales Representative	Printing companies. Contact: head of firms, other sales reps.	Any job with printing company and/or production department of ad agency.
Property Maker	Free-lance for production companies; prop shops; appropriate union. Contact: scenic designers.	Most prop people are trained by another prop person who is seasoned in the trade and a member of NABET or the IA. However, any related job, even that of production assistant, is good.
Research Jobs (Independent)	Research suppliers. Contact: head of operations.	Junior analyst; field operator; telephone solicitor.
Retoucher	Free-lance; printers; retouchers.	Any artwork experience.
Script Person	TV production companies; appropriate union. Contact: TV directors, producers, other script clerks.	As with other union jobs, you must be trained by a union member; therefore, any job is good which puts you in contact with such a person—for instance, production assistant.
Set Designer	Free-lance; appropriate union. Contact: TV directors.	Stylist; production assistant.
Stock Photo and Music House Jobs	Stock photo and music houses. Contact: head of firm.	Clerk.
Stylist	Free-lance for production companies, still photographers, and on staff for large production companies, photographic studios, retail stores; appropriate union. Contact: TV directors, TV production coproducers.	Assistant to photographer.

Job	Where to Apply for Job and/or Information	Related Middle- and Entry-Level Jobs
Talent Payment (Independent)	Talent payment firms. Contact: head of company.	Talent payment clerk.
TV Commercial Crew	Free-lance for production companies and directors; appropriate unions. Contact: TV directors, producers, production managers.	Traditional entry-level production job is that of production assistant. There are some entry-level jobs for particular crew jobs—for example, many would-be cameramen begin their careers by working for equipment rental companies.
TV Commercial Director	TV production companies; some large ad agencies; appropriate union. Contact: head of firm.	First assistant director; second assistant director; editor; production assistant.
TV Commercial Production Manager	Production companies; free-lance for same; the Directors Guild of America (see Appendix B). Contact: producer, director.	Assistant to production manager; production assistant; office coordinator; secretary with production company.
TV Production-Company on-Staff Jobs	Production company. Contact: head of firm.	Producer, assistant producer, casting director at ad agency, production assistant, gofer.
Video Technician	Video production and rental houses. Contact: head of firm, production managers.	Any work with such houses, including that of messenger.

Appendix B: Resources

In the next few pages you will find a collection of names, addresses, telephone numbers, books, periodicals, employment agencies, personnel representatives, schools, miscellaneous information and a review of some of the major advertising agencies, as well as the names and addresses of others. Some of the information is provided to help you in your job search and some will be useful to you once you get a job. None of the lists are complete, but they are comprehensive enough to give you a good start—the idea being that as you progress in your own research, your personal list of resources will also expand. Obviously, not all the resources provided will be useful to everyone, so choose what *you* need and can use. Also, things in advertising tend to change quickly and frequently, so this appendix should be updated by you often. Periodicals and trade papers stop being published, books go out of print, people change jobs and clients change agencies—so always check and make certain your information is current.

Schools

Today there are literally thousands of colleges, universities and professional schools offering courses in the diverse areas of advertising and marketing. Every kind of program is available, from noncredit one-time workshops to professional training courses to graduate programs. You can study graphic design, copywriting, public relations techniques, lettering, typography, pasteup and mechanical preparation, illustration, TV production techniques, marketing, media magazine advertising sales . . . just about anything you are interested in. For those interested in programs at the college level, a booklet is put out each year by Texas Tech University, entitled *Where Shall I Go to Study Advertising.* At last edition, the number of schools with advertising programs was ninety. For those interested in short-term and nonmatriculated study, there are professional schools as well as continuing education programs at virtually every major school in the country. For example, New York University's School of Continuing Education offers several courses and even diploma programs (e.g., the diploma in direct marketing, an intensive credit program designed to provide individuals who have already earned their B.A. or B.S. with the knowledge and skills needed to successfully apply direct marketing strategies to a marketing effort). In addition, NYU offers a free seminar on marketing and advertising careers, open to the public, usually in September. (For information, call 212 598-2100.) A more intensive course on careers in advertising is offered by NYU and taught by this author. (For information, call the Management Institute, School of Continuing Education, New York University, (212) 598-2100, and/or send for the New York University Bulletin, School of Continuing Education, 100 Washington Square East, New York, NY 10003.)

Other schools offering a wide array of noncredit courses and programs in advertising are: the School of Visual Arts School of Continuing Education, 209 East 23rd Street, New York, NY, (212) 683-0600; Parsons/New School for Social Research, 66 West 12th Street or 560 Seventh Avenue, (212) 741 7576; New York Institute of Technology, Old Westbury Campus, Old Westbury, NY 11568, (516) 686-7778; Metropolitan Center, 1855 Broadway, New York, NY 10023, (212) 399-9669. Also, many of the professional associations listed in this appendix offer a variety of courses. For example, the Ad Club of New York's advertising and marketing course—and the American Management Association's wide variety of noncredit courses.

For those in need of guidance in preparing their portfolio or "book" of ad campaigns, sometimes an evening course or two will do the trick. For those interested in marketing or account work, an MBA might be called for. Everyone must make his own decision on how much and what type of education he is in need of, but as a general rule, in a tight job market where on-the-job training is scarce, it is a good idea to gain better credentials and learn as much as you can. Also, since many of these classes are taught by professionals, it gives you an opportunity to meet and communicate with the professional community. As with finding a job, don't jump in blindly. If you're not sure what area you wish to enter, take an overview course first; and once you do know your goal, take the courses designed for your needs. With so many being offered, you probably will find one exactly tailored for you.

Personnel Representatives at the Major
New York Advertising Agencies

Below you will find the names, addresses, telephone numbers and, wherever possible, personnel representatives of the major New York ad agencies. It is always advisable to confirm names and addresses before you get in touch, in case the contact has moved from one agency to another or changed jobs within. Also, the contact mentioned here may not be the appropriate person for you to deal with. Most agencies employ a number of personnel people, each responsible for a specific area. For instance: executive recruitment, creative, traffic, media, secretarial. Before sending off your letter and resumé, find out the name and correct spelling of the personnel representative *you* should be contacting; a simple phone call to the number provided will get you the information you need. Also, as previously stated in Part VI, "Finding a Job," it's advisable at the same time to also send your resumé with another cover letter to the on-line person at the agency—that is, the person you would be working for.

Agency	Number of Employees (NY)	Telephone	Contact
Ally & Gargano, Inc. 805 Third Avenue New York, NY 10022	225	688-5300	Jerilyn Caesar—VP, personnel/office services Mary Chapman—personnel assistant Pat Weber—personnel assistant
BBD&O, Inc. 383 Madison Avenue New York, NY 10022	910	355-5800	Sandy Greiser—personnel manager
Benton & Bowles 909 Third Avenue New York, NY 10022	1,200	758-6200	Karen McClain—employment manager
Bozell & Jacobs One Dag Hammarskjold Plaza New York, NY 10017	250	705-6000	Susan Law—personnel manager
Compton Advertising 625 Madison Avenue New York, NY 10016	650	350-1837	Jeanne Sakas—personnel manager
Cunningham & Walsh 260 Madison Avenue New York, NY 10016	333	683-4900	Evelyn Hunt—benefits administrator
D'Arcy-MacManus & Masius, Inc. 360 Madison Avenue New York, NY 10017	175	850-7300	Merri Ferber—director of office services

Agency	Number of Employees (NY)	Telephone	Contact
Della Femina, Travisano & Partners, Inc. 625 Madison Avenue New York, NY 10022	200	421-7180	Juanita Gallo—personnel manager Elizabeth Alley—assistant to manager
Doyle Dane Bernbach 437 Madison Avenue New York, NY 10022	1,100	826-2000 415	Marian Faytell—personnel manager, training/MBA program Jane Folds—personnel manager
Foote, Cone & Belding 101 Park Avenue New York, NY 10178	300	907-1000	Claire Sullivan—personnel manager
Grey Advertising 777 Third Avenue New York, NY 10017	1,200	546-2000	Joyce Casey—personnel manager Cindy Springer—assistant personnel manager
Interpublic Group of Companies 485 Lexington Avenue New York, NY 10017	300	883-1050 Ext. 4204	Eilleen Giraci—recruiter Peter Tafti—VP, personnel
Kenyon & Eckhardt, Inc. 200 Park Avenue New York, NY 10017	420	880-2000	Mary Anne Schiffer—personnel manager
Ketchum Communications, Inc. 1133 Sixth Avenue New York, NY 10015	125	536-8800	Ricki Fein—personnel manager

Company / Address		Phone	Personnel Contacts
Leber Katz Partners, Inc. 767 Fifth Avenue New York, NY 10022	250	826-6816	Mindy Lester—personnel supervisor
Marschalk Company, Inc. 1345 Sixth Avenue New York, NY 10105	320	708-8747	Pat Peltola—personnel manager
Marsteller, Inc. 866 Third Avenue New York, NY 10022	800	752-6500	Linda Sobel—personnel representative
McCaffrey & McCall, Inc. 575 Lexington Avenue New York, NY 10022	310	421-7500	Debbie Sulcer—personnel director Robin Miller—assistant personnel director
McCann-Erickson 485 Lexington Avenue New York, NY 10017	400	697-6000	Terry Harkin—personnel manager
Needham, Harper & Steers, Inc. 909 Third Avenue New York, NY 10022	310	758-7600	Pat Cremin—personnel director Eileen Ceccarelli—personnel manager Marina Brant—personnel assistant
N W Ayer, Inc. 1345 Sixth Avenue New York, NY 10015	1,030	708-5000	Linda Potts—employment manager Lynn Friedman—employment manager
Ogilvy & Mather, Inc. 2 East 48 Street New York, NY 10017	1,000	907-4155	Marge Gordon—VP, personnel Kim Tracey—personnel coordinator

Agency	Number of Employees (NY)	Telephone	Contact
Scali, McCabe, Sloves 800 Third Avenue New York, NY 10022	300	421-2050	Margaret Gomez—VP, personnel director Becky Keogh—personnel supervisor
SSC&B/Lintas One Dag Hammarskjold Plaza New York, NY 10017	575	605-8000	Patti Ranson—personnel assistant
Ted Bates Advertising 1515 Broadway New York, NY 10036	770	869-3131	Ursula Mathers—recruiter Nora Connors—employment interviewer
J. Walter Thompson 466 Lexington Avenue New York, NY 10017	1,200	210-7000	Gail Warshaw—employment manager
Waring & LaRosa, Inc. 555 Madison Avenue New York, NY 10022	130	755-0700	Marsha Weil—personnel manager
Wells, Rich & Greene, Inc. 767 Fifth Avenue New York, NY 10022	540	758-4300	Rosemary Peters—personnel director
Wunderman, Ricotta & Kline 575 Madison Avenue New York, NY 10022	250	909-0256	Eileen Dale Marquis—VP, manager office services

Young & Rubicam, Inc.   1,300   909-0256   Madeline Madden—personnel assistant
285 Madison Avenue   Irene Johnson—personnel representative
New York, NY 10017   Betsy Gilbert—director of training

Executive Recruiters Specializing in Advertising and Public Relations Jobs

Following, you will find the names, addresses and telephone numbers of executive recruiters that specialize in the communications fields, particularly advertising, marketing and public relations. Most of these have divisions within their organization to handle the various disciplines. For instance, copy, art, account services, marketing, research, color, etc. A phone call will get you the name of the appropriate person for you to contact. Each has its own way of being reimbursed, and you should certainly find out what that is before you sign up with them.

While most of these recruiters do not handle entry-level people, it is important for you to know who they are and perhaps it is even worth your while to give them a call . . . as one recruiter said, "There're exceptions to every rule, particularly when a candidate is brilliant!"

Jerry Fields Associates, Inc.
714 Fifth Avenue
New York, NY 10019
(212) 307-1212

Handles all areas of communications and advertising, including art, copy, account services, media, research, production, marketing and traffic jobs. Also handles some PR jobs.

Judy Wald Agency, Inc.
110 East 59th Street
New York, NY 10022
(212) 421-6750

Handles all areas of advertising but specializes in senior-level creative and TV production jobs. Has offices in New York, Los Angeles, Chicago, London, Paris, with affiliates in Sydney and Toronto.

Judd-Falk
124 East 37th Street
New York, NY 10016
(212) 686-1500

The nation's largest executive search firm specializing in marketing and advertising executives. There's a branch office in Chicago.

Toby Clark
655 Madison Avenue
New York, NY 10022
(212) 752-5670

Specializes in marketing, public relations and communications jobs, not entry-level.

Schapper-Phillips, Inc.
310 Madison Avenue
New York, NY 10017
(212) 490-1211

Handles all areas of public relations jobs from not-for-profit organizations to Fortune 500 companies to public relations agencies.

Some agencies do handle entry-level secretarial and assistant jobs within advertising and other communications type firms. Here are two:

Forum Personnel, Inc.
342 Madison Avenue
New York, NY 10017
(212) 687-4050

Sometimes has jobs in the media field, traffic, sales promotion.

Smith Fifth Avenue Agency
17 East 45th Street
New York, NY 10017
(212) 682-5300

Handles all levels of research, media, account management and sales promotion jobs.

Publications in Advertising, Marketing, Public Relations and Related Fields

There are many books, directories, trade magazines and newspapers published having to do with advertising and the professional community. Some are very important for you to read because they keep you up to date and aware of trends; others can be read at your discretion and leisure. (Those marked with an asterisk should get your particular attention.) Many of the trade periodicals include agency and executive profiles, which could prove most beneficial to anyone researching potential employers. Also, many periodicals include help-wanted sections as well as positions-sought sections where, in some cases for free, you can advertise yourself. For those wanting further information, contact the publications below. For a list of books about advertising, contact the Advertising Distributors of America, 400 Madison Avenue, New York, NY 10021.

Periodicals and Directories

Ad East
AdEast Enterprises, Inc.
907 Park Square Building
Boston, MA 02116
(617) 423-1122

Ad East contains articles covering advertising and marketing strategy, advertising campaigns, company profiles, etc. Special features include columns which address local, state interests, industrial advertising and marketing and public relations practitioners. This publication could be useful to those residing in the Boston area. Circulation: 11,789.

Ad Forum
Agency File, Inc.
18 East 53rd Street
New York, NY 10022
(212) 751-2670

Ad Forum contains articles on issues and trends in the advertising and marketing of consumer products and services. Frequently includes executive and company profiles. Circulation: 5,384.

Advertising Age*
Crain Communications
740 N. Rush Street
Chicago, IL 60611
(312) 649-5200

This publication is read by most everyone having anything to do with the advertising industry. It is probably, more than any other, *the* trade publication. It is available at many newsstands in New York, and at most libraries. It covers all phases of the industry and will keep you up to date on the goings-on. Special features include descriptions of the 100 leading national advertisers, and financial profiles of the major ad agencies. It has increased its frequency to twice a week. Circulation: 79,417.

Advertising and Communications Yellow Pages*
New York Yellow Pages, Inc.
113 University Place
New York, NY 10003
(212) 675-0900

An excellent and inexpensive reference tool for the job-seeker. Includes listings of advertising agencies, production companies, printers—virtually everything needed by the job-seeker. Also provides a phone information service. Available only through publisher.

Advertising/Communications Times
121 Chestnut Street
Philadelphia, PA 19106
(215) 629-1666

Advertising Communications Times is for those in the Philadelphia, eastern Pennsylvania, New Jersey and Delaware areas. Columns focus on regional developments, personnel changes (good for job-seekers to know!) and other facets of the advertising industry. Circulation: 23,978.

Advertising World
(Published 6 times a year)
Directories International
150 Fifth Avenue
New York, NY 10011
(212) 807-1660

Advertising World is devoted to international advertising, with articles on the international advertising scene, research, campaign management, U.S. rep appointments, media buying, who's who and more. This is an excellent publication for those interested in a career in international advertising. Available only through the publisher. Circulation: 5,060.

Adweek*
ASM Communications, Inc.
820 Second Avenue
New York, NY 10017
(212) 661-8080

Comprising *Adweek/East*, *Adweek/Southeast*, *Adweek/Midwest*, *Adweek/West*, *Adweek/Southwest*, this is a group of magazines devoted to advertising news and information. Each magazine is edited in the region it serves. Of particular interest to job-seekers is the annual agency review, where agency billings, gross income, major account changes and media placements are profiled, and the special career issues. Available only through the publisher, contact above for regional addresses. *Adweek* has both help-wanted and positions-wanted posted. (The positions-wanted ads are run free of charge for two weeks!)

American Newspaper Markets Circulation
P.O. Box 994, 2701 Barrymore
Malibu, CA 90265
(213) 456-1863

This directory, published annually, could be useful to those interested in a comprehensive list of magazines and newspapers—for instance, those interested in media sales.

Art Direction
10 East 39th Street
New York, NY 10016
(212) 889-6500

Art Direction is for visual professionals—reporting events, people, shows, awards and new techniques. Good for those interested in becoming an art director. Circulation: 10,275.

Art Product News
In-Art Publishing Company
P.O. Drawer 117
St. Petersburg, FL 33731
(813) 821-6064

Art Product News is for the professional artist and designer. Interesting features include interviews with leading art directors and graphic designers. Circulation: 47,369.

Backstage* and *The Backstage TV, Film & Tape*
Backstage Publications
330 West 42nd Street
New York, NY 10036
(212) 947-0020

Backstage is for the communications industry, with regular stories and columns covering TV commercial-industrial, film and tape production. The annual directory includes agency listings for New York, Hollywood and Chicago and includes the names of the commercial producers at each listed company. Both these are a must for anyone interested in TV commercial production or industrial filmmaking. Circulation: 32,000.

Broadcasting
Broadcasting Publications, Inc.
1735 DeSales Street, N.W.
Washington, DC 20036

Broadcasting is a business news magazine editorially directed to broadcasting managers and those interested in broadcasting management. Articles include those on advertising, programming, broadcast and cable journalism. Good for those interested in TV advertising sales. Circulation: 36,935.

Business Marketing
Crain Communications
740 N. Rush Street
Chicago, IL 60611
(312) 649-5260

Good for those interested in business-to-business advertising. Circulation: 32,948.

Communication Arts
Coyne & Blanchard
P.O. Box 10300
410 Sherman
Palo Alto, CA 94303
(415) 326-6040

Communication Arts is edited for professionals in graphic design and advertising. Articles and interviews feature individuals, studios and agencies, with examples of their work. Circulation: 51,673.

Communications World
IABC
870 Market Street
Suite 940
San Francisco, CA 94102
(415) 433-3400

Communications World provides professional information for public relations executives, photographers and audiovisual specialists. Good for those interested in corporate communications. Circulation: 11,576.

Creative: The Magazine of Promotion and Marketing
Magazines/Creative, Inc.
37 West 39th Street
New York, NY 10018
(212) 840-0160

Creative is edited for the advertising, sales promotion and merchandising managers of corporations. Feature articles include trends in the various areas of promotion and marketing. Circulation: 10,265.

*The Creative Black Book**
Friendly Press, Inc.
401 Park Avenue South
New York, NY 10016
(212) 684-4255

The acknowledged "bible" for advertising people around the world. The 1984 edition is the fourteenth annual *Creative Black Book*. It is three volumes and includes 25,000 listings of major suppliers in nineteen countries, including most every advertising agency, production company, employment agency, photographer, union, school, organization. Also includes samples of the work of top commercial photographers, illustrators, designers, film people, etc. The *Black Book* is truly the essential reference book for the working and would-be working professional in advertising, design and related fields. In 1984, a condensed version of the standard *Black Book* was created; however, for job-seekers the standard is still the best. The books are rather expensive, but available at some libraries. Use them.

Direct Marketing
A Hoke Communications, Inc., Publication
224 Seventh Street
Garden City, NY 11530
Direct Marketing deals with how direct mail is used by business. Columns include: Mail Order Markets & Methods, Letter Copy, etc. Circulation: 13,892.

The Direct Marketing Market Place
Hilary House Publishers, Inc.
1033 Channel Drive
Hewlett, NY 11557
The directory of the direct marketing industry. It is a reference and mailing list source to find new business, to locate suppliers, and to find free-lancers specializing in direct marketing. (Free-lance direct marketing copywriters might want to list themselves here.) Published annually.

DM News: The Newspaper of Direct Marketing
Mill Hollow Corporation
19 West 21st Street
New York, NY 10010
(212) 741-2095
Just what the title implies. Circulation: 20,635.

The Folio: 400
Folio Publishing Corporation
P.O. Box 697
125 Elm Street
New Canaan, CT 06840
(203) 972-0761
Folio is the ranking and media analysis of the business and consumer publications. Interesting to those interested in magazine sales. Circulation: 24,832. Published annually.

Food & Beverage Marketing
Charleson Publications
124 East 40th Street
New York, NY 10016
(212) 953-9322
Food & Beverage provides news and how-to information for marketing and advertising executives in the food, beverage, liquor and tobacco industries. Good to look at if interested in working on the client's side or for packaged goods ad agency account services department. Circulation: 18,077.

The Gallagher Report
230 Park Avenue
New York, NY 10017
(212) 661-5000
A weekly newsletter geared toward top management in the industry.

Graphic Design: USA
Kaye Publishing Corporation
120 East 56th Street
New York, NY 10022
(212) 759-8813
Provides news and ideas of graphics, people, trends, etc., in the graphic arts field.

International Advertiser
Roth International
615 West 22nd Street
Oak Brook, IL 60521
(312) 986-0064
Includes profiles of international advertisers, agencies, and personalities. Another publication for those interested in international. Circulation: 5,713.

Journal of Advertising Research
The Advertising Research Foundation
3 East 54th Street
New York, NY 10022
(212) 751-5656
Edited for users and practitioners of advertising research. Circulation: 4,727.

Journal of Marketing and *Journal of Marketing Research*
The American Marketing Association
250 S. Wacker Drive
Chicago, IL 60606
(312) 648-0536
Publications of the American Marketing Association, contains articles on the science of marketing. Circulation: 17,358/10,465.

*Madison Avenue**
Madison Avenue Publishing Corporation
369 Lexington Avenue
New York, NY 10017
(212) 972-0600
For national advertisers and their agencies. Articles include studies of major ad campaigns, debates on controversial issues and personal career advice. Circulation: 31,674.

Magazine Age
Freed Crown Lee Publishing, Inc.
225 Park Avenue
New York, NY 10169
For advertisers and agency personnel, focusing on the effective use of advertising in magazines.

Marketing and Media Decisions
Decisions Publications, Inc.
1140 Avenue of the Americas
New York, NY 10036
(212) 391-2155
Examines, evaluates, and chronicles in depth the factors involved in deciding where national and regional ad dollars go. Includes some interesting articles for would-be media, account executive and marketing people. Circulation: 24,682.

Marketing Communications
United Business Publications
Media Horizons
475 Park Avenue South
New York, NY 10016
(212) 725-2300
Reports on marketing strategies and campaigns. Written for marketing executives and those concerned with advertising, media, public relations, promotion, direct mail, premiums and incentives, point-of-purchase, packaging.

Marketing News
The American Marketing Association
250 S. Wacker Drive
Chicago, IL 60606
(312) 993-9504
The AMA newsletter, this reports on the activities of the association, as well as the marketing field in general.

Media People
Media People Magazine
P.O. Box 3905
Grand Central Station
New York, NY 10163
(212) 573-8582
Media People deals with various aspects and personalities associated with the various forms of media. Circulation: 41,000.

Medical Advertising News
Engel Communications
150 Fifth Avenue
New York, NY 10010
(212) 929-6400

Medical Advertising News is a news and information magazine for the medical advertising industry, reporting on events, trends, etc., that affect pharmaceutical manufacturers and ad agencies in the medical advertising community. Circulation: 10,000.

Millimeter
Millimeter Magazine, Inc.
826 Broadway
New York, NY 10003
(212) 477-4700

For production professionals in motion pictures, television and TV commercials. A regular column covers news on TV commercial production with frequent profiles of commercial directors and other technicians. Circulation: 22,000.

Moody's Industrial Manual
Moody's Investors Service Inc.
99 Church Street
New York, NY 10007
(212) 553-0300

An annual directory of thousands of companies, providing history, description of business and products, top management and financial data. Good research tool.

New England Advertising Week
100 Boylston Street
Boston, MA 02116
(617) 482-0876

Edited to serve the New England advertising community.
Circulation: 12,860.

*New York Times**
229 West 43rd Street
New York, NY 10036
(212) 556-1234

Certainly this publication should be scoured by anyone interested in advertising. But particular attention should be paid to Philip Dougherty's daily advertising column in the Business Day section, Mondays through Fridays. Also the Sunday Business section and classifieds should be read religiously.

O'Dwyer's Directory of Public Relations Firms/O'Dwyer's Profiles:
25 Largest PR Operations
J. R. O'Dwyer Company
271 Madison Avenue
New York, NY 10016
(212) 679-2471

Good research tool for anyone interested in public relations work.
O'Dwyer also publishes a newsletter.

Perspectives, Trends in Health Care Promotion
CPS Communications, Inc.
P.O. Box 488
31 Baily Avenue
Ridgefield, CT 06877
(203) 438-9301

Just what the title indicates. Circulation: 2,000.

Potentials in Marketing
Lakewood Publications
731 Hennepin Avenue
Minneapolis, MN 55403
(612) 333-0471

News of new products, services, and market data, covering premiums,
incentives, audiovisual aids and training, business gifts, etc. Circulation: 67,000. The company plans on publishing a directory.

Premium/Incentive Business
Gralla Publications
1515 Broadway
New York, NY 10036
(212) 869-1300

Contains news articles and features which report on merchandising
and product trends affecting the premium marketing field. Circulation: 30,000.

Print
America's Graphic Design Magazine
R. C. Publication
355 Lexington Avenue
New York, NY 10017
(212) 682-0830

Edited for creative specifiers in print and other forms of visual communications. Covered are creative trends, promotion design, advertising graphics, etc. Circulation: 26,000.

The Publicist
P. R. Aids, Inc.
330 West 34th Street
New York, NY 10001
(212) 947-7733

Includes interviews with professionals, occasional news of internships, and sections on the craft of doing public relations. Comes out bi-monthly.

Public Relations Journal and Public Relations Journal Directory Issue
Public Relations Society of America
845 Third Avenue
New York, NY 10022
(212) 826-1757

The *Public Relations Journal* is the official publication of the Public Relations Society and is edited for public relations practitioners and educators. The *Directory* lists members of the Society, and could be a good research tool; it is published annually. Circulation: 16,500/ 10,000.

Public Relations News
127 East 80 Street
New York, NY 10021
(212) 879-7090

Just what it says it is.

Signs of the Times
ST Publications
407 Gilbert Avenue
Cincinnati, OH 45202
(513) 421-2050

For those interested in outdoor advertising. Circulation: 15,300.

Specialty Advertising Business
Specialty Advertising Association International
1404 Walnut Hill Lane
Irving, TX 75062
(214) 258-0404

Includes news of the activities of the association, reports on sales-training programs, education, etc., and is edited for distributors and suppliers of the specialty advertising industry.
Circulation: 3,935.

Standard & Poor's Register of Corporations,
Directors and Executives
Standard & Poor Corporation
25 Broadway
New York, NY 10004
(212) 248-2525

There are three volumes of *Standard & Poor's Register.* Volume I is an alphabetical listing of over 36,000 U.S. and Canadian companies, providing officers, etc. Volume II is a list of executives and directors with brief data about each—an indispensable research tool before you go on that interview. Volume III includes an index of companies by location. The company also publishes a semimonthly publication, *Standard Corporation Descriptions,* detailed, timely information on corporate background, operations, key personnel changes and important news concerning many thousands of companies.

*Standard Directory of Advertisers**
(classified and geographical edition)
National Register Publishing Company, Inc.
5201 Old Orchard Road
Skokie, IL 60077
(312) 470-3100

Lists more than 17,000 advertisers, with names of key personnel, their titles, budgets and advertising agency. This is a must-see for anyone interested in working on the client side; also a good research tool for anyone interested in learning about a potential client. The classified edition is arranged by category, the geographical by state and city. There is a weekly supplement, *Ad Change Weekly.* Known as the *Advertiser Red Book,* this and its sister book, which follows, are two of the most-used directories by those seeking employment and/or researching potential clients. Most libraries have the directories and the weekly supplement. Circulation: 11,000.

*Standard Directory of Advertising Agencies**
(known as the *Agency Red Book*)
same as above

This is the number-one tool for anyone looking for a job with an advertising agency. The *Red Book* lists over 4,000 agencies and includes the year they were founded, number of employees, specialization, names and titles of key personnel, regional offices and accounts. The *Red Book* is published every February, June and October, with supplements published monthly. Available at most libraries and a marvelous tool for you. Take advantage of it! Circulation: 9,000.

Standard Rates and Data Service
Old Orchard Road
Skokie, IL 60077
(312) 583-1333
Business Publication Rates and Data-Classified
Change Bulletin Group
Co-op Source Directory
Community Publication Rates and Data
Consumer Magazine and Farm Publication Rates and Data
Direct Mail Lists Rates and Data
Newspaper Circulation Analysis
Newspaper Rates and Data
Print Media Production Data
Spot Radio Rates and Data
Spot Radio—Small Markets Edition
Spot Television Rates and Data

While these directories may not be of much use to the job-seeker, everyone interested in advertising should know of their existence. Most advertising agencies subscribe to at least one or two of the above, which include personnel listings of the various media, advertising rates and circulation; and other accurate, up-to-date information on hundreds of thousands of media availabilities from print to broadcast to direct marketing media. If you want to know what your potential client reads, look through the Business Publications Rates and Data. You'll learn.

Television and Radio Age
Television Editorial Corporation
1270 Avenue of the Americas
New York, NY 10020
(212) 757-8400

Provides coverage of the broadcast business for both buyers and sellers of radio and TV time. Circulation: 18,000.

Television Cable and Factbook
Television Digest
1836 Jefferson Place NW
Washington, DC 20036
(202) 872-9200

A two-volume reference work containing information of relevance to those working in the television and cable industries.

Variety
154 West 46th Street
New York, NY 10036
(212) 869-5700

Edited for those in the entertainment, broadcast and advertising trades. Circulation: 43,000.

Wall Street Journal
420 Lexington Avenue
New York, NY 10170
(212) 285-5000

Besides business news, the *Wall Street Journal* has a very good classified job openings sections—scour it. Circulation: 1,900,000.

Zip/Target Marketing
North American Publishing Company
401 N. Broad Street
Philadelphia, PA 19108
(215) 574-9600

For direct marketers, focusing on the creation, printing and mailing of promotional, sales and informational material. Circulation: 37,000.

Books

As with periodicals, there are literally hundreds of books written about advertising and the related fields. Some are how-to books, actually describing ways to design, or to write copy. Others are personal sagas about life in advertising. Others are more career-oriented. Still others provide insight into the role of advertising in general. My basic advice is to read as much as you can, particularly if you are unemployed, because while there is nothing like hands-on experience, learning secondhand is better than not learning at all. Look at your reading and research as preparation for future interviews and jobs. As new books on advertising come out frequently, it's a good idea to check your local bookstore now and again; browse through the marketing, advertising, career and artbook sections for the latest titles. Also, use your library. Many are well stocked with the "classics" on advertising as well as some of the new books. Below you will find enough books to get you started. This is by no means a complete list—for that, you'll have to do your own research. And, every time you go on an interview or have a meeting with someone in the field, ask them to recommend a book. This will not only get you a relevant title, it will give you a good reason to contact that person again . . . to thank them for their suggestion!

Advertising Procedures, by Otto Kleppner. This book is on many a
    school's reading list. It has been revised twice and is being re-
    vised again. It is about what the title indicates, advertising proce-
    dures.
Ayer Glossary of Advertising and Related Terms (Ayer Press, NY, 1977).
    Useful to have and review, it is just what the title indicates.
The Best Thing on TV—Commercials, by Jonathan Price (Penguin, NY,
    1978). For anyone interested in writing, designing and/or pro-

ducing TV commercials. See also award annuals in this appendix for other reviews of excellent commercials.

Blood, Brains and Beer: An Autobiography, by David Ogilvy (Atheneum, NY, 1978.) Also by the same author, *Confessions of an Advertising Man* (Atheneum, 1963). By the founder of Ogilvy & Mather, provides great insight into the industry and provides a good, forthright approach to advertising. "Eleven Lessons Learned on Madison Avenue" should prove particularly useful. Mr. Ogilvy's third book, *Ogilvy on Advertising* (Crown, NY, 1983), is also worthwhile.

The Compleat Copywriter, by Hanley Norins (McGraw-Hill, NY, 1963). For would-be copywriters.

Creative People at Work, by Edward Buxton (Executive Communications, Inc., NY, 1976). Emphasis is the step-by-step paths upward from getting the first job to attaining high-salaried top management positions.

Critical Issues in Public Relations, by Hill & Knowlton executives (Prentice-Hall, Englewood Cliffs, NJ, 1975). A good overview of PR, including history. Also, different sections written by an expert in the field he or she is writing about.

Does She or Doesn't She, by Shirley Polykoff (Doubleday, NY, 1975). About the author's life in and out of advertising, who is the creator of the great slogan "Does She or Doesn't She . . . Only Her Hairdresser Knows. . . ." The book is out of print but available at libraries.

From Those Wonderful Folks Who Gave You Pearl Harbor, by Jerry Della Femina (Simon & Schuster, NY, 1970). By the last great eccentric creative, the president and founder of Della Femina, Travisano & Partners, Inc. Provides lots of advertising "stories" and is fun to read too.

Getting Hired, by Edward Rogers (Prentice-Hall, Englewood Cliffs, NJ, 1982). A good book on resumés by the director of personnel of N W Ayer.

How to Advertise, by Ken Roman and Jane Mass. (St. Martin's, NY, 1977). Provides a good description of each area of advertising, e.g., positioning a product, print advertising, direct mail, television production. In the foreword to the book, David Ogilvy says, "When you have read it, you will know what it took me twenty-four years to learn on the job." So read it.

How to Put Your Book Together and Get a Job in Advertising, by Maxine Paetro (Executive Communications, Inc., NY, 1979). A good book for creatives, i.e., would-be copywriters and art directors who are in the process of creating portfolios. Ms. Paetro is a creative manager in charge of hiring creatives based on their "book," so she knows what the agencies are looking for.

The Language of Graphics, by Edward Booth-Clibborn and Daniele

Baroni (Harry N. Abrams, NY, 1983). An anthology of advertising product design translated from an Italian book. Includes text on traditional Japanese packaging, British product design, etc. Should be fascinating to graphic designers, art directors and students.

The Photographer's Market, Writer's Digest. Updated annually. Lists over 3,000 places where you can sell your photos—including advertising agencies, public relations firms, stock photo agencies.

Pocket Pal (International Paper Company, NY, updated annually). Since its debut in 1934, the *Pocket Pal* has served as an introduction to the graphic arts for many in the advertising and graphics fields. Great for anyone interested in print production. Only available through the publisher, at 77 West 45th Street, NYC 10036.

Reality in Advertising, by Rosser Reeves (Knopf, NY, 1961). A solid marketing concept: USP (the Unique Selling Proposition) is explained in this classic advertising book.

The Right Angles (*How to Do Successful Publicity*), by Babette Hall (Ives Washburn, Inc., NY, 1965). A book on the strategies and techniques of public relations.

Selling Smart, How Magazine Pros Sell Advertising, by Ira Ellenthal (Folio Publishing Corporation, CT, 1982). Just what the title indicates and a good introduction to anyone interested in media sales. The book is rather expensive, so try to borrow a copy.

Slogans in Print (Doyle Dane Bernbach, NY). The agency compiles advertising slogans for the previous year, which will help you to answer such questions as who said what for which client. Available through the agency's library.

Systematic Approach to Advertising Creativity, by Stephen Baker (McGraw-Hill, NY, 1979). Also interesting by this author: *Advertising Layout and Art Direction* and *Visual Persuasion*.

Thirty Seconds, by Michael Arlen (Farrar, Straus and Giroux, NY, 1981). Originally a *New Yorker* piece, this fascinating little book traces every step in the making of one :30 television commercial. You'll meet the A.E., producer and others from N W Ayer advertising agency, as well as the crew from one of the most prestigious production companies (Steve Horn, Inc.) and, of course, the client.

Walking the Tightrope: The Private Confessions of a Public Relations Man, by Henry Rogers (Morrow, NY, 1980). A light look at the PR field, by a forty-year veteran.

What Color Is Your Parachute, by Richard Nelson Bolles (Ten Speed Press, Berkeley, CA, 1983). By now everyone knows of this marvelous manual for job-seekers and career-changers. Read it slowly and let it soak in. Author has also written other good career books: *Where Do I Go From Here With My Life?* with John C. Crystal, whose work in career guidance *Parachute* is based on; and *The Three Boxes of Life, and How to Get Out of Them*.

Who's Hiring Who, by Richard Lathrop (Ten Speed Press, Berkeley, CA, 1977). One of the better books on resumé writing and job-hunting techniques.

Professional Associations

There are hundreds of professional associations that can help you one way or another in your job search: in learning more about a particular area of advertising and even in learning about your potential client's business. Below you will find the names and addresses of some of those which are advertising-related. However, a complete listing of all professional organizations does exist in a directory entitled *Career Guide to Professional Associations, A Directory of Organizations by Occupational Field* (The Carrol Press, Cranston, RI). Many of the associations have literature available for the career seeker; others publish periodicals and books that could be of help and interest to you. By all means call whichever organizations you believe can offer you information and ask for literature, names of employment agencies, dates for seminars—anything they have or can do for the career seeker.

The Advertising Club of New York
3 West 51st Street
New York, NY 10019
(212 541-4350

The Advertising Club sponsors the Andy Awards, an annual competition to honor outstanding examples of advertising. It also sponsors the Advertising and Marketing Course, a twenty-two-week course designed for those newly engaged in advertising. The club is also a gathering place for those in the professional community, offering various seminars, cocktail parties and occasional galas. The club also publishes a monthly newsletter. Membership in the Advertising Club qualifies you for membership in the American Advertising Federation.

The Advertising Research Foundation
3 East 54th Street
New York, NY 10022
(212) 751-5656

This 46-year-old foundation was established by the 4 A's and the Association of National Advertisers to ensure a professional approach to advertising research applications to business problems. And, to advance the science and practice of advertising research. The foundation has approximately 360 members; advertisers, agencies, media companies and independent research firms make up the largest numbers, but academics and other associations are among their members.

Advertising Women of New York, Inc.
153 East 57th Street
New York, NY 10022
(212) 593-1950

Advertising Women of New York was founded in 1912. Today it is a
professional organization of approximately 800 women in executive
positions in the communications industry: advertising, marketing,
merchandising, research promotion, public relations and media. Its
goals are equal-opportunity development of the management and professional skills of their members, the improvement of the status of
women and contributions to the development of future professionals.
They conduct seminars, luncheon programs—and an annual college
career conference created for students in advertising and communications. They also established, in 1958, the Advertising Women of New
York Foundation, a separate tax-exempt entity to develop educational,
philanthropic, community and cultural activities. Write and/or call for
information on the College Career Conference and other related career activities and literature.

American Advertising Federation
1225 Connecticut Avenue, NW
Washington, DC 20036

This grass-roots organization has individual as well as corporate
members from all facets of the industry. (While the members of the 4
A's are the country's leading ad agencies, and the members of the
ANA are national advertisers, the local and club members of the AAF
can be everyone with any connection to the industry—advertisers,
ad agencies, the media, printers, photographers, production companies, etc.) In all, there are some 25,000 members belonging to 203
clubs in the fifty states. The AAF does have an educational foundation; literature encouraging people to consider a career in advertising
is available.

American Association of Advertising Agencies (known as the 4 A's)
666 Third Avenue
New York, NY 10017
(212) 682-2500

This is probably the most prestigious of all advertising associations,
with all the large and important advertising agencies in the country
and world belonging to it. The objectives of the 4 A's is, according to
them, "to promote and further the interests of advertising agencies by
increasing their usefulness to advertisers, to media and to the public."
And, to collect and disseminate information and ideas affecting advertising and advertising agencies among members of the Association and
others interested; to cooperate with government on matters affecting
advertising; to foster and stimulate scientific research and investiga-
tion in connection with advertising; to maintain and safeguard honesty,

fairness and good taste in advertising copy; to maintain friendly relations with other associations and promote friendly relations among all advertising agencies. The 4 A's also helps educators who teach advertising, and is sometimes called upon to help member agenices in solving management and operational problems. They also are the ones who recruit member agencies to do voluntary public service campaigns. The 4 A's was founded in 1917, and as of June, 1982, there were 550 member agencies in various cities of the U.S., in Puerto Rico and other countries. The association maintains an education, employment and development committee and does publish several guides to careers in advertising. If you are working for a member agency, you can take advantage of the association's research department and other resources. Until then, you are limited. However, everyone interested in advertising should make himself familiar with this organization.

American Management Associations
135 West 50th Street
New York, NY 10020
(212) 586-8100

For professional managers in various areas of business. The twelve divisions include: Finance; General Management; Manufacturing; Insurance & Employee Benefits; Marketing; Information Systems and Technology; Research and Development; Human Resources; Packaging; International Management; Purchasing, Transportation and Physical Distribution; General & Administrative Service. Courses in the above are offered; also, AMA publishes various business management books, periodicals, handbooks and reference material. For further information and/or application literature, contact as above.

Art Directors Club, Inc.
488 Madison Avenue
New York, NY 10022
(212) 838-8140

A trade organization for graphic arts professionals, and the producer of a key advertising reference annual on the year's best creative work. Also a social club and meeting place, promoter of art education (ask for their marvelous booklet on job descriptions in the business world of art and design), an information center on industry issues. Serves the professional community, art students and faculties, the government and corporations. Begun in 1920, the club has four goals: to develop and maintain the highest standards of design practice in the profession of art direction, to improve the creative climate for communicators where they work, *to aid students coming into the field*, and to promote an awareness and understanding of the position of art director in industry. A constantly expanding educational program is high on the club's list of priorities, and the Portfolio Review is something every would-be art director should take advantage of. That's for graduating students and would-be art directors, and is a one-to-one encounter between practicing art directors and the neophyte. Call and ask for details and take advantage of this worthwhile organization's interest in you.

Association of National Advertisers, Inc.
155 East 44th Street
New York, NY 10017
(212) 697-5950

The ANA consists of about 400 members, most of them major advertisers—that is, "the client." It is the only organization concerned solely with the interests of the *users* of advertising. The ANA assists in the training and development of member-company advertising and of marketing executives, and communicates advertisers' practices and attitudes to agencies, media and other suppliers of advertising services, as well as providing its members with other information and services. While no literature about careers on the client side *per se* is available, the ANA does publish reports, studies and books on all phases of advertising and marketing management. While these publications are primarily for the use of ANA members, some are available and useful to nonmembers. Especially good are a series of sixteen essays available separately or as a complete set ($14.80). Some of these essays are: "The Role of Promotion," "The Role of Marketing Research," "The Client-Agency Relationship." Write and ask for a free listing of marketing and advertising publications available from the ANA.

Business/Professional Advertising Association
205 East 42nd Street
New York, NY 10017
(212) 661-0222

A 60-year-old association of some 4,000 advertising, marketing, communications and marketing professionals in companies engaged in business-to-business selling; in advertising agencies serving such companies; with business magazines, etc. There are chapters located in various cities throughout the country, including a student chapter at Boston University, with other student chapters to be added. A good resource for anyone interested in business-to-business advertising. Ask about their handbooks, seminars, educational programs and student membership.

Cabletelevision Advertising Bureau, Inc.
767 Third Avenue
New York, NY 10017
(212) 751-7770

A nonprofit association supported by the cable industry. CAB's main goal is to establish cable as a major factor in advertising by providing information and services relating to cable as a medium. As of now they have no educational foundation; however, they are a young organization and this might change, so if this is your area of interest, touch base with them.

> The Clio Organization
> 336 East 59th Street
> New York, NY 10022
> (212) 593-1900

The Clio Organization was founded in 1959 to conduct the first annual CLIO Awards Competition in 1960. CLIO, the Award for Advertising Excellence, is known as the "cousin of Oscar." While the organization does not have an educational program *per se*, it would be worthwhile for those interested in the creative side of the business to look through Clio's publications and their latest pamphlets.

> Direct Mail/Marketing Association, Inc.
> 6 East 43rd Street
> New York, NY 10017
> (212) 689-4977

The Direct Mail/Marketing Association operates the Direct Mail/Marketing Educational Foundation at the same address and telephone listed above. They publish several career pamphlets on direct mail copywriting, career opportunities in mailing lists, careers in direct marketing, etc. Write or call for information on careers in direct marketing, for information on week-long scholarship programs for college seniors to study direct mail/marketing. Also, contact the association for information on direct marketing institutes, seminars, conferences; for a bibliography of direct marketing books and magazines; and for help in compiling your own list of potential direct marketing employers.

> Institute of Outdoor Advertising
> 342 Madison Avenue
> New York, NY 10173
> (212) 986-5920

The Institute of Outdoor Advertising is the marketing, research, and promotion arm of the outdoor advertising industry. Supported by outdoor companies and affiliates of the industry, it provides the advertising community with information needed for a more thorough understanding of the medium. For anyone interested in the field, the institute publishes a brochure, including a glossary of terms, facts on purchasing outdoor advertising, on designing it, and other facts.

> Magazines Publishers Association
> 575 Lexington Avenue
> New York, NY 10022
> (212) 752-0055

MPA is the umbrella trade association of the consumer magazine industry. It sponsors several seminars and conferences on various topics concerning magazine selling. It also maintains a library/information center for members. If you are interested in magazine advertising sales, contact MPA for further information.

The One Club
251 East 50th Street
New York, NY 10022
(212) 935-0121

The One Club is a craft guild solely for copywriters and art directors and aspiring copywriters and art directors. (They do have a Junior/ student membership.) Some of their programs include career counseling (a private thirty-minute meeting with a counselor); a portfolio review clinic, offered monthly, and various workshops. The club also conducts a bimonthly series entitled "Evening with the Gold Winners" (the One Club Award) and a job placement service. All aspiring copywriters and art directors should contact the One Club at the above and ask for a newsletter and membership information. This one is really interested in you.

Public Relations Society of America, Inc.
845 Third Avenue
New York, NY 10022
(212) 826-1750

The society, which was founded in 1948, has more than eighty chapters located throughout the United States. Its members total more than 10,000. In 1968, PRSA established the Public Relations Student Society of America (PRSSA) to cultivate a favorable and mutually useful relationship between students and professional public relations practitioners. The society publishes the monthly *Public Relations Journal* and the annual *Public Relations Register*. For further career information, send $1.00 for a copy of *Careers in Public Relations* to the above. In addition to this booklet, the society provides an annual selected public relations bibliography and a list of American colleges and universities whose public relations sequences have been accredited.

Society of Illustrators
128 East 63rd Street
New York, NY 10021
(212) 838-2560

This professional association offers a terrific little booklet entitled *Society of Illustrators' Career Guidance in Illustration and Graphic Design*, in which such questions are answered as: How to prepare a professional portfolio? How many samples should be shown? How does one get in to see an art director? Also, the various types of jobs available to illustrators are described in detail; the jobs available with advertising agencies (i.e., pasteup man, mechanical man, lettering man, sketch man, art director) are also described. Seminars and other educational programs are available, so anyone interested in the "art" side of advertising should touch base with this very worthwhile organization.

Unions

There are a few jobs in advertising, mostly in the television production free-lance area, where it will be necessary for you to become a member of a union in order to work on "professional crews." Gaining entrance into these unions is often a frustrating and difficult task. Admission information is best gotten directly from each local listed below, but in some cases even that won't be an easy matter. If there is any way for you to meet and ingratiate yourself with union members, do so and let it be known that you wish to join their local—for more often than not, you will have to be sponsored to gain entrance. Below is a listing of most of the unions involved.

American Federation of Television and Radio Artists (AFTRA)
1350 Avenue of the Americas
New York, NY
(212) 265-7700

The union for actors working in commercials. Those of you in talent payment, while not members, will come in contact with this union often.

Directors Guild of America (DGA)
7950 Sunset Blvd, Hollywood, CA 90046 (213) 656-1220
110 West 57th Street, New York, NY (212) 581-0370

The DGA negotiates minimum salaries and working conditions for directors, assistant directors and unit production managers working in television commercials (as well as theatrical films). They do have an internship program in film directing, but not in commercials. (For further information see *The Business of Show Business*, by this author).

International Alliance of Theatrical Stage Employees and Moving Picture Machine Operators of the United States and Canada (IATSE—pronounced "yatsee"—a.k.a. the IA) The IA is the largest entertainment union in the country, with over 900 locals representing film crews. Below are the names, addresses and phone numbers of the locals involved with television commercial production:

New York—area code (212)

Local 52—represents studio mechanics. 221 West 57th Street, NYC 10019 (765-0741)

Local 161—represents script supervisors. 251 E. 50th Street, NYC 10022 (686-7724).

Local 304—represents film projectionists and audiovisual workers. 745 Seventh Avenue, NYC 10019 (586-4018)

Local 644—represents cameramen. 250 West 57th Street, NYC 10019 (247-3860)

Local 771—represents film editors. 630 Ninth Avenue, NYC 10036 (581-0771)

Local 798—represents makeup artists and hairstylists. 1790 Broadway, NYC 10019 (757-9120)

For corresponding Los Angeles and other regional locals contact the national office, IATSE, 1515 Broadway, NYC 10036. (212) 730-1770. Or see *The Business of Show Business*, by this author.

National Association of Broadcast Employees and Technicians (NABET)
Local 15
1776 Broadway
New York, NY 10019
(212) 265-3500

NABET
Local 531
1800 Argyle
Los Angeles, CA 90028
(213) 462-7485

NABET
80 East Jackson Boulevard
Chicago, IL 60604
(312) 922-2462

NABET consists of forty-five local unions across the country, representing film and tape personnel, broadcast technicians, newswriters. Of the forty-five locals, five represent film and tape personnel and are in direct competition with the IA for members. NABET represents free-lance grips, hairstylists, makeup artists, stylists, script clerks, camera operators, sound people and electricians, etc. NABET prides itself on being an "open" union, and in fact was originally started in the 1950s in response to the closed-door policy of the IA. Call and/or write asking for admission information. (An exam in each discipline is required.)

United Scenic Artists, Local 829
1540 Broadway
New York, NY 10036
(212) 575-5120

Local 829 is an autonomous local of the Brotherhood of Painters and Allied Trades. Local 829 has labor jurisdiction over scenic designers, set designers and costume designers working on TV commercials (as well as film and theater). Entrance to the union is achieved through an intensive exam given annually, usually in June.

Internships

An internship is a period of time spent learning while working in a professional environment. For their work, some interns earn a small stipend, others college credit, others on-the-job training, education and contacts. At its best, an internship bridges the gap between school and the professional world; at its worst it provides labor for exploitive companies and individuals. To avoid the latter, make sure from the start that you will be getting something (money, experience, entrance into a union, college credits) in return for your work. A number of schools allow their students (graduate and undergraduate) to intern with a relevant professional organization for college credit, so inquire at your school. Generally, in those cases, the school will arrange for and supervise the internship. Those out of school can also, if they so desire, participate in an internship. From time to time, an advertising agency will offer such an opportunity. For example, McCaffrey & McCall offers an eight-week summer internship. A public relations firm, Anthony M. Franco, Inc., offers one student internship each summer; the work period is ten weeks and a stipend is provided. The best way to learn of internships is to call the major agencies and PR firms and *scour* the trades listed in this appendix.

Workshops

For those of you still not certain of what you want to do, the John C. Crystal Creative/Life Work Planning Course might be something to consider. It's this workshop that *What Color Is Your Parachute* is based on, and basically helps you discover what work you are best suited for. For more information, contact: John C. Crystal Center, 111 East 31st Street, NYC 10016. (212) 889-8500.

Appendix C: A Review of the Top Forty Advertising Agencies

Following is a listing of the top forty advertising agencies, their addresses, phone numbers, major clients and number of offices and employees. In some cases, some history and information on training programs, etc., is also included. Please keep in mind that while the top ten agencies tend to remain the same, the others change frequently, as do their lists of clients. To keep current, read the trades and all agency reviews listed in the appendix. Also, because an agency is not in the top forty billing-wise does not mean it is not a major agency. For instance, one of the most popular places to work is Ally & Gargano, not mentioned here at all. (When this list was compiled, it was number 45; more recently it has moved way up the ladder.)

As mentioned in the overview, an advertiser often employs the services of more than one agency, so if you see repeats in the client listing, that's the reason.

These forty companies are just the tip of the iceberg as far as future places of employment are concerned . . . so please don't stop here. Look into smaller agencies, production companies, media buying firms (some of which are listed at the end of the agency review), public relations firms, etc.

Agency/Address	Some Major Clients*	Personnel/Offices
Young & Rubicam, Inc. 285 Madison Avenue New York, NY 10017 (212) 210-3000	AT&T; American Home Products; Peter Paul Cadbury; Clorox; Colgate-Palmolive; Continental Group; Del Monte; Dr Pepper; Eastman Kodak; Gillette (Personal Care Division); Frito-Lay; Gannett; General Foods; Gulf Oil; Hallmark; Holiday Inns; Jamaica Tourist Board; Johnson & Johnson; Kentucky Fried Chicken; Lipton; Manufacturers Hanover Trust; Merrill Lynch; Metropolitan Life; Motorola; National Distillers; New York Telephone; Philip Morris; Miller Brewing Co.; Rank Xerox; RCA (C.I.T. Financial Services); Richardson-Vicks; Southland Corp. (7-Eleven Food Stores); Time, Inc.; Twentieth Century–Fox; Union Carbide; Uniroyal; United Vintners; U.S. Postal Services; Warner Communications (Atari); Warner-Lambert.	3,957 employees in 35 U.S. offices and 2,904 employees in 91 foreign offices.

Young & Rubicam is always among the top ten agencies. It is also one of the few agencies interested in entry-level people and is considered an excellent place to work if you are a would-be A.E., creative or research person. It is known as a copywriters agency. Also, the agency is known to promote from within and does have some training

Note: For a yearly update of the fifty biggest agencies, see *Adweek's* yearly agency directory available through the publisher. (See Appendix B.) Also *Advertising Age's* agency review; and for further information on all agencies, see the *Agency Red Book* (see Appendix B for details) and its monthly supplements.

* As previously stated, clients change frequently in advertising, and many of these already have! If you wish to use this information for any reason, check to make sure it is current. You can use the space around the client lists to do your own updating.

Agency/Address	Some Major Clients*	Personnel/Offices
	programs. The agency was founded in 1923 and today consists of consumer agencies, specialty shops, international offices and one of the largest public relations firms in the world.	
Ted Bates Worldwide, Inc. 1515 Broadway New York, NY 10036 (212) 869-3131	American Cyanamid Inc. (Breck, Shulton); Brown-Forman/Jos. Garneau Co.; Cadbury Schwepps USA, Inc.; Carter-Wallace, Inc.; Colgate-Palmolive; Adolph Coors Co.; Electrolux Corp.; General Foods; Home Box Office Inc.; ITT Continental Baking; Kal Kan Foods, Inc.; Leeming/Pacquin Division, Pfizer, Inc.; M&M/Mars; Matsushita Electric; Maybelline Co.; the Prudential Insurance Co.; RCA Corp.; Richardson-Vicks Inc.; U.S. Navy Recruiting; Warner-Lambert, American Circle Division; Warner-Lambert Product Division.	2,054 employees in 13 U.S. offices and 2,193 employees in 60 foreign offices.
	Started in the late 1940s by Ted Bates, who had previously handled the Colgate account at Benton & Bowles. The agency is famous for its USP (the Unique Selling Proposition), an approach to advertising that gives emphasis to a product's unique consumer benefits. Bates is known for the "hard sell" rather than "soft sell" creative" approach to advertising. They do have training programs and have been recruiting at several graduate schools. Contact the various departments (account management, creative, media and research) as well as the appropriate personnel person for interview and/or more information.	
J. Walter Thompson & Co. 466 Lexington Avenue New York, NY 10017 (212) 210-7000	Activision, Inc.; American Federation of State, County & Municipal Employees; Beatrice Foods Co., Manufacturing Division; H&R Block, Inc.; Booth Newspapers, Inc.; Burger King Corp.; Capitol Broadcasting Co.; Castle & Cooke Foods; Champion Spark Plug Co.; Chevron U.S.A., Inc.;	3,102 employees in 61 U.S. offices and 4,317 employees in 42 foreign offices.

Cutter Laboratories; Dart & Kraft Inc. (corporate, Kraft Retail Food Group, Food Trade, Military, new products, Food Service and Industrial Group); Dunlop Sports Co.; Eastman Kodak Co. (Consumer Professional & Finishing Marketing Division, Motion Picture & Audio Visual Markets Division, Business System Markets Division, Graphic Markets Division, Customer Equipment Service Division, International corporate, sports promotion, Epcot Center at Disney World); Eaton Automotive Components Group; Eaton Truck Components; Esselte Pendaflex Corp.; Ford Motor Co. (dealer advertising associations, Export Corp., cars, trucks); the R. T. French Co.; Genesco, Inc.; Gerber Products Co.; Hart Schaffner & Marx; Hewlett-Packard Co.; Hyatt Hotels Corp., Hyatt International Corp.; Jacuzzi Whirlpool Bath, subsidiary of Walter Kidde & Co.; S. C. Johnson & Son, Inc.; Jovan, Inc.; Kawasaki Motors Corp.; Kellogg Co. (Nutri-Grain cereals, food service); Kemper Group; Lever Brothers Co. (Close-up, Denim cologne, Dove, Drive detergent, Lux, Shield, Rinso, new products); McDonnell-Douglas Corp.; Miles Laboratories (One-A-Day vitamins), new products; Motion Picture Association of America; Munsingwear, Inc.; Nabisco Brands, Inc. (Fleischmann's Yeast, International, new products); National Association of Home Builders; the Nestle Co. (Nestea, Sunrise); Northern Telecom; Northwestern Mutual Life In-

Agency/Address	Some Major Clients*	Personnel/Offices

surance Co.; Orkin Exterminating Co., Inc., division of Rollins, Inc.; Oscar Mayer & Co., division of General Foods; Pepsi-Cola Co. (On Tap, Teem); the Quaker Oats Co.; Rolex Watch U.S.A., Inc.; Rollins Protective Services Co.; Samsonite Corp; Jos. Schlitz Brewing Co.; Scott Paper Co.; Sears, Roebuck & Co.; Six Flags over Georgia; Southern Communications (SPRINT); W. A. Taylor & Co.; Tenneco Automotive; the Terson Co.; Uncle Ben's Foods, Frozen Foods; Warner-Lambert Co.; Wedgewood, Inc.; W. F. Young Inc.

Begun in 1864 as a space brokerage firm, the agency today is one of the biggest worldwide and has a fine reputation in the advertising community. In 1980 the JWT Group, a holding company, was formed to correct the companies' reputation as being "too big." JWT Group, Inc., consists of: J. Walter Thompson Co. (itself consisting of other units: J. Walter USA; J. Walter International; J. Walter Canada; Brouillard Communications; Thompson Recruitment Adv.); Hill and Knowlton, a major PR firm; and Euro Advertising Holding, B.V. (7 European agencies).

Ogilvy & Mather International, Inc.
2 East 48th Street
New York, NY 10017
(212) 688-6100

American Bell; American Express Co.; Avon Products; Campbell Soup Co. (Swanson, Pepperidge Farm, Inc.); Chesebrough-Pond's, Inc. (Health & Beauty Products Division, Packaged Foods Division); Cotton, Inc.; Ex-Lax Pharmaceutical Co.; Foremost-McKesson, Inc., Grocery Products Division (C. F. Mueller Co.); General Foods Corp.; Hallmark Cards, Inc.; Hershey Chocolate Co.; In-

2,010 employees in 15 U.S. offices and 3,300 employees in 100 foreign offices.

ternational Paper Co.; International Playtex (Danskin, Inc.); Kimberly-Clark Corp.; Lever Brothers Co.; Longines-Wittnauer Watch Co.; Marriott Corp.; Menley & James Laboratories, Division of SmithKline Corp.; Nimslo Corp.; Owens-Corning Fiberglass Corp.; Par Parfums, Ltd.; Peugeot Motors of America; Publishers Clearing House; R. J. Reynolds Tobacco Co.; Smith Barney, Harris Upham & Co.; Thompson Medical Company Co., Inc.; Trans World Airlines, Inc.; Warnaco; Warner Amex Cable Communications, Inc.; Mattel, Inc.; E. & J. Gallo Winery; E. Tech.

Ogilvy & Mather was started in 1948 by legendary adman David Ogilvy. For years Ogilvy has been thought of as one of the best training grounds for A.E.'s and creatives; and in fact, one of the best agencies to work for. The agency owns other agencies, including Ogilvy & Mather Direct Response; Sussman & Sugar, specialists in book publishers; Scali, McCabe, Sloves, a small "highly creative" shop; North American Advertising, recruitment specialists; Ogilvy & Mather/2; and Cole & Weber, Pacific Northwest. If interested in Ogilvy & Mather, read David Ogilvy's books (see Appendix B). You'll gain much insight into the agency philosophy.

McCann-Erickson Worldwide
485 Lexington Avenue
New York, NY 10017
(212) 697-6000

American Express Co.; Bache Halsey Stuart Shields, Inc.; Brown-Forman Distillers Corp.; Brown & Williamson Tobacco Corp.; Chevron Chemical Co.; the Coca-Cola Co.; Cosmair, Inc.; Del Monte Corp.; Exxon Co. USA; General Motors Corp.; Gillette; the Great Atlantic & Pacific Tea Co.; Heublien, Inc.; Hilton Hotels Corp.; Lockheed Corp.; Nabisco Brands, Inc.; the Nestle Co.; Pabst Brewing Co.; Sears, Roebuck & Co.; Sony Con-

1,225 employees in nine U.S. offices and 5,000 employees in 89 foreign offices.

Agency/Address	Some Major Clients*	Personnel/Offices

sumer Products Co.; Specialty Brands Inc.; Texas Instruments; United States Borax and Chemical Corp.; Wells Fargo & Co.; Western Airlines.

McCann is the principal agency in the Interpublic Group of Companies, the large communications holding company. While McCann has some strong accounts in this country, it is really strong overseas. Certainly their work, all over, is excellent, particularly the Coke advertising. While it wouldn't hurt contacting McCann's personnel department, Interpublic's personnel department and the person you'd like to work for, it should be noted that the Interpublic way of finding people is through recruitment. In other words, they like to discover you.

BBD&O International, Inc.
383 Madison Avenue
New York, NY 10017
(212) 355-5800

American Cyanamid Co. (Pine-Sol, new products); Armstrong World Industries; Avis, Inc.; the Black & Decker Manufacturing Co.; Campbell Soup Co.; Dean Witter Reynolds Inc.; Dow Jones & Co. (*The Wall Street Journal*); E. I. Dupont De Nemours & Co., Inc. (corporate, Textile Fibers Division, Automotive Products Division, Organic Chemicals); Firestone Tire & Rubber Co.; General Electric Co.; Gillette (corporate, Personal Care Division, Safety Razor Division), Hammermill Paper Co.; Lever Brothers Co.; National Distillers & Chemical Corp.; PepsiCo, Inc. (Pepsi-Cola Co., PepsiCo International, Pepsi-Cola bottlers); the Pillsbury Co.; the Quaker Oats Co.; Joseph Schlitz Brewing Co.; Scott Paper Co.; Thom McAn Shoe Co.; the Timken Co.; Tupperware Home Parties, division of Dart Industries; Burlington Northern, Inc.; Cargill, Inc.

1,997 employees in 25 U.S. offices and 999 employees in 66 foreign offices.

(corporate); Honeywell, Inc. (corporate, Commercial Division, Building Services Division, Protective Services Division); George A. Hormel & Co.; 3M Co. (Data Recording Products Division, Electronic Products; Home Entertainment Products Department); James B. Beam Distilling Co.; Booth Fisheries, Inc.; Boyle-Midway, division of American Home Products (Pam, Wizard); E.J. Brach & Sons; Church's Fried Chicken; William Wrigley, Jr., Co.; Del Monte Corp.; Fisher Corp.; Hunt-Wesson Food Inc.; Los Angeles Tribune Co.; Delta Air Lines.

BBD&O was founded in 1891 and originally called the George S. Batten Company, but the real star was Bruce Barton, who remained active in the agency for quite some time and developed a fine reputation as a solid advertising man. Today the agency has a reputation for a strong, disciplined and conservative approach to advertising. The agency has several training programs, including one of the best in media. They own several subsidiaries including: Tracy-Locke in Dallas; a business and financial agency, Doremus & Company; GM DuBois, a sales promotion agency; two health care agencies: Frank J. Corbet, Inc., Chicago and Lavey/Wolff/Swift, Inc. New York and Franklin Spier, Inc., NY, specializing in book publishing.

Leo Burnett Co., Inc.
Prudential Plaza
Chicago, IL 60601
(312) 565-5959

Allstate Insurance Companies; American Bankers Association; Commonwealth Edison Co.; General Motors Corp.; Green Giant Co.; Harris Trust & Savings Bank; H. J. Heinz Co.; Keebler Co.; Kellogg Co.; Kimberly-Clark Corp.; Maytag Co.; McDonald's Corp.; Memorex Corp.; Nestle Co., Inc.; Philip Morris, Inc.; Pillsbury Co.; Procter & Gamble Co.; RCA Consumer Electronics Division;

1,557 employees in 41 U.S. offices and 1,679 employees in 36 foreign offices.

Agency/Address	Some Major Clients*	Personnel/Offices

Schenley Industries, Inc.; Star-Kist Foods, Inc.; Union Carbide Corp.; Union Oil Co. of California (Union 76 Division); United Airlines; Wilson Sporting Goods Co.; Salada Foods, Inc.

One of the few top agencies located outside of New York, Leo Burnett was started in 1935 by the man himself, a powerhouse of energy. Known for its ability to handle packaged goods accounts, and for its sound marketing, Burnett is an ideal place for would-be account executives. In general, it's known as a good place to work offering excellent opportunities for advancement. They are known to respond to letters and resumés, so give them a try. Their personnel department is divided into the various departments and they do employ a manager of creative services who reviews books.

Saatchi & Saatchi Compton Worldwide, Inc.
625 Madison Avenue
New York, NY 10022
(212) 754-1100

American Motors Corp.; Austin, Nichols & Co.; Borden; Buitoni Foods; Cunard Lines; Harlequin Enterprises; General Electric, Hotpoint Division; International Business Machines Corp.; Johnson & Johnson; Jones Dairy Farm; *National Enquirer*; McNeill Consumer Products Co.; New York Life Insurance Co.; Personal Products Co.; Phelps Dodge Industries; Procter & Gamble Co.; Sheraton Corp.; Thompson Medical Co.; United States Steel Corp.; British Leyland; Cadbury-Schweppes; Dupont; Gillette.

2,630 employees in U.S. and foreign offices.

Founded in 1908, Compton has gone on to be a consistently successful agency with major clients. It's a good place to work because it has so many top-notch clients and because it is an agency with integrity. Its conservative but positive image is well earned. It owns several subsidiaries, among them Ross Roy–Compton, an agency which specializes in collateral material; Rumrill-Hoyt, a small, full-service agency in upstate New York; Cadwell Davis

Savage, a new-product development agency; Klemtner Advertising, a medical agency; Hoffman York, a strong midwestern agency. In 1982, the hot, young (1970) British agency Saatchi & Saatchi bought Compton to form Saatchi & Saatchi Compton Worldwide, Inc.

Foote, Cone & Belding
Communications Inc.
401 North Michigan Avenue
Chicago, IL 60601
(312) 467-9200

British Airways; Clairol, Inc.; Frito-Lay, Inc.; Life Savers, Inc.; Lorillard, division of Loews Theatres; Adolph Coors Co.; Amana Refrigeration, Inc.; First National Bank of Chicago; S. C. Johnson & Son, Inc.; Kitchens of Sara Lee; Kraft Retail Food Group, division of Kraft, Inc.; Lanier Business Products, Inc.; Pearle Vision Center, Inc.; Pizza Hut; Sears Roebuck & Co.; Sunkist Soft Drinks, Inc.; Swift & Co.; Zenith Sales Co., division of Zenith Radio Corp.; Clorox Co.; Levi Strauss & Co.; Atlantic Richfield Co.; Mazda Motors of America, Inc.; Volume Shoe Corp.; Corning Glass; Woodside Travel; Knapp Communications; Lipton Tea; California Milk Advisory Board; First Interstate Bank of Oregon; INA Ross Loos Healthplan, Inc.; Dreyer's Grand Ice Cream; Alaska Tourism; Armour-Dial; Pacific Telephone; International Harvester; Denny's; Renault; Brown & Williamson; Hallmark; Gillette/Braun; ICI; Rembrandt Group.

2,250 employees in eight U.S. offices and 1,540 employees in 27 foreign offices.

Begun in 1893 as a space brokerage firm known as Lord & Thomas, the agency took on its present name in 1942. Today it owns several smaller companies including Carl Byoir & Associates, a large public relations firm; Albert Franl/FC&B, a financial agency; Deutsch, Shea & Evans, a recruitment agency. They do good work and have training programs for A.E.'s, creatives, media and research people. Contact the human resources person in charge of the area that interests you.

Agency/Address

Grey Advertising, Inc.
777 Third Avenue
New York, NY 10017
(212) 546-2000

Some Major Clients*

Acme Boot Co., Inc., subsidiary of Northwest Industries, Inc.; AMAX, Inc. (corporate); American Broadcasting Co.; American Council of Life Insurance; American Motors Corp.; Beecham Products; Block Drug Co., Inc.; Bloomingdale's (broadcast); Boehringer Ingelheim Ltd., O-T-C Marketing Unit; Borden, Inc. (Cheese Products Group, Confectionary Products Group, Grocery Products Group); Bristol-Myers Products; Brown & Williamson (Viceroy); Bullock's Department Stores; Canada Dry Corp.; Canon U.S.A., Inc. (cameras); Carter-Wallace, Inc. (Pearl Drops tooth polish, Rise shave cream, new products); Champion International Corp., Building Products Division; Congoleum Corp. (Home Furnishings Group, Bath Iron Works); David Crystal, Division of General Mills Apparel Corp.; Doubleday & Co., Inc., Book Club Division; the Drockett Co.; Filene's Basement Stores; General Foods Corp.; B. F. Goodrich Co., Tire Group; Gordon's Dry Gin Co., Ltd.; Health Insurance Association of America; H. J. Heinz Co.; Holly Farms Poultry Industries, Inc.; Huffy Corp.; International Playtex, Inc.; ITT Continental Baking Co. Inc. (Beefsteak Rye, Town Talk breads, new products); Kayser-Roth Corp. subsidiary of Gulf + Western Industries (No-Nonsense Fashions, Inc.); Kenner Products; the Mennen Co.; B. S. Moss En-

Personnel/Offices

725 employees in U.S. offices and 560 employees in 30 foreign offices.

terprises; National Alliance of Business; Northwest Orient Airlines Inc.; Panasonic Co.; the Procter & Gamble Co. (Bold 3, Downy, Duncan Hines Cookie Mix, Jif, Joy, Puffs facial tissues); RCA Corp. (records and tapes); Remington Products, Inc.; Revlon, Inc.; Sentry Insurance Co.; Shearson/American Express, Inc.; Spanish National Tourist Office; STP Corp.; Swift & Co.; Timex Corp.; Trans-Lux Corp.; Turco Manufacturing Co.; Union Underwear Co.; U.S. Consumer Product Safety Commission; U.S. Department of Defense (joint recruiting program); Warner Bros., Inc.; Division of Warner Communications; B. Dalton Bookseller; the Center Companies; Dayton's, Dayton Hudson Jewelers; Diamonds Department Stores; Horizon Industries; J. B. Two Corp.; King Koil Sleep Products; Kroy, Inc.; Pickwick Books; Bank of America; Computer-Land; Continuous Curve Contact Lenses; Kikkoman International, Inc.; Princess Cruises; Taco Bell; Westin Hotels; American Express Co. (special projects); Campbell Soup Co. (Champion Valley Farms); Eli Lilly & Co. (corporate); U.S. Education Department; Jewel Companies, Inc.

Grey was started in 1917 and the story is it got its name from the color of the building where it was then situated. For years it has had a reputation for being a tough place to work but a good place to get training. They have one of the best research departments of any agency. Their subsidiaries include: Grey Direct, a direct marketing agency; Grey, Conohay & Lyons, for smaller clients; Grey Meidal; and Grey & Davis, a public relations firm.

Agency/Address	Some Major Clients*	Personnel/Offices
Doyle Dane Bernbach International, Inc. 437 Madison Avenue New York, NY 10022 (212) 826-2000	Allied Corp.; American Greetings Corp.; American Tourister Luggage, Inc.; Atari, Inc.; Bankers Trust Co.; Borden, Inc. (Consumer Products Division); Bristol-Myers Products Division; Bulova Watch Co.; W. Atlee Burpee Co. (Retail Division); CBS Broadcast Group; Celanese Fibers Marketing Co.; Chanel, Inc.; Ciba-Geigy Corp. (Airwick Industries, Inc.); Citicorp; Clairol, Inc.; the Continental Insurance Companies; Foodways National, Inc. (Subsidiary of H. J. Heinz Company); Gagliardi Brothers, Inc. (Affiliate of H. J. Heinz Company); General Telephone and Electronics Corp.; H. J. Heinz (Camargo Foods, Inc., Foodways National, Inc., Gagliardi Brothers, Inc., Ore-Ida Foods); Hershey Foods Corp.; International Business Machines Corp. (IBM Office Products Division, corporate); ITT, Continental Baking Co. (C&C Cola); International Gold Corp., Ltd.; Lehman Brothers Kuhn Loeb, Inc.; MCA/Universal; Miles Laboratories, Inc. (Grocery Products Division, Consumer Products Division); Mobil Oil Corp. National Federation of Coffee Growers of Colombia; North American Philips Consumer Electronics Corp.; Paine Webber, Inc.; Polaroid Corp.; the Procter & Gamble Co. (Gain, Coast, Puritan oil, Rejoice liquid soap); O. M. Scott & Sons Co.; Joseph E. Seagram & Sons, Inc. (Browne Vintners Co., Calvert Distillers Co.,	1,850 employees in 11 U.S. offices and 1,000 employees in 21 foreign offices.

General Wines & Spirits Co., Seagram Overseas Sales Co.); Sheaffer Eaton Division, Textron, Inc; The Stroh Brewery Co.; Volkswagen of America, Inc.; CBS (Entertainment Division); Celestial Seasonings; The Southern California Gas Co.

Doyle Dane Bernbach was started in 1949, and along the way is said to have changed the face of advertising. Bill Bernbach is credited for putting the art director on the advertising map and creating ads that people really *looked* at—hence starting a "creative revolution" that continues even today. Known as a "creative agency," it remains one of the most sought-after places of employment. They have offices throughout the world and control several subsidiaries. For creatives, this is an excellent place to train.

SSC&B:Lintas Worldwide/
SSC&B, Inc.
One Dag Hammarskjold Plaza
New York, NY 10017
(212) 644-5000

American Brands, Inc. (American Tobacco Co., American Cigar Co.); American Can Co., Dixie Consumer Products Division; Amstar Corp., American Sugar Division; Carnation Co. (Contadina Division, Instant Division, Pet Foods Divisions, Specialty Foods Division); Citicorp (Citibank, New York Banking Division, Citicorp Person-to-Person); the Dun & Bradstreet Corp. (corporate); Johnson & Johnson (Baby Products Co., Chicopee, Personal Products Co.); Lego Systems, Inc.; Lever Brothers Co. (Autumn margarine, concentrated, dishwasher and liquid All, DX toothbrushes, Pepsodent toothbrushes and toothpaste, Lifebuoy, Lever Puerto Rico, new products); Thomas J. Lipton, Inc. (Beverage Division, Foods Division, Good Humor Corp.); the Mennen Co.; Monet Jewelry; Noxell Corp. (Cosmetic Division, Toiletry/Household Division);

623 employees in three U.S. offices and 3,098 employees in 62 foreign offices.

241

Agency/Address	Some Major Clients*	Personnel/Offices
	Olympus Camera Corp.; Renfield Importers, Ltd.; Scannon, Ltd.; Steak & Ale Restaurant Corp.; Sterling Drug, Inc. (Glenbrook Laboratories, Lehn & Fink Consumer Products Division); Textron, Inc., Homelite Division; Van Munching & Co., Inc.; Bearing Engineer, Inc.; California Association of Winegrape Growers; California Avocado Commission.	

SSC&B started in 1946 with Noxzema and some Lever Brothers accounts. In 1979 they became part of the Interpublic Group of Companies. With some solid accounts, this is a good agency to work for and they do have a management development program. Write the personnel director for details. SSC&B:Lintas is one of the leading agencies in Europe, Argentina, India and South Africa and the largest in Thailand.

D'Arcy-MacManus & Masius 360 Madison Avenue New York, NY (212) 850-7300	Advertising Council National Comm.; CPC International, Inc.; Edison Electric Institute; Heublin, Inc.; Leeming/Pacquin Division of Pfizer, Inc.; Mars, Inc.; Pitney Bowes; RCA; S. B. Thomas, Inc.; U.S. Air Force; U.S. Treasury.	1410 employees in 17 U.S. offices and 2069 employees in 53 foreign offices.

Founded in 1973, this agency is not as well-known as other top agencies. It owes its size to its many mergers. Though main headquarters are in New York, there are several major offices throughout the country, namely, in Chicago, St. Louis, San Francisco, L.A., Atlanta, and Minnesota.

Dancer Fitzgerald Sample, Inc. 405 Lexington Avenue New York, NY 10174 (212) 661-0800	Advertising Council, Inc.; American Cyanamid (Shulton); American Insurance Association; Blue Bell, Inc.; CBS Publications; CPC International, Inc. (Best Foods Division, S. B. Thomas, Inc.); Con-	1194 employees in five U.S. offices and 1536 employees in 41 foreign offices.

solidated Edison Co. of New York, Inc.; Consolidated Foods Corp. (Bali Co. Hanes Corp., L'erin Cosmetics, Popsicle Industries, Inc.); Dart & Kraft, Inc. (Duracell Products Co., Duracell, Inc., Canada); Ethan Allen, Inc.; Fresh Air Fund; General Entertainment Corp.; General Mills, Inc. (Big G Division, Fundimensions, Toy Group International, Kenner Products, New Business Division, Parker Brothers—U.S. and Canada, Sperry Division, Yoplait USA, Inc.); Glass Packaging Institute; Life Savers, Inc.; Lorillard Division of Loews Theatres, Inc.; Norton Simon, Inc. (Somerset Importers, Ltd.); Olympia Brewing Co.; Peninsular Distributing Co.; Peter Paul Cadbury; Procter & Gamble (Oxydol, Dreft, Solo, White Cloud bathroom tissue, Bounty paper towels, Luvs disposable diapers); Procter & Gamble Co. of Canada Ltd. (Luvs); RCA (Selecta Vision VideoDisc software); State of Florida, Department of Citrus; Toyota Motor Sales USA, Inc. (Abdul Latif Jameel Establishment, Saudi Arabia); Wendy's International; J. B. Williams Co. (Femiron vitamins, P.V.M. diet aids); Ciba-Ceigy Corp., Agricultural Division; MSD AGVET, division of Merck & Co. (animal health products); Actimart S. A.; Barratt American, Inc.; Bridgestone Tire Co. of America, Inc., Bridgestone Tire Co., Ltd. (Japan); Crown Atlantic Corp.; Los Angeles Public Theatre; Occidental Petroleum; 3M Co. (personal care products, home stationery).

Agency/Address

Some Major Clients*

Personnel/Offices

Started in 1923 as Blackett-Sample-Hummert, the agency grew steadily and dramatically in the 30s when it became heavily involved in radio soap operas. The agency took its present name in the 1940s when major interest was sold to Dancer and Fitzgerald. Today it is considered one of the better places to work and is known for a low turnover among personnel, something rather rare in the ad game. They are said to be more receptive to new people entering the business than most large agencies.

Benton & Bowles, Inc.
909 Third Avenue
New York, NY 10022
(212) 758-6200

AMF, Inc. (corporate, Hatteras Yachts, Robalo Powerboats, Marine Products International); Anderson-Clayton Foods (New Age Sandwich Slices); Caltex Petroleum Corp.; Computer Sciences Corp. (Information Services, recruitment); Crum & Forster (property and casualty insurance); Digital Equipment Corp. (computers, related products); Emery Worldwide; Estech, Inc., Division of Esmark (Vigoro Lawn & Garden Products); FirstBank Evanston; Peter Eckrich & Sons Inc.; Jos. Garneau Co., Inc. (Ambassador Scotch, Cella Wines, Martell Cognacs); General Foods Corp. (Brim ground and freeze-dried decaffeinated coffees, Cool Whip Non-Dairy whipped topping, Gaines Gravy Train, Orange Plus, Yuban coffee); Hardee's Food Systems Inc.; Home Savings & Loan Association; E. F. Hutton & Co., Inc.; Jensen Sound Laboratories; Magic Pan Restaurants; Marriott Hotels; Marine Midland Bank; McCulloch Corp.; Milliken & Co. (Visa Fabrics); Nicholas International, Ltd.; Norwich-Eaton Pharmaceuticals, Inc. (Encare Contra-

1464 employees in U.S. offices and 426 employees in 4 foreign offices.

ceptive, Necta Sweet artificial sweetener, NP-27 athlete's foot remedy, Ocusol eye drops and lotion, Pepto-Bismol stomach remedy, Unguentine burn remedy); Pinkerton Tobacco Co., division of the Liggett Group; the Procter & Gamble Co. (Attends disposable briefs, Bounce dryer-added fabric softener, Charmin toilet tissue, Crest toothpaste, Dawn dishwashing liquid, Ivory Snow laundry soap, Pampers disposable diapers, Scope mouthwash, Wondra skin-conditioning lotion, Zest); RCA Music Service, division of RCA Records; Jos. Schlitz Brewing Co. (Schlitz Malt Liquor); Showtime; Standard Brands, Inc. (Planters peanut oil and popcorn oil, Planters Snacks); the Stiffel Co.; Texaco, Inc. (Havoline motor oil, Texaco anti-freeze and coolant, batteries, oil filters, air filters, wiper blades, Texaco gasolines); Texas Commerce Bancshares; Van de Kamp's Frozen Foods Division (batter-dipped fish, Mexican specialty products, pizza); Richardson-Vicks (Clearasil acne medication, Fixodent cream adhesive, NyQuil nighttime colds medicine, Sinex decongestant nasal spray, Topex acne medication, VapoRub decongestant ointment, Vicks Blue extra-refreshing cough drops, Vicks Inhalers nasal decongestant, Victors nasal action cough drops); MacDowell Colony; Muscular Dystrophy Association; UNICEF.

Agency/Address	Some Major Clients*	Personnel/Offices

Benton & Bowles was begun in 1929 and is today considered a good place to work, particularly if you're interested in media. For those interested in the agency, read *Our Kind of People, the Story of the First 50 Years at Benton & Bowles*—difficult to get hold of but worthwhile—written by Gordon Webber, a former creative head. The book provides much insight.

1,213 employees in the U.S. offices.

N W Ayer, Inc.
1345 Avenue of the Americas
New York, NY 10105
(212) 708-5000

ABC; Alexander & Alexander, Inc.; American Telephone & Telegraph Co.; Avon Products, Inc.; Bahamas Government Ministry of Tourism; Cannon Mills; Carrier Air Conditioning Co.; Chemical Bank; De Beer Consolidated Mines, Ltd.; E. I. Du Pont de Nemours & Co. (Consumer Products Group, Industrial Group); Edison Electric Institute; Federal National Mortgage Association; First Boston Corp; Gillette (Personal Care Division); Globe Life and Accident Insurance Co.; Harlequin Enterprises, Ltd.; Howard Johnson's; Lehn & Fink Products Group, division of Sterling Drug, Inc.; Menley & James Laboratories; National Council on Alcoholism; Pinkerton's, Inc.; Ralston Purina Co. (new products); the Seven-Up Co.; *TV Guide* magazine; Time-Life Books; U.S. Army Recruiting; Univac Division of Sperry Corp; Van Camp Sea Food Co.; Xerox Learning Systems; Kraft, Inc. (Dairy Products Group, Retail Food Products Group, corporate marketing).

One of the oldest agencies in the country, Ayer has long been considered a good solid agency . . . and a fine place to work. Once considered stodgy, that is no longer true. Creatively, they are certainly "with it." Contact the personnel department . . . and, as always, the person inside the agency you'd like to work for.

William Esty Co., Inc.
100 East 42nd Street
New York, NY 10017
(212) 697-1600

American Home Products Corp. (Whitehall Laboratories, Ayerst Laboratories, Ekco Housewares Co.); Chesebrough-Pond, Inc. (Health & Beauty Products Division, Prince Matchabelli Division, corporate); Colgate Palmolive Co.; the Genesee Brewing Co., Inc.; Marriott Corp. (Great America Theme Park Division); MasterCard International; Minolta Corp., Photographic Division; Nabisco Brands, Inc., Nabisco Foods, Inc.; Nissan Motor Corp. in U.S.A.; Noxell Corp. (Noxzema shave cream); R. J. Reynolds Tobacco Co.; Jos. E. Seagram & Sons, Inc.; Tampax, Inc.; Union Carbide Corp., Battery Products Division; Warner-Lambert Co., Consumer Products Division.

619 employees in two U.S. offices.

Marsteller, Inc.
866 Third Avenue
New York, NY 10022
(212) 752-6500

Alfa Romeo, Inc.; Armstrong World Industries, Inc.; Arthritis Foundation; Ashland Chemical Co. Barnes Group, Inc.; Beatrice Foods Co. (Canada), Ltd.; Chicago Title Insurance Co.; Colt Industries; Continental Corp.; Dannon, Inc.; Ethyl Corp.; Exxon Office Systems; FMC Corp.; Grumman Corp.; Hoffman-LaRoche Inc.; ITT, Telecommunications Division; Keep America Beautiful, Inc.; McGraw-Hill Publications Co.; New American Library; Sunshine Biscuits Inc.; Tobacco Institute; U.S. JVC Corp.; United Technologies Corp.; Abbott Laboratories; Armour Foods Co., Food Service Systems

967 employees in five U.S. offices and 525 employees in eight foreign offices.

Agency/Address	Some Major Clients*	Personnel/Offices
	Division; James B. Beam Distilling Co.; Beatrice Foods Co. (corporate, John Sexton & Co., Vogel-Peterson Co., Beatrice Foods Co. [Canada] Ltd.); Spiegel Publishing, Inc.; USA cable network; Singer Co.	
Wells, Rich, Greene, Inc. 767 Fifth Avenue New York, NY 10153 (212) 758-4300	Philip Morris, Inc.; Ralston Purina Co.; Procter & Gamble Co.; Miles Laboratories; Warnaco; J. C. Penney; National Geographic Society; Wolverine World Wide; New York State Dept. of Commerce; Savin Corp.; Pan American World Airways; National Multiple Sclerosis Society; Junior Achievement, Inc.; Council on Family Health; Juvenile Diabetes Foundation; Ford Motor Co.; Max Factor; Miles Laboratories; St. Louis National Baseball Club.	910 employees in 10 U.S. offices and 43 employees in one foreign office.

Headed up by the best-known woman in advertising, Mary Wells, this agency was at one time considered *the* place to work; today it's still a glamorous, important agency. Unfortunately, Wells Rich has never been very interested in entry-level people. Still, give them a try.

| Needham, Harper & Steers Advertising, Inc. 909 Third Avenue New York, NY 10022 (212) 758-7600 | Alexandra de Markoff; American Honda Motor Co., Inc.; American International Group Inc.; Amtrak; Amurol Products Co.; Anheuser-Busch Companies, Inc.; Armour Dial Co.; Atlantic Richfield Co.; Atari, Inc.; Charles of the Ritz; Crocker National Bank; Dayton Newspapers, Inc.; Deloitte Haskins & Sells; Dorsey Laboratories, division of Sandoz | 592 employees in six U.S. offices and 786 employees in 23 foreign offices. |

Inc.; Frigidaire Co.; White Consolidated Industries, Inc.; Gas Appliance Manufacturers Association; General Mills, Inc.; Household Finance Corp.; Israel Gov't. Ministry of Tourism; Kraft, Inc.; Kubota Tractor Corp: Land's End; Morton Salt; National Automobile Dealers Association; National Guard Bureau; Quasar Co.; Rubbermaid, Inc.; Shasta Beverages, Inc., a subsidiary of Consolidated Foods; State Farm Insurance Companies; *Southern Living* magazine; the Leadership Network; the Washington Post; Third National Bank & Trust Co. of Dayton; Union Carbide Corp.; William Wrigley, Jr., Co.; Xerox Corp.

Bozell & Jacobs, Inc.
One Dag Hammarskjold Plaza
New York, NY 10017
(212) 644-7200

Allied Corp.; Savings Bank Life Insurance Co.; Union Carbide; Days Inn of America; Jockey International; Johnson & Johnson (Patient Care Division); Stauffer Chemical; Mutual of Omaha Insurance Co.; Paramount Pictures; Peat, Marwick, Mitchell & Co.; Poppin Fresh Pie Shops; Quaker Oats Co.; Rossignol Ski Co., Inc.; Sun Giant; Tenneco, Inc.; Union Pacific Railroad; Avis; Borden Co.; New Jersey Bell; Celentano Bros., Inc.

1,300 employees in 13 U.S. offices and 93 employees in 5 foreign offices.

Kenyon & Eckhardt Inc.
200 Park Avenue
New York, NY 10166
(212) 880-2045

Air France; Bristol Myers Co.; Coca Cola Co. (the Wine Spectrum, Ramblin' root beer); Colgate-Palmolive; Alfred Dunner, Inc.; Government of Puerto Rico (Rums of Puerto Rico, Industrial De-

772 employees in 15 U.S. offices and 1,806 employees in 50 foreign offices.

Agency/Address	Some Major Clients*	Personnel/Offices
	velopment Admin.); Prudential-Bache Securities; Quaker State Oil Refining Corp.; Holiday Inns.	
Ketchum Communications Four Gateway Center Pittsburgh, PA 15222 (412) 456-3500 In New York: 1133 Avenue of Americas New York, NY (212) 536-8800	Alcoa; Calgon Corp.; C&P Telephone Companies; Colonial Penn Group, Inc.; Consolidated Natural Gas Co.; Dravo Corp.; Gulf Oil Corp; H. J. Heinz Co.; Mine Safety Appliances Co.; Penn Athletic Products; Commonwealth of Pennsylvania (tourism); Pittsburgh National Bank; PPG Industries, Inc.; Rubbermaid, Inc.; Thermo King Corp.; Wear-Ever Aluminum, Inc.; Westinghouse Electric Corp.; Acco Industries; Air Jamaica; BWIA International; Carrier International Corp.; Eurailpass; General Foods Corp.; Japan Air Lines Co.; New York Air; Schering Corp.; Melitta, Inc.; Pizza Hut, Inc.; Firestone Tire & Rubber Co.; Little Tikes Co.; White Motor Truck Group; ACF Industries, Inc.; Gordon Jewelry Corp.; Humana; PRE Corp.; Clorox Co.; From & Schiel; Hunt-Wesson Foods, Inc.; Kikkoman International, Inc.; Levi Strauss & Co.; Oregon Freeze Dry Foods, Inc.; the Pillsbury Co.; the Potato Board; Cooper Labs; Cutter Medical; Safeway Stores.	835 employees in nine U.S. offices and 255 employees in five foreign offices.
Campbell-Ewald Co. 30400 Van Dyke Warren, MI 48093	Advertising Council; Eastern Air Lines; First Federal Savings of Detroit; Goodyear International Corp.; the Goodyear Tire & Rubber Co.; Gulf-	595 employees in ten U.S. offices.

stream American; Kelly Services.

Amil Gargano started here. Read his profile (pages 110–125) for details.

Cunningham & Walsh, Inc.
260 Madison Avenue
New York, NY 10016

American Brands, Inc., the Andrew Jergens Co.; American Home Products Corp. (Boyle-Midway, American Home Foods, Household Research Institute); American Telephone & Telegraph Co. (Bell System Yellow Pages, Long Lines); the Bank of New York Co., Inc.; Beecham Products, Inc.; C. B. Fleet Co., Inc.; "21" Brands, Inc., division of Foremost-McKesson Inc.; Kayser-Roth Corp. (No Nonsense Fashions, Inc.); Mitsubishi Motors Corp. (corporate), Mitsubishi Motor Sales of America, Inc. (passenger car, trucks); Mrs. Paul's Kitchens, Inc. (Arthur Treacher's Seafood Restaurants); Procter & Gamble Co. (Folger Coffee Co., Crush International Inc., Paper Products Division); St. Regis Paper Co.; Schieffelin & Co. (wines, champagnes); Southern Railway System; Sterling Drug, Inc. (Glenbrook Laboratories, Winthrop Laboratories Division).

630 employees in five U.S. offices.

Backer & Spielvogel, Inc.
11 West 42nd Street
New York, NY 10036
(212) 556-5200

Bon Jour International, Ltd.; Campbell Soup Co.; Helene Curtis Industries, Inc. (Suave line of toiletries, new products); Miller Brewing Co. (Miller High Life Beer, Lite Beer, Lowenbrau Beer, Magnum Malt Liquor, new products); Noxell Corp. (Lestoil, new products); Paddington Corp. (J&B

429 employees in one U.S. office.

Agency/Address	Some Major Clients*	Personnel/Offices

Rare Scotch, Royal Ages Scotch, Catto's Scotch, Crofts Ports and Sherries, Knockando Scotch, Bailey's Original Irish Cream, new products); the Savings & Loan Foundation; the Seven-Up Co. (new products).

A new agency (started in 1979 when the two partners split from McCann), its growth rate is unheard-of—already they are considered one of the best in the world. Competition for jobs here is fierce.

Campbell-Mithun, Inc.
1000 Northstar Center
Minneapolis, MN 55402
(612) 339-7383

Andersen; General Mills; Land O'Lakes; 3M Corp; Republic Airlines; Ray-O-Vac; Control Data Corp.; County Seat; Dairy Queen; Beatrice Foods (Fisher Nuts); Better Homes and Gardens (Real Estate Division); Crown-Zellerbach; Honeywell; Kohler; Mirro; Northwestern Banco System; Tonka toys; Trane; Uniroyal; Tombstone Pizza; Kroger; Cryovac; American Egg Board; Chicago Oldsmobile Dealers Association; Chicago & Northwestern Railroad; A. B. Dick; Dow Chemical; Dubuque Packing; Eaton Corp.; Exchange National Bank; S. C. Johnson; Norand; Rich Products; Universal Foods; McGraw-Edison; Ashley's; SuperAmerica; Allis Chalmers; Branigar Organization; Drake Hotel; Fred S. James Co.; Larsen Co.; Kellwood Co.; Sap's Foods; St. Charles Manufacturing; Quaker Oats; Welch Foods.

600 employees in two U.S. offices.

Scali, McCabe, Sloves, Inc.
800 Third Avenue
New York, NY 10022
(212) 421-2050

American Can Co.; Buckingham Corp.; Bulova Watch Co.; GAF Corp.; Hebrew National Kosher Foods, Inc.; Hertz Corp.; Maxell Corp.; Mrs. Paul's Kitchens; Nikon, Inc.; Perdue, Inc.; Playboy Enterprises, Inc.; Chesebrough-Pond (Prince Matchabelli Division); Singer Co.; Sperry Corp.; E. R. Squibb & Sons, Inc.; Texas International Airlines; U.S. Pioneer Electronics Corp.; Volvo of America; Warner Amex.

45 employees in one U.S. office and 455 employees in eight foreign offices.

Geers Gross Advertising
220 East 42nd Street
New York, NY
(212) 916-8000

American Cyanamid; Buxton, Inc.; Cuisinarts, Inc.; ESPN Cable Sports Network; Fortunoff, Inc.; Fuji Photo Film; General Mills (fashion group); Gold Seal Company; the Hearst Corporation; Kraft Dairy Group; Loewe, Inc.; Ludens, Inc.; New Zealand Lamb Co., Inc.; Purolater-Courier Corp.; Ralph Lauren Licensees; Schenley Industries, Inc.; W. J. Sloane; Topps, Inc.; Ventura Travelware, Inc.; Warner Communications.

193 employees in NY, 290 worldwide.

Leber Katz Partners
767 Fifth Avenue
New York, NY 10153
(212) 826-3900

Apollinaris Mineral Water; Bongrain International (American) Corp.; Campbell Soup Co. (Prego Spaghetti Sauce); Chipwich, Inc.; the Wineries of Earnest & Julio Gallo (E&J Brandy); Hans Holterbosch, Inc. (Hofbrau Beer); Pepperidge Farm, Inc.; R. J. Reynolds Tobacco Co. (Vantage, More, NOW, Vantage Ultra Lights, More Lights); DiscoVision Associates; International Business Machines (General Systems Division, Information Records Divi-

249 employees in one U.S. office.

253

Agency/Address	Some Major Clients*	Personnel/Offices

sion); Bonne Bell, Inc.; Hoffman-LaRoche, Inc. (Pantene Hair Care Products); Hanes, division of Consolidated Foods Corp. (Hanes Knitwear Division, Hanes Printables Division); M. Lowenstein Corp., Inc. (Lowenstein Division, Wamsutta Mills, Pacific Home Products); Henry I. Siegel Co.; U.S. Shoe Corp.; the American Fur Industry; Art-Carved, Inc.; Birger Christensen, Inc.; Hartman, Inc.; Lenox, Inc.; Netherlands National Tourist Office; Stern's Garden Products, Inc. (Miracle-Gro); Casual Corner Retail Chain; Kay Jewelry, Inc.; American Stock Exchange; Utica Mutual Insurance Co.; Majestic Industries, Inc.; Conde Nast Publications (*Vanity Fair* magazine).

Ross Roy, Inc.
2751 East Jefferson Avenue
Detroit, MI 48207
(313) 568-6000
In New York:
635 Madison Avenue
New York, NY
(212) 350-7999

Bacardi Imports; Detroit Edison Co. (corporate); Federal-Mogul Corp.; Federal Screw Works; General Electric; K Mart Corp.; Kelsey-Hayes Co., subsidiary of Freuhauf Corp.; La-Z-Boy Chair Co.; Libbey Division, Owens-Illinois, Inc.; McDonald's Restaurants; Michigan Bell Telephone Co.; Michigan Milk Producers Association; National Yellow Pages Service Association.

104 employees in our U.S. offices and 20 employees in one foreign office.

Owned by Saatchi & Saatchi Compton Worldwide, Inc.

254

TBWA Advertising, Inc. 292 Madison Avenue New York, NY 10017 (212) 725-1150	Anheuser-Busch; Avianca; Braemar; Carillon Importers; Cartier; Eminence; Evian Water; Fairchild Publications; Ferragamo; Food and Wines From France; Fro Bel, Inc.; Girard Perregaux; Granada TV Rental; Pirelli-Superga Footwear Division; Roche-Bobois; *Venture* magazine; Wilkes Group; Ralston Purina Co.; Air 1, Inc.	45 employees in one U.S. office and 455 employees in eight foreign offices.
Creamer, Inc. 1633 Broadway New York, NY 10019 (212) 887-8000	Sheraton; Stouffer's; Speidel; ALCOA; Raytheon; Duffy-Mott; San Giorgio; Hercules Corp.; Maidenform; Rado Watch Co.; McDonald's (Pittsburgh, Hartford); Etonic; Equibank; Rhode Island Hospital Trust Bank; Chef Pierre Pies; Mobil Corp; Raybestos Corp.; Carlisle Tire & Rubber Co.	512 employees in six U.S. offices.
Della Femina, Travisano & Partners, Inc. 625 Madison Avenue New York, NY 10022 (212) 421-7180	Airborne Freight Corp.; Airwick Industries; Ale-8-One Bottling Co.; American Automobile Association; American Broadcasting Co. (WABC-TV); American Isuzu Motors, Inc.; American Isuzu Dealer Advertising Associations; BSR (USA), Ltd.; Beech-Nut Nutrition Corp.; Campus Sweaters & Sportswear; Chemical Bank; Connecticut General Insurance Corp.; CooperVision Optics, Inc.; CooperCare, Inc.; Dow Chemical U.S.A.; Dribeck Importers; Einstein Moomjy; Goody Products, Inc.; Lloyds Bank California; WNBC Radio; NBI, Inc.; New York Mets; Parr Securities; Ralston Purina Co.; Remy Martin Amerique, Inc. (new products); Schenley Industries; Sharp Electronics Corp.; Sin-	321 employees in three U.S. offices.

Agency/Address	Some Major Clients*	Personnel/Offices
	gapore Airlines; Singapore Tourist Promotion Board; Six Flags Magic Mountain; Weight Watchers International, Inc.; Treesweet Products; Monarch Importing Co.; Pacida Harbour; London Town Co. (Hush Puppies, coats & jackets); Rolls-Royce Motors; Sunshine Biscuit Co.	

One of the tops as far as creative work is concerned. Jerry Della Femina is one of the most visible in his profession—also somewhat of a creative great.

The Marschalk Co., Inc. 1345 Avenue of the Americas New York, NY 10105 (212) 974-7700	ABC Radio Enterprises, Bob Evans Farms, Inc.; Citicorp; Coca-Cola Co. (Sprite, Sugar-Free Sprite, Mr. Pibb, Foods Division); Cone Mills, Inc.; Economics Laboratory, Inc.; *Family Circle* magazine; Formfit Rogers, Inc.; The Gillette Co. (Personal Care Division, Safety Razor Division, Paper Mate Division); Glenbrook Laboratories, division of Sterling Drug; Gorham Division Textron, Inc.; W. R. Grace & Co.; Heublein, Inc. (Grocery Products, Spirits Group); IBM World Trade Americas/Far East Corp.; Maybelline, Division of Schering-Plough Corp.; Mutual of New York; NL Industries, Norcliff Thayer, Inc.; Revlon, Inc.; Richardson-Vicks, Inc.; Upjohn Co.; Victor F. Weaver, Inc.; Bernzomatic; Chessie System; Ohio Bell Telephone Co.; Richman Brothers Co.; Sentry Hardware; Standard Oil Co. of Ohio; State of Ohio Tourism;	370 employees in two U.S. offices.

Vistron Corp.; WJKW-TV; William Penn.

Wunderman, Ricotta &
Kline, Inc.
575 Madison Avenue
New York, NY 10022
(212) 909-0100

239 employees in two U.S. offices and 135 employees in 11 foreign offices.

L. L. Bean Inc.; Book-of-the-Month Club; C.I.T. Financial Corp.; Columbia House, division of Columbia Broadcasting System; Government Employees Insurance & Co. (GEICO); Grolier Enterprises, Inc.; Margrace Corp.; Merrill Lynch, Pierce, Fenner & Smith, Inc.; Metropolitan Museum of Art; Monex International, Ltd.; New York Telephone Co.; Procter & Gamble Co.; Reader's Digest Association; Shillcraft Importers; Swiss Colony; Time, Inc., Circulation Division, Time-Life Books; Times Mirror Magazines, Inc.; Warner Amex.

Vistron Corp.; WJKW-TV; William Penn.

A subsidiary of Young & Rubicam, and one of the tops in direct marketing advertising.

Dailey & Associates
3055 Wilshire Boulevard
Los Angeles, CA 90010
(213) 386-7823

260 employees in two U.S. offices and 288 employees in 11 foreign offices.

Air New Zealand; American Honda Motor Co., Inc.; Beatrice Foods Co. (Rosarita Mexican Foods); California Apricot Advisory Board; Canlis' Restaurants, Inc.; KNXT-TV; Craig Corp.; Crown Zellerback Corp.; Curtice-Burns, Inc.; Fairmont Hotel Co.; Ford Dealers Advertising Association of Southern California; Foremost-McKesson; Fuller-O'Brien Paints; Great Western Financial Corp.; Guild Wineries and Distilleries; Hunt-Wesson Foods, Inc.; Knudsen Corp.; Lawry's Restaurants; Thomas J. Lipton, Inc.; Manila Hotel; Mexicana Airlines; New Zealand Government Tourist Office; Olympic Valley Association; Pacific Area Travel As-

Agency/Address	Some Major Clients*	Personnel/Offices
	sociation; Philippine Airlines, Philippine Convention Bureau; Purex Corp., Ltd. (military sales); Reckitt & Colman; San Francisco Convention & Visitors Bureau; Taco Bell; the Arizona Bank; Transamerica Corp. (Occidental Life Insurance Co. of California); TraveLodge International, Inc.; Trusthouse Forte Group (Colony Foods); Warnaco, Inc. (White Stag); Westours.	

The latest acquisition of the Interpublic Group of Companies.

Agency/Address	Some Major Clients*	Personnel/Offices
Tracy-Locke Advertising Plaza of the Americas South Tower, P.O. Box 50129 Dallas, TX 75250 (214) 742-3131	AMF Ben Hogan Co.; Associates First Capital Corp.; Beaird-Poulan; Best Products, Inc.; Borden, Inc., Consumer Products Division, Dairy Groups; First National Bank in Dallas; Haggar Co.; Imperial Sugar Co.; Inter-First Corp.; Marion Laboratories, Inc.; Mrs. Baird's Bakeries, Inc.; Nichols-Kusan, Inc.; Pepsi-Cola Bottling Group; Phillips Petroleum Co.; Preview, Inc. (subscription TV); Weed-Eater, Inc.; American TV & Communications Corp.; Columbia Savings & Loan Association; Frontier Airlines; Gates Rubber Co.; Group One Broadcasting; Mile-High Equipment Co., Sunbeam Ice-O-Matic; Mountain Bell Telephone Co., Mountain Bell Yellow Pages; Snowmass Companies, Ltd., Snowmass Resort Association; Taco John's; Walker Group; Warsteiner Importers Agency; Young Realty Corp.	287 employees in two U.S. offices.

258

McCaffrey & McCall, Inc.
575 Lexington Avenue
New York, NY 10022
(212) 421-7500

Air Canada; American Broadcasting Companies, Inc.; Del Taco Corp.; European American Bank; Exxon Corp.; Hartford Insurance Group; Hiram Walker, Inc.; Mercedes-Benz of North America, Inc.; North American Phillips Corp.; J. C. Penney Co.; Pfizer, Inc.; St. Joe Minerals Corp.; Texize; Westvaco.

301 employees in one U.S. office.

Chiat/Day Inc. Advertising
517 South Olive Street
Los Angeles, CA 90013
(213) 622-7454

Aames Home Loan Co.; Alaska Airlines; Allstate Savings & Loan; Apple Computer Services, Inc.; Ask Computer Systems; Asphalt Roofing Manufacturers Association; Biltmore Hotel; Gilbert H. Brockmeyer's Natural Ice Cream; California Brandy Advisory Board; California Cling Peach Advisory Board; Clearprint Paper Co.; ENI Companies; Fafco; Fotomat Corp.; Genstar Corp.; Robert Half of New York; Holland America Cruises; Illinois Tool Works, Inc.; Intel Corp.; KING-TV, Seattle; Kiron Corp.; Mitsubishi Electric Sales America, Inc.; *The Newporter*, Olympia Brewing Co.; Oregon Bank; Pacific Northwest Bell Telephone Co.; Pioneer Electronics of America; Saffola Products, Division of Wilsey Foods; Seattle Aquarium; Sharkey's, Inc.; Shugart Associates; Skipper's Suntory International; TOM Inc.; Times Mirror Co.; Transamerica Corp.; Wienerschnitzel Restaurants, Wienerschnitzel Operators Association; Winston Tire Co.; Woodland Park Zoo; Yamaha Motors Corp.; Ziff-Davis Publishing.

297 employees in four U.S. offices.

259

Index